THE FIVE WEEKS OF GIUSEPPE ZANGARA

THE FIVE WEEKS OF GIUSEPPE ZANGARA

THE MAN WHO WOULD ASSASSINATE FDR

BLAISE PICCHI

ACADEMY CHICAGO PUBLISHERS

Published in 1998 by
Academy Chicago Publishers
363 West Erie Street
Chicago, Illinois 60610

Printed and bound in the U.S.A.

Library of Congress Cataloging-in-Publication Data

Picchi, Blaise.
    The five weeks of Giuseppi Zangara : the man who would assassinate
F.D.R. / Blaise Picchi.
        p.   cm.
    Includes bibliographical references.
    ISBN 0-89733-443-4
    1. Roosevelt, Franklin D. (Franklin Delano), 1882–1945—
Assassination attempt, 1933. 2. Zangara, Giuseppe, 1900–1933.
3. Assassins—United States—Biography. I. Title.
E807.3.P53   1998
973.917'092—dc21   98-11938
                                                              CIP

TO I.H.M. AND LAURA PICCHI

CONTENTS

ACKNOWLEDGMENTS

F irst of all, I must acknowledge the invaluable assistance of Gen. Leonard F. Chapman, Jr., USMC (Ret.), whose father, L.F. Chapman, was warden of the prison where Giuseppe Zangara was incarcerated and executed. Gen. Chapman went through his father's papers and found, not only Zangara's memoirs, but a box containing manuscripts, photograph albums and a scrapbook that his father had kept during his twenty-five years as warden of the state penitentiary. Without this material, which I was allowed to keep over a year, no book about Giuseppe Zangara could have been written. These papers are now historical treasures housed in the Florida State Archives in Tallahassee, where they were received from Gen. Chapman in an official ceremony presided over by the Florida secretary of state. Needless to say, I am deeply grateful to Gen. Chapman for his generosity and his trust.

The list of names of those who contributed to the research for this book is too long to include here. But I particularly want to thank Dr William Straight, medical historian; Dr George W. Barnard, Professor Emeritus of Forensic Psychiatry at the University of Florida;

Dr John A Spencer; Dr Rajender Reddy; Dr Robert A. McNaughton and Dr Joseph Davis, Dade County Medical Examiner Emeritus. These men gave freely of their time to read the material and provide their expert medical and psychiatric analyses.

I wish to thank also Dr Thomas Armour, Jr., who may be the only living witness of the shooting, for both his and his father's account of the event; Robert Graham, Anton Cermak's grandson; R.P. McClendon, retired prison inspector; Lt. Enoch Griffis of the Raiford Union Correctional Institute; Milton Gustafson of the National Archives and Kenneth Driggs, Esq., Tallahassee attorney and legal historian.

Kathleen Karr of the Interlibrary Loan Department of the Broward County Public Library provided rare microfilms and books from around the country; she and her staff worked tirelessly to help me. Luci Santi of New York researched and helped translate Italian microfilms and records at the New York Public Library. I wish to thank also Mary Kathleen Thomas and my mother, Laura Picchi, who called on her years of editorial experience, to assist in the proof-reading of this manuscript.

Finally, I have to mention the many kind and cooperative people who went out of their way to assist me. These include former presidential advisors, officials, journalists, archivists and researchers who combed through old cartons and files in libraries from Los Angeles to New York. The FBI searched through J. Edgar Hoover's private files for anything that would be helpful. I owe them all a great debt of gratitude.

PREFACE

At about 9:15 on Wednesday, February 15, 1933, during a crowded political rally in Miami's Bayfront Park, Giuseppe Zangara, an unemployed Italian immigrant bricklayer, fired five pistol shots at the head of Franklin Delano Roosevelt, then the president-elect. Although Zangara was no more than twenty-five feet away from his target, his shots went wild, missing Roosevelt by inches, and hitting five bystanders, one of whom was Anton J. Cermak, the mayor of Chicago. Most of the witnesses agreed that Zangara's first shot was free, clear and unobstructed. This little bricklayer from Calabria could have changed the history of the United States, if not the world.

A little more than three weeks after this shooting, the would-be assassin was sentenced to death, and electrocuted seven days later. From the shooting of Anton Cermak to the execution of Giuseppe Zangara, only five weeks had passed. It was the swiftest legal execution in America in the twentieth century.

Because of this very real rush to judgment, little was known about Zangara and his motives. As could be expected, many theories arose: that Zangara was actually aiming at Cermak and not Roosevelt, that he had been sent by the Black Hand, that he was an anarchist, a Communist—or simply a madman. Now, more than six decades later, Zangara remains a political, medical and psychological enigma. There was little discussion of the case at the time, and only a few magazine articles were written about it considerably later. The incident is mentioned in passing in biographies of FDR.

Reactions to the shooting at the time tell much about American insularity, xenophobia and class prejudice in the first decades of this century. Zangara was defined by his dark skin and curly hair and his propensity to emotional outbursts and gesticulation. In 1933, he was perceived as a stereotype by the largely WASP society of Miami, of Florida, indeed of the entire country. It can be noted that until after the Second World War, one would be hard pressed to find men—to say nothing of women—of Mediterranean, African or Asian ancestry in positions of responsibility in government, the military or the commercial or social Establishment.

I have assembled this account from government files, state archives, court transcripts and exhibits and the combined reportage of seven daily newspapers. The reader will be able to hear Zangara's voice for the first time: I was able to retrieve his jailhouse memoir from the warden's files where it had lain unread for all these years. Zangara's crudely expressed thoughts throw some light on the whole man, if anything can do that. There arises the question of Zangara's physical and mental condition. His consistent explanation of his act was that he wanted to kill Roosevelt because he blamed all heads of state for a class system which he thought had caused the searing abdominal pain from which he had suffered all his life. But it is not only his physical condition which raises questions here: there is his mental condition as well.

Did the state of Florida execute an insane man? Although he was pleasant, cooperative and apparently intelligent, Zangara espoused a wild theory which seems to have been entirely his own: that regicide is a valid instrument of political policy. And from the first minute of pandemonium following his attack until the switch activated the electric current, he did not show the slightest sign of remorse or acknowledge that he had behaved in any way that was morally wrong.

Giuseppe Zangara, whatever we may think of him in the end, deserves his day in court. If he had been given a fair hearing and if, after his execution, all the known facts—including his diary—had been objectively revealed, there would not now be a cloud of confusion over this bizarre case.

History owes both this killer and his killers a sober analysis. I hope I have at least partially succeeded in giving that to them here.

1

"A SORT OF RECEPTION"

At about seven o'clock on the evening of February 15, 1933, Vincent Astor's yacht, the *Nourmahal*, anchored at Pier One of Miami's municipal docks, near Bayfront Park. Vincent Astor, the son of John Jacob Astor—who had died in the *Titanic* disaster—was one of the richest men in America. The five-year-old German-made *Nourmahal*, 263 feet long , was one of the largest private yachts in the world. It had a cruising range of 19,000 miles and a maximum speed of sixteen knots. For twelve days, it had been leisurely cruising the Bahamas, stopping here and there for fishing and excursions while February snow covered the northern states and blizzards raged on the Great Lakes. Among the guests on board was Franklin Delano Roosevelt, who, in seventeen days, would succeed Herbert Hoover to become the thirty-second president of the United States.

The nation stood at a crossroads. In 1929, the booming U.S. stock market had suddenly collapsed, precipitating the worst depression in American history. Countless thousands of homeless men—"bindle stiffs" they called themselves—drifted from place to place, sleeping in "Hoovervilles": makeshift collections of lean-tos and tents in woods, dumps and near railroad tracks throughout the country. People were hungry and there was no organized method of feeding them: there were only bread lines where private charities and, to a lesser extent, local governments, doled out food.

American intellectuals, as well as millions of workers and union members, had become convinced that capitalism was a failure. Some were looking with hope at Russia, where the Communist revolution was now fifteen years old. Others wanted an American Mussolini. Huey Long, "Kingfisher," had built a political empire in Louisiana on his motto of "Soak the Rich" and was working to establish a national constituency. Father Charles Coughlin, for one, was gaining a wide following by preaching his brand of fascism. Americans could not see a way out of the Depression. Some prominent business leaders were even suggesting that the new president take office with "dictatorial powers." In November 1932, the Great American Experiment was in deep trouble and many Americans were truly afraid. On election day that November, the people officially placed their hopes of salvation in the hands of the Democratic nominee for president, Franklin Roosevelt, and his running mate, the Speaker of the House of Representatives, John Nance Garner of Texas.

Roosevelt, born into a wealthy, aristocratic New York family, was a distant cousin of Theodore Roosevelt. He was not well known outside the northeast, although he had been elected governor of New York in 1930, had run in 1920 as the vice presidential nominee on the Democratic ticket with James M. Cox, and had served from 1913 to 1920 as assistant secretary of the Navy. When Cox lost the election to Warren G. Harding, FDR had retreated to his home at Hyde Park to assess his future. It was then that this young, physically active patrician was stricken with polio and lost the use of his legs. He rallied from this blow and began a regimen of physical therapy which included bathing in the hot pools of Warm Springs, Georgia, and reentered politics to win the governorship of New York.

Everyone knew that Roosevelt was handicapped (in Italy he was called *"Il Paralitico"*) but Americans made very little of it, perhaps because they were never shown the extent of the paralysis. At that time, the country saw political figures only in newsreels in movie theaters: Roosevelt was never filmed in motion, nor was he photographed being helped to stand or "walk" by his son James, or by aides and Secret Service men. He was able to stand in public for posed shots and to "walk" to a podium with heavy leg braces hidden under his trousers, and with the help of these men. Roosevelt's affliction was known to the American public, but only as an intellectual abstraction..

In early February 1933, the president-elect conferred with advisors at Warm Springs, preparing for his March fourth inauguration—the last time, incidentally, that a presidential inauguration would be held in March. His plan was to go to Jacksonville, Florida, for a rally and board the yacht *Nourmahal* there for a two-week fishing vacation in the Caribbean, after which he would return to Jacksonville where he would entrain for New York and finish work on his inauguration.

Roosevelt traveled in his private railway car to Jacksonville. His party, in addition to his entourage of secretaries, aides and Secret Service men, consisted of four guests: Theodore Roosevelt's son Kermit, Judge Frederick Kernochan, George St. George and Dr Leslie Heiter. These were what the press called FDR's "boon companions." Roosevelt's reception in Jacksonville was enthusiastic: the newspapers had been heralding his arrival for days, describing in detail his itinerary and parade route. Thousands of citizens met him at the train station where he entered an open car with the city's mayor, John T. Alsop, Jr. (who turned out to be FDR's distant cousin), and David Sholtz, the governor of Florida. The motorcade wound its way through the Riverside residential section to Hemming Park in the city's center; cheering crowds lined the route. A crowd estimated at 25,000 had gathered at the park; a police band and the American Legion drum and bugle corps played "Happy Days Are

Here Again." The next morning Roosevelt delivered a short im-promptu speech in front of the Windsor Hotel, thanking the citizens for their courtesy and praising the city. Then he was driven off to the docks to board the *Nourmahal.*

During the voyage, Robert H. Gore, publisher of the *Fort Lau-derdale Daily News*, suggested that, on the yacht's return, Roosevelt attend a grand rally in Miami , where the president-elect could meet influential party leaders and leave for New York from there instead of from Jacksonville. Roosevelt thought this was a good idea: the weather in Miami was balmy and he could use the elegant Coral Gables Biltmore Hotel as a base. Robert Gore had ruled out Fort Lauderdale as a site for the rally, because it could not accommodate large political events.

The Jacksonville *Florida Times-Union* reported that Mayor Anton Cermak of Chicago was one of the out-of-state politicians who planned to meet with Roosevelt in Jacksonville before the presi-dent-elect boarded the yacht. Cermak was not able to arrange this, but, since Roosevelt was now going to conclude his vacation in Miami, the mayor decided to travel there with James Farley, na-tional chairman of the Democratic Party, who was soon to be named Roosevelt's Postmaster General.

After twelve days of cruising, the *Nourmahal* sailed into Miami's Biscayne Bay just as the winter sun was setting. As the ship was tied up to the municipal docks, the passengers were enjoying a fes-tive farewell dinner. Then, while the staff cleared the table, report-ers were ushered into the dining room. FDR, in high spirits, told the press he had done "a lot of fishing and a lot of swimming and I didn't even open the briefcase!" They had visited a different place each day and he had spent a whole day bone-fishing off Andros Island. He had hooked "a whale of a fish" but lost it when it dived and the line broke. He had had twelve "perfectly grand" days, he said. But he did not want to talk about politics. He was asked whether Senator Carter Glass of Virginia was to be named Secretary of the Treasury; whether James Farley would be Postmaster General and

Cordell Hull of Tennessee would become Secretary of State. Roosevelt said that he was holding to the tradition that presidents-elect did not name their cabinets until twenty four hours before inauguration.

After the reporters left, Roosevelt conferred about his cabinet appointments with Professor Raymond Moley, his chief economic advisor. This was a quick conference, because Roosevelt had to leave shortly for "a sort of reception" at the Bayfront Park amphitheater. The mayor of Miami, Redmond Gautier, had come on board to escort FDR to the park. The city had planned a rousing welcome-home party with concerts, speeches and parades featuring the American Legion Honor Guard and the drum and bugle corps from the Harvey Seeds Post as well as a contingent of Shriners, units of the drum and bugle corps of the Miami Junior Chamber of Commerce and the Riverside Military Academy band. Roosevelt was to deliver a short, impromptu speech from the bandstand, as he had done in Jacksonville, and to accept a telegram signed by several thousand Miami well-wishers.

After that he was to be driven to the train station several blocks west of the park, followed by a parade of the American Legion Honor Guard, the Shriners and the bands. From the rear platform of his railway car he would bid a brief farewell to the crowd: already 2,000 people had gathered at the station. Then, by ten P.M., he would be en route to New York. The local newspapers had been publishing the precise details for days: the times of the events, the convoy's route, which motorcar Roosevelt would be riding in and who would be riding with him. National political figures and presidential advisors would attend the festivities, as well as many members of the south Florida political establishment, including mayors and judges.

This was an important event for Miami. In 1933, the city had existed as an incorporated entity for little more than thirty-seven years, having been carved from the wilderness in 1896 when Henry M. Flagler's Florida East Coast Railway first steamed into the set–tlement. The city's growth had been rapid, buoyed by a growing tourism base and the unbridled activity of real estate agents. Several presidents had visited the area on fishing holidays, but no official visit had been paid by an incumbent president. In January 1928, Herbert Hoover, then president-elect, had paraded in triumph down Flagler Street , the main thoroughfare: he was the first Republican to carry Florida in a presidential election. His opponent had been Al Smith, a Catholic, and the Republican campaign had profited from anti-Catholic sentiment.

The population of southern Florida was white Anglo-Saxon Protestant in religion and Democratic in politics. There were few Jews, Hispanics or Republicans, and blacks did not vote. Some beach hotels were openly "Gentiles Only" and all public accommodations were labeled for "Whites" or "Coloreds." Since 1921, the Ku Klux Klan had been a force in Miami, cooperating with police and "guarding" the city against Bolsheviks, Socialists, labor leaders, Jews, Catholics and foreigners in general. Columns of hooded, robed Klansmen marched for blocks during parades, funerals and other public displays in the city. Many prominent citizens are believed to have belonged to the Klan in the 1930s, including high-ranking public officials and at least one chief of police.

In 1931, after one of the wildest sessions in its history, the Florida legislature voted to permit on-track gambling at horse and dog races. The conservative governor, Doyle Carlton, Sr., raised in a strict Protestant family in this Bible-belt state, considered this legislation immoral and vetoed it, but his veto was overridden. The conservative northern counties had originally backed the governor, but they accepted a compromise: all of the state gambling revenue would be distributed equally to each of Florida's sixty-seven counties. Thereafter, for decades, some rural Florida counties would impose low taxes or none at all, supporting themselves entirely on income from the southern Florida racetracks. So, with its sandy beaches, luxurious hotels, warm winter weather and racetrack gambling, Miami in 1933 was already one of the country's most popular tourist meccas. The permanent population of the county was only about 150,000, but one million visitors were said to have come to the city in that year. Nineteen-thirty-three was, in fact, a particularly busy tourist year; rents had been lowered to a quarter of their pre-Depression rates.

On that balmy February evening, newspapers advertised four-day tours of Havana, Cuba, for $42.50, including hotel, meals, sightseeing in new Packard automobiles and excursions to the Prado and Sloppy Joe's. For twenty-five cents, one could attend Elizabeth Van Dyke's lectures on feminine hygiene, including herb formulas and beauty tips, and there was "nude sunshine bathing" in a private solarium at the Dallas Park Hotel on the Miami River. Sears Roebuck was selling ladies' silk dresses for $2.95, spring hats for $1.00 and a genuine two-point diamond ring mounted in fourteen karat white gold for $1.98. A carton of Old Gold cigarettes cost ninety-nine cents.

In the second race at Hialeah that day, "Roosevelt" came in first, paying $3.35. In local news, Edward W. Overmiller pleaded guilty in court to possessing two barrels of moonshine at his Brickel Avenue home; he was sentenced to a $500 fine or six months in the county jail. He did not have $500. Morning radio featured "Little Jack Little" on the CBS affiliate WQAM and "Betty Crocker" on NBC's WIOD. Each evening at six P.M., H.V. Kaltenborn read the news for CBS. And Miami radio signed off at one A.M. after each day of offering fare like "Amos 'n' Andy," "Spy Story," "Buck Rogers in the 21st Century" and "Just Plain Bill."

Then there was the Olympia, the most impressive movie palace ever built in Miami, with Elizabethan balconies and rococo appointments, housed under a celestial ceiling sparkling with stars when the lights were turned down. And it was air conditioned at a time when air conditioning was a rare luxury. The Olympia stage offered vaudeville acts and big bands along with movies. That February day, Eddie Cantor and George Jessel performed to a packed house, "Even if you don't understand Jewish you'll gurgle with merriment," a reviewer wrote the next morning. Films playing that evening were

Hard to Handle starring James Cagney, and *42nd Street* with Warner Baxter, George Brent, Ruby Keeler and 150 Busby Berkley chorus girls.

But that night most people were not at the movies. They were gathered at Bayfront Park, a forty-acre strip of land about a hundred yards wide and a quarter of a mile long, sandwiched between Biscayne Bay on the east and Biscayne Boulevard, lined with palm trees, on the west. The park had been created from Biscayne Bay in the late 1920s at a cost of $2.5 million. The mouth of the Miami River lies a few hundred yards to the south of the park; parking lots for fishermen and docks for yachts formed its northern boundary, and just across Biscayne Boulevard stood the eastern edge of the downtown business district.

At the southern end of the park was the amphitheater and bandstand: an elevated stage with a concave back wall. These structures were, in a time before the perfection of microphones and amplifiers, useful venues for concerts and political speeches. The Bayfront Park bandstand was exceptionally ugly: a gaudy three-story yellow stucco structure with a concrete open-air stage protruding from its front and center, facing north. About four feet above this outdoor stage was an interior stage, extending into the building. Overhanging the protruding stage was a large, cumbersome portico painted green, yellow, orange, silver and red. From the center of the stage, steps descended to a semicircular paved area, and it was on this pavement that Roosevelt was to speak from his car, which was parked parallel to the bandstand and facing west.

Topping this architectural nightmare were three onion domes, one on each end of the roof and the third on top of the portico. The amphitheater had been constructed in the 1920s for a Shriner's convention, which might explain the intended Oriental look of the building, although Byzantine buildings were popular in Miami at that time. (Opa Locka, a suburb to the north of Miami, consisted of structures with onion domes, minarets and balconies on streets named Ali Baba and Schaharazade.)

There were semicircular rows of seats facing the amphitheater on a slightly inclined concrete apron. These slatted wood and metal folding seats, which could accommodate 7000 people, were permanently fastened to each other and to the ground.

At nine in the evening, Roosevelt's party left the yacht and boarded three waiting vehicles: two open police cars and a small sedan. Hatless, wearing a grey suit, FDR was helped down the gangplank and into the lead car, a big open Buick, by his private aide and bodyguard, Gus Gennerich. For these public appearances, Roosevelt wore ten-pound leg braces which allowed him to walk with canes and assistance while the knee hinges were locked, and to sit when the hinges were unlocked. After helping FDR into the back seat, next to Miami mayor Redmond Gautier, Gennerich got into the car along with Secret Service agent Robert Clark and Marvin McIntyre, who was to be the president's appointments secretary. The driver was Fitzhugh Lee, a Miami policeman. The second vehicle, also a convertible, held several Secret Service men, and in the last car were Roosevelt's associates: Raymond Moley, Vincent Astor, Judge Kernochan and Kermit Roosevelt.

By ten minutes after nine, the small motorcade had driven the hundred or so yards to Biscayne Boulevard, a wide highway divided by a large median with parking for hundreds of cars. As the motorcade proceeded, it was joined by several other vehicles occupied by prominent people. The parking areas in the median and on either side of the boulevard were filled. People had begun to gather in the park since six P.M. and by seven o'clock there was standing room only. Hundreds of people were still walking toward the bandstand as Roosevelt passed slowly in his open car, waving and smiling, greeted by cheers and applause. Roosevelt had told the national press corps that his comments would be inconsequential, so most of them had decided to skip the park rally and go directly to the depot to wait for him. Consequently, there were only local reporters at the bandstand, along with a few wire service stringers and one newsreel team.

Roosevelt's green Buick convertible began slowly nosing its way through the largest crowd assembled in the history of the city, estimated at 25,000. Vincent Astor, riding in the last car, commented that this was a dangerous situation. There was the president-elect, exposed in the rear seat of an open car that was moving at walking pace through a massive crowd. Moley agreed, but noted that the situation was better now than it had been during the campaign, when they had had to rely only on local police and Roosevelt's personal bodyguard. At least now, Moley said, the president-elect was protected by the Secret Service.

In fact, according to best estimates, the president-elect had six Secret Service operators with him, together with several dozen policemen, acting as motorcycle escort, drivers and crowd control. This contrasted with protection afforded outgoing President Herbert Hoover who, two days earlier, had attended a political dinner in New York City with an entourage of eight hundred Secret Service agents and local police.

This would be the last time FDR was to have such relatively scant protection. When he returned to New York from Miami he was met by a thousand-man police guard.

2

"STOP THAT MAN!"

The president-elect's car came to a stop directly before the steps to the stage, where dignitaries were seated, among them Mayor Anton Cermak of Chicago, Joseph H. Gill, president of the Florida Power and Light Company, with his young wife, Mabel; Joseph Widener, founder of the Hialeah racetrack; Colonel Henry Doherty, owner of the Biltmore and Roney Plaza hotels; Frank B. Shutts, publisher of the *Miami Herald*, and Robert H. Gore, publisher of the *Fort Lauderdale Florida News*. All 7000 seats in front of the stage were filled, and thousands stood in the aisles and all around the seating area.

It was a warm February evening. The tall royal palms surrounding the amphitheater area were illuminated with red, white and blue lights, and a battery of floodlights were switched on to shine on FDR's car as it stopped. All the light was concentrated on the car and the stage; the crowd stretched back into the darkness. The air was filled with the blaring music of the chrome-helmeted American Legion drum and bugle corps and the sounds of thousands cheering and applauding. Those who were lucky enough to have seats rose to their feet as the people on the stage came down the steps to greet Roosevelt.

In the crowd was a short, slight Italian immigrant dressed in brown slacks and a brown print shirt. This was Giuseppe Zangara, known to acquaintances (he said he had no friends) as Joe. Several days earlier, Zangara had gone to a downtown pawnshop on North Miami Avenue and bought a five shot .32 calibre revolver for $8.00. This gun, the equivalent of a modern Saturday night special, was in Zangara's pocket that night, along with a newspaper clipping detailing FDR's schedule in Miami.

H.L. Edmunds, visiting Miami from Ottumwa, Iowa, was standing in the mass of people just a few rows from the front. He had been waiting over two hours to get a glimpse of Roosevelt. An hour and a half before FDR's arrival, Edmunds noticed a small man in a brown shirt pushing his way toward him. When the man began to shove some women standing directly behind Edmunds, the Iowan asked him, "Where do you think you're going?"

"I go right down to front," Zangara said.

"Well," Edmunds said, "I'm sorry, but you can't go down there. It's full."

"It no look to me like it full."

"There are many people sitting on the ground, ladies and children sitting on the ground," Edmunds replied, "and it isn't proper, it isn't right for you to go and stand out and push yourself in front of someone else."

Zangara appeared to accept this, and went no further. He was now in or behind the third row, only twenty-five or thirty feet from where Roosevelt was going to speak. He needed to be close to his target, because he was too small (not quite five feet, one inch tall and weighing only 105 pounds) to see over the crowd.

■ ■ ■

George E. Hussey, chairman of the reception committee, urged the spectators to quiet down, and introduced Mayor Gautier, who in turn introduced Roosevelt. The city was listening to a broadcast of the proceedings as WQAM announcer Fred Mizer described what was happening as though it were a sporting event.

"We welcome him to Miami," the mayor said. "We wish him success and are promising him cooperation and support, and we bid him Godspeed. Ladies and gentlemen, the president-elect of the United States of America."

Once more the crowd rose, cheering and applauding. The microphone was handed to Roosevelt, who had been hoisted atop the back seat of his car. "I certainly appreciate the welcome of my many friends here in Miami, but I am not a stranger here," FDR said, delivering what was certainly an inconsequential speech, as he had told the press it would be. "It is true that I haven't been here in seven years, but I have often visited here. I am firmly resolved that this will not be the last time I will come here to Miami." Interrupted by applause, he went on, "I have had a wonderful twelve-day fishing trip in Florida and Bahamian waters. I have had a wonderful rest and caught a great many fish. However, I will not attempt to tell you a fish story." When the laughter died down, he continued: "The only fly in the ointment is that I put on ten pounds during the trip—" more laughter "—and one of my first official duties will be taking the ten pounds off. I hope that I am able to come down next winter, see you all, and have another ten days or two weeks in Florida waters."

He handed the microphone back to Gautier. He had delivered a 145-word speech in less than a minute. A member of a newsreel team which had been slow to set up its equipment climbed on the back of the convertible and asked Roosevelt if he would repeat his little speech to the camera. Roosevelt refused. The man protested that the team had come a thousand miles to film this event. "I'm very sorry," Roosevelt said, "But I can't do it." He was helped down in his seat so that he could talk to the dignitaries who had left the stage to greet him.

One of these was Anton Cermak, the mayor of Chicago, who was with his friend Jim Bowler and L.L. Lee, Miami city manager, who had been assigned to escort Cermak for the reception. Cermak came down from the stage and walked over to shake hands with Roosevelt; the two men exchanged a few words. They had a good relationship: Cermak had helped FDR by calling the delegates to order at a critical moment during the Democratic Convention that past summer, when pandemonium had broken out on the floor among opponents of Roosevelt's nomination. Cermak had some important Chicago business to discuss with the president-elect; Roosevelt suggested they talk on the train. Cermak nodded, smiling, and walked toward the back of the car—and at the same time toward Giuseppe Zangara. Others standing near the car were Joseph Widener, Joseph Gill and the two newspaper publishers Frank R. Shutts and Robert H. Gore. Robert Clark, the Secret Service agent, was standing next to the rear car door on the right.

Just slightly to the rear of the convertible, about twenty-five feet away, Lillian Cross was standing. She was the forty-eight-year-old wife of Dr William Cross, a Miami physician. Zangara was directly behind her. Since she was only a little over five feet tall, Mrs Cross climbed onto one of the seats to get a better look at the president-elect. Her friend, Mrs Willis McCrary, was standing in front of her. Dr Cross and Mr McCrary were somewhere back in the crowd. They planned to meet at their car when the festivities ended, a meeting that would be long delayed on this night.

Thomas Armour, a forty-six-year-old Miami carpenter, was standing behind Zangara. He had earlier traded places with his fifteen-year-old son Tommy, so that the boy would have a better view and could tell his own children that he had seen Franklin D. Roosevelt and heard him speak. Now it was the father's turn to use the vantage point. Both Mrs McCrary and the elder Armour would later tell reporters that they had seen Zangara approach an hour and a half before the shooting; another man was with him, they said, but they did not know what had become of that other man. H.L. Edmunds of Ottumwa, Iowa, who had told Zangara not to push his way through the crowd, did not mention that Zangara was with anyone.

In his death-row memoir, Zangara commented on these moments before the shooting:

> I tried to get close to him [Roosevelt], but there were too many people around him. I wanted to get in front of him in order to get a good shot at him, but the people kept on pushing me back further all the time and I could not get to see him. . . . When I saw I could not get near him I decided to shoot him from the distance. While he was talking I could not get to see him because all of the people were crowded around him. He only spoke for about a minute from the car and sat down immediately after. When he did I only could see his head, although by that time I was standing on a park chair. However, the rest of his body was hidden by the car.

As Cermak moved away from the car, A.B. Willis, the Dade County Democratic executive committeeman, was being helped to bring a six-foot-long telegram of welcome to Roosevelt, signed by 2,800 citizens of Miami. FDR leaned toward him but Willis never presented his telegram.

Five shots rang out: "pop," then "pop, pop," like a motorcycle backfiring, or the sound of firecrackers. Then "pop, pop" again.

A woman screamed. Someone cried, *"Stop that man!"* And someone else shouted, *"Don't let him kill Roosevelt!"*

The city of Miami listened in shock to the sounds of gunfire and shouts and cries broadcast over Fred Mizer's open microphone.

Immediately, there was a jumble of bodies and a flurry of activity as six uniformed American Legionnaires—World War veterans—charged into the crowd, shoving people back. Willis was pushed aside with his telegram. Roosevelt's driver, Fitzhugh Lee, started the engine. Roosevelt, at first confused, looked back; behind him he saw Mayor Cermak doubled over, and to the left a man dressed in white bleeding from his forehead and crying, "Help me, I'm hurt." Mabel Gill had collapsed on the amphitheater steps. Gus Gennerich, the bodyguard who had been sitting in the front seat, leapt over it and hurled himself against Roosevelt's chest, to protect him from the front. Joseph Tomaszewski, a spectator, was standing directly behind FDR, holding a box camera on a tripod. Quickly he put the camera down and placed his hands on Roosevelt's shoulders from behind, urging him to get down, which Roosevelt did, slumping in his seat. Tomaszewski shielded him from behind with his body.

The Secret Service men rushed up, guns drawn, to lock arms and encircle the back of the car. The chief agent, George Broadnax, pounded the fender and shouted at Fitzhugh Lee, "Get him the hell out of here!" Lee threw the car into gear and began moving through the crowd toward the northwest corner of the bandstand. When Gennerich removed himself, FDR turned to look around and, having seen wounded people, ordered Lee to stop the car, which he did, but Broadnax shouted at him to move forward again. The car crept on.

L.L. Lee, the city manager, was linking arms with Cermak when the shooting began. The mayor sagged to his knees, but Lee and County Committeeman W.W. Wood helped him to his feet. There was a growing bloodstain on Cermak's white shirt, and his trouser knees were stained from the fall. The bullet had hit him in the right rib cage. He later said that he felt a severe jolt which reminded him of a heart attack he had suffered several years earlier. He cried, "The President—get him away!" Committeeman Wood called after the moving car, "Cermak's been hit!" Someone else shouted, "For God's sake, a man's been shot, get an ambulance!" FDR heard this and turned to see Cermak supported by the two men. Leaning forward, so that Fitzhugh Lee could hear him over the din and confusion, Roosevelt calmly commanded him to stop a second time. Then the president-elect motioned to Lee and Wood to put Cermak in the back seat of the convertible. They put him on the seat to Roosevelt's left; Mayor Gautier was sitting on his right. Roosevelt raised his right arm and waved to the crowd, saying loudly and calmly, "I'm all right. Tell them I'm all right."

Those who could hear him began to cheer. Now the convertible started to move again, more quickly this time. Motorcycles roared and sirens shrieked as the motorcade edged its way through the crowd. Fitzhugh Lee turned left at the northwest corner of the bandstand and headed for the roadway behind it. A voice came over the loudspeaker telling everyone to evacuate the park.

■ ■ ■

Seconds before the shots were fired, Lillian Cross had been standing on her seat in the second row, in the midst of the crowd, watching FDR speak twenty-five feet in front of her. Suddenly someone climbed onto the small chair next to her; it teetered and nearly collapsed. Turning, she saw a small swarthy man about her size sharing the chair on her right. "Don't do that, please," she said. "You're going to knock me off." At that point the man, standing on tiptoe, extended his right arm high over her right shoulder; he was holding a pistol. Mrs Cross said later that she immediately saw what was happening. She could literally sight down the gun barrel and knew that it was pointed at the back of Roosevelt's head. At that moment, she told reporters, she thought, "Oh, he is going to kill the president!" The muzzle of the gun was so close to Lillian Cross that when Zangara fired, the powder burned her cheek. Marion Fountain of Miami was standing directly in front of Mrs Cross as Zangara fired; his ear was burned by the powder. Lillian Cross was to say later that she had pushed Zangara's arm up and deflected his aim; she was to be credited with saving FDR's life, although her claim would be disputed by Thomas Armour, the Miami carpenter who had been standing behind Zangara and Mrs Cross. He said that the first shot was unimpeded and missed Roosevelt on its own, and that after that he, Armour, grabbed for the gunman's forearm. Zangara resisted, still firing, his face contorted with effort. Trying to force his arm back down, he crooked his hand downward. But even so his bullets were hitting people on the steps and toward the front of the convertible. Armour said he could feel the recoil of each shot as it was fired. As Armour struggled with Zangara's arm, Guy Proctor of Tampa, standing next to Armour, also reached to seize Zangara's arm over Armour's hands, as he shouted "Don't!"

Young Tommy Armour was standing a few feet away in the aisle. Sixty years later, now a seventy-five-year-old retired physician, he still remembered vividly the hand extended above the crowd and the flashes of gunfire in the darkness. He saw the crowd in front of the shooter ducking, dropping to the ground almost in unison, as though they were genuflecting. "After the first shot, at least by the second shot, everyone was down practically," he recalled. He faintly remembered that after the first shot there was a pause. He was terribly afraid that his father had been hit. "I could not see him, I kept looking where the flashes were and then, all of a sudden, I realized that Dad wasn't coming out. So I started yelling for Dad. I had a feeling he was involved. I was real afraid that he had gotten shot or something. Then he came out and finally got to me. I wanted to go home, but Dad said, 'We'll stay for a while.'"

Ed Ridolf, a resident of northwest Miami, was standing against the right rear fender of the convertible. After Roosevelt had finished his speech and had signed a paper that someone had given him, Ridolf heard several rapid reports which he thought were backfires. Standing behind FDR, he looked into the crowd and saw Zangara with spurts of fire coming from the barrel of his gun. "The gun was aimed directly at the back of Roosevelt's head," Ed Ridolf said. "The man that was doing the shooting was standing on his tiptoes and had his arm outstretched over the crowd." Roosevelt slumped down into his seat as Ridolf jumped between him and the gunman. The last shot, he said, passed between his head and Roosevelt's, burying itself in the ground in front of the convertible.

John Sewell, a former mayor of Miami, was on the stage with his wife and some friends. When he heard the first shot, he saw Zangara not forty feet in front of him with the pistol in his hand: Zangara's arm was raised above the heads of the spectators, but his hand was bent downward as he shot. Some bystanders, Sewell said, were shoving Zangara's arm up. Then, according to various bystanders, two Legionnaires and three Miami policemen all crashed into Zangara, Armour and Proctor "like a ton of bricks."

Thomas Armour said that it was a single policeman who first attacked, leaping from the front onto the gunman.

"Lynch him!" someone cried out. "Kill him, cut his throat!"

Dade County Sheriff Dan Hardie jumped from the stage with two of his deputies and entered the fray, amid the shouting and screaming. Those close to Zangara tried to move away from him, while those farther away, who did not understand what was happening, pressed in closer out of curiosity. Two large women were trying to shove the crowd back, shouting at the top of their lungs, to prevent the small children at their feet from being crushed.

The three Miami policemen—Lester G. Crews, N.B. Clark and Raymond H. Jackson—had been standing behind the cars. When the shooting began, Officer Clark, seeing Zangara standing on the folding chair with a smoking gun, rushed with officers Crews and Jackson behind him, to leap over people and seats to slam into Zangara, Mrs Cross and the senior Armour just as the Legionnaires appeared from the other side. Zangara was soon at the bottom of a tangle of attackers: Guy Proctor was attempting to strangle the shooter, while others were pummeling him.

One of the policemen was hitting him with a blackjack. In the struggle, Zangara's clothes were literally ripped from his body; Officer Raymond Jackson lost his revolver and his pay envelope containing $89.00 dollars, his salary for two weeks. Zangara was silent while all this was going on.

Five shots had been fired and five people had been hit. Mabel Gill, the wife of the president of the power company, was sitting on the steps in evening dress, bent over holding her abdomen. There was blood on her hands; her eyes were glazed. She was bleeding internally and going into shock. She was to be near death for weeks.

Margaret Kruis, a pretty twenty-three-year-old visitor from New Jersey, had sunk to the ground. A bullet had pierced her hand and another had penetrated her hat to graze her head. That bullet bounced off and was later found in Mayor Cermak's collar, with a piece of Ms Kruis's hat attached to it. Robert Gore, who had been standing next to FDR's car with his foot on the rear bumper, heard the bullet that hit Cermak whiz past his ear. The bullets that hit Margaret Kruis passed Roosevelt's head, he thought, by just two feet. Gore scooped the injured girl in his arms and handed her to someone before he rushed over to the struggling pile on top of Zangara. He said that it was Mrs Cross who was trying to strangle Zangara. Gore said, too, that he heard Zangara shout, "I want to kill the president—I kill the president. Too many people are starving to death. I'm glad I got Cermak." No one else heard Zangara say this, or anything else at that time. Mrs Cross was certain he did not speak. "If he said anything, I didn't hear it," she said later. "And I'm sure he didn't shout because he was right in back of me." It is in fact unlikely that Zangara uttered these words, because it is doubtful that under the circumstances Zangara would have known whether he had hit anyone, let alone recognized the mayor of Chicago.

There were minor injuries. Bill Sinnott, a hefty forty-six-year-old New York policeman had come up to pay his respects to FDR, whom he had guarded when the latter was governor of New York. Sinnott suffered a glancing wound to his forehead and scalp. Russell Caldwell, age twenty-two, a chauffeur who lived in Coconut Grove, a suburb of Miami, was hit squarely in the forehead by a spent bullet which embedded itself under the skin. Then there was Secret Service agent Robert Clark, who was standing next to the convertible. A bullet, thought to be the one that hit Cermak, supposedly grazed the back of his right hand. He did not report this wound and was not listed among the wounded. It was Roosevelt who mentioned that the agent had been wounded. Several reporters who saw Robert Clark at the hospital said that it was not a wound on his hand, but a streak of someone else's blood. But to this day he is listed by the Secret Service as an agent wounded in the line of duty.

3

WHO SAVED ROOSEVELT?

Officer Lester Crews took possession of the pistol and, together with other policemen, lifted the bedraggled Zangara and carried him to the third vehicle—the sedan which had been used by Raymond Moley, Vincent Astor and Kermit Roosevelt. It was imperative that Zangara be gotten away immediately because the mood in the park was growing ugly. There were shouts of "Kill him, kill him!" and "Lynch him!" There was no room in the sedan for Zangara because Russell Caldwell, with his superficial forehead wound, had been brought there, so Zangara was hoisted up and handcuffed to the luggage rack above the car's trunk. Two policemen stood on the bumper, leaning against the prisoner, while the third rode on the running board with the sheriff of Dade County. The car nosed its way through the crowd and sped wildly down Biscayne Boulevard toward Jackson Memorial Hospital, where FDR's convertible was also headed with Cermak.

Later Zangara wrote, "The people tried to kill me, but the police surrounded me at once and put me in a car and took me to the Miami jail. On the way to the jail the police abused me, and one of them had me by the collar and kept on squeezing my neck very hard."

Tom Armour's son remembers that they carried Zangara horizontally. "I think they just picked him up and carried him. They held him by his head and feet. They took him to the car. It had two doors and a humped trunk with a rack. They threw him on the rack and tied him down."

Fitzhugh Lee drove FDR's car north, past the groups of people still coming to and from the park. Lee leaned on the horn, racing through the red light at Flagler Street and Biscayne Boulevard, then roared north along the boulevard to Northeast 11th Street, turned left and headed west to Northwest Seventh Avenue and on to the hospital at Tenth Avenue. Roosevelt said later that this trip seemed endless. He did not think Cermak would make it to the hospital. Roosevelt's left arm was around Cermak, whose head slumped against Roosevelt's chest.

The county investigator, Detective J.B. Rowland, had jumped on the car's left running board and was sitting on the rear fender. He told Roosevelt he didn't think Cermak was going to make it. "I'm afraid he isn't," Roosevelt replied. He could not find a pulse at first and thought that Cermak was dead. But he did find a pulse, and began to talk to the mayor, who had in fact never lost consciousness. "Tony, keep quiet," FDR said. "Don't move. It won't hurt you if you keep quiet." During the drive, Cermak's pulse became stronger and he began to perk up. Doctors later credited Roosevelt with keeping the mayor from going into shock by his encouraging words during the seemingly endless trip to the hospital.

The second vehicle, rushing to the hospital behind Roosevelt's car, was driven by Miami policeman Raymond N. Sullivan; it was carrying Bill Sinnott, with his superficial head wound, Margaret Kruis, whose hand had been pierced, and Mabel Gill, who was seriously wounded and whose condition had become critical. The sedan, the third car in this frantic motorcade, was holding not only

Russell Caldwell, who lay in the back seat with the spent bullet embedded in his forehead, but Raymond Moley, Judge Kernochan, Vincent Astor and Kermit Roosevelt. Zangara was on the trunk rack, secured by officers N.B. Clark and Raymond Jackson, while Sheriff Hardie and Officer Lester Crews clung to the running boards, with Professor Moley holding onto Crews's belt. Thus there seem to have been eleven people in and on that sedan. As the car took a sharp turn at a corner, N.B. Clark flew off the car and onto the pavement. The driver stopped and Clark was picked up, uninjured.

When the cars arrived at Jackson Memorial, Caldwell was rushed to waiting attendants. Zangara was moved to a police car to be taken downtown to the Dade County courthouse and its jail, towering twenty-four stories above the city. Judge Kernochan and Raymond Moley went with him.

According to local legend, the night resident in the emergency room of Jackson Memorial Hospital—then a small, municipally operated facility—was sitting with his feet propped up on his desk, reading a "girlie" magazine. He had no radio, so he did not know what had happened at the park. Since the door to the emergency room was solid, with only a small glass window at eye level, he could not see the hallway nor could he hear the commotion of the motorcade's arrival. He was aroused by a loud, imperious voice demanding, "Open the door for the president of the United States." Annoyed, and thinking it was a stupid joke, the young resident shouted, "Tell him to piss on the floor and swim in under it." At that moment, a Secret Service agent opened the door and Roosevelt was wheeled in. There is no record of what happened after that. The resident became a prominent Miami physician who, when asked years later if the story was true, would only smile and say, "Maybe."

Roosevelt spent over four hours at the hospital that night, monitoring the condition of the victims. He visited each of them except Mrs Gill, who was in surgery. He was driven back to the *Nourmahal* at two in the morning where he spent the rest of the night, having postponed his departure from Miami to the next day.

The people around FDR were watching him to see how this man who was about to lead a troubled nation would react to the attempt on his life. That February evening he was still an unknown quantity. In the immediate aftermath of the assassination attempt, virtually every word and action of the president-elect was reported to the nation over the radio and in newspapers. Was he frightened? Nervous? Relieved that he had escaped unhurt? Was he rattled or petulant? He was none of those things. He appeared unfazed, calm, deliberate, cheerful—throughout the shooting itself as well as during its aftermath. He said and did all the right things at the right times: he stopped the car twice to pick up the wounded; he assured the crowd that he was all right; he calmly talked Cermak out of shock and he visited the victims that night and returned to the hospital the next day with flowers, cards and baskets of fruit. He had met his first test under fire, and had impressed not only his associates, but the press and the nation. It was on this note of personal courage, graciousness and self-confidence that he was to assume the reins of government seventeen days later.

■ ■ ■

It is interesting that Zangara was taken to the county, rather than the city, jail. His crime had occurred on Miami city turf and the arresting officers were Miami policemen, so technically this case belonged to the city police. Policemen are always jealous of their turf and the public credit that goes with making an arrest. But Dan Hardie, who had taken office as sheriff of Dade County only six weeks earlier, was a seasoned politician who was not about to let this important case, attracting worldwide attention, slip out of his grasp. The three patrolmen were young beat cops; they would have been no match for the sheriff who decided that the city jail would not be secure enough for Zangara. That decision made it Dan Hardie's case.

Hardie was a colorful character who had dropped out of school in his native St. Louis after the third grade, but had learned shorthand and typing in business school. He had come to Miami just before the turn of the century, when outlaw bands, opium dens and bawdy houses flourished there. Often taking the law into his own hands in the flashy frontier style of a natural showman, Hardie served two terms as sheriff in Miami, from 1908 to 1916; he ran promising to arrest suspicious-looking persons first and ask questions later. In 1916 he owned a "casino" business on Miami Beach: this was actually a swimming resort which also featured dancing and refreshments; it had nothing to do with gambling. By the 1920s, Hardie had become a millionaire, but he lost everything in the 1929 market crash.

When Hardie was elected sheriff again in 1932 at the age of fifty-three, he was an anachronism. His brash, outspoken syle, which reflected his third-grade education, no longer suited an increasingly cosmopolitan Dade County. His predecessor had been removed for corruption. No one could accuse Hardie of dishonesty, but he was hot-headed and melodramatic and, as his grandson later said, "stepped on too many toes," arresting prostitutes and their clients, many of whom were respectable citizens, closing betting parlors and in general, some said, making the city look bad and hurting tourism. Frank Shutts, the powerful editor of the *Miami Herald*, was an outspoken critic of the sheriff. Once, after he had performed his grisly duty as executioner, Hardie was asked by *Herald* reporters if he had had any qualms about throwing the switch. The sheriff replied that his only regret was that Shutts was not sitting in the condemned man's lap.

Eight months after Zangara's arrest, Governor Dave Sholtz removed Hardie for misfeasance and nonfeasance because of a "lack of sound judgement and mental stability." The papers called it "incompetence." At the time, Sholtz wished to remove not only Hardie, but Columbia County sheriff Rex Sweat; it has been suggested that this was because Sweat opposed gambling interests in his north Florida county. Hardie said he was removed because "the gamblers want to run this county and I haven't allowed it. I guess the old methods are out of date. When I was sheriff before, I showed gamblers the way out of town at the end of a .38. Apparently, they don't do it that way anymore." Hardie was eventually exonerated, but by then his political career was over.

Less than twenty years later, Senator Kefauver's crime commission would virtually set up shop in Miami to investigate gambling and organized crime which was open and unchecked in Dade County.

■ ■ ■

A local controversy arose about who actually spoiled Zangara's aim and saved Roosevelt's life. At first the press credited Thomas Armour, but then it began to credit Lillian Cross, whom Roosevelt personally thanked. South Florida Congresswoman Ruth Bryan Owen (the daughter of William Jennings Bryan) suggested that Mrs Cross be awarded the Congressional Medal of Honor and North Florida Congressman Green agreed that "she should have, and she will have, a Congressional Medal of Honor." Roosevelt invited Mrs Cross to sit with his family and other important persons at the inauguration. She accepted, and brought her friend Mrs McCrary with her, telling reporters that she hoped to be invited by Mrs Roosevelt to tea at the White House. Young Tom Armour remembered that on her return she told the local press that Roosevelt had waved at her during the ceremonies. She later sold her story to a true crime magazine.

But in his sentencing testimony in court, Zangara said that no one attempted to stop him until after the shooting, although Mrs Cross had spoiled his aim by shaking the chair. "Nobody had my arm," Zangara testified. "Nobody take my arm, sure; one lady over there on my side when I try to shoot president on a little iron chair and when I try to shoot him the chair move because the lady, she move, and I missed the first shot and the lady try to get away. She no try to touch me because she was scared. She try to get away." About Armour, whom the state called to testify against him (they did not call Mrs Cross), Zangara said, "I no see a man. He told you I was in the bench; I was in an iron chair." Later he would blame the death of Cermak and the injuries of others on the woman who spoiled his aim.

In his death-house memoir, he writes:

> When I fired the first shot, the chair I was standing on moved and the result was that it caused me to spoil my aim, and at the distance of at least thirty feet to miss by one foot. I then tried to get my aim again but after I had fired the first shot the people crowded around the car and I could hardly see Roosevelt's head. I saw two heads in front of the President's and figured on firing another shot between those two heads but the bullet struck them both in the head. And this is what saved his life. This was also the reason for me shooting six people with a five shot gun.

Of course, he was inaccurate about hitting two victims in the head with one bullet, but he was hardly in a position to know the extent of his victims' injuries.

Months after the shooting, supporters of Armour wrote to their Congressmen, and even to Roosevelt, to contend that Mrs Cross had lied. Roosevelt was barraged with at least eight eyewitness affidavits. Even Armour's pastor at the Riverside Baptist Church wrote to former Congresswoman Ruth Bryan Owen, vouching for Armour's honesty. Armour himself signed an affidavit saying that he, not Mrs Cross, had grabbed Zangara's arm and that Mrs Cross had never touched the shooter. He had, in fact, he said, had to extricate her because she had gotten her foot caught in the chair.

> I sprang [Armour said in his affidavit] but before I could get him he fired the first shot. I grabbed his right arm, which held the gun, between the wrist and the elbow with my right

hand before the second shot exploded. I then pushed the arm which held the gun up in the air. An officer jumped over the benches from the front and knocked Zangara off the bench. . . . [I] then grabbed Zangara by the left arm and pulled him to his feet at the same time another man grabbed Zangara around his neck and began choking him and pulling him to the ground, which also caused me to fall down with Zangara. The officers then took charge of Zangara. [I] then noticed that a woman who was standing between me and Zangara at the beginning had fallen or been knocked from the bench and her foot was caught in the bench some way, and I assisted her in getting her foot from the bench, as she seemed about to break her ankle.

The day after the shooting, Armour was interviewed by the press. "Seeing that the policeman had him," he told reporters, "I got up in the confusion, with everyone mixed up trying to beat him and kick him, I thought they were killing the man as he quit struggling. Several more policemen came and I had an idea of walking out of it altogether, but several people pointed me out as the man who had 'saved the president.' So they took me up on the stage and made some pictures."

Raymond Jackson, the policeman who had lost his gun and his pay packet during the melee, later swore in an affidavit that it was a man who pushed Zangara's arm up. He said he did notice a woman to Zangara's immediate left, who, he thought, "had her hands up in the air waving as if she was about to fall."

Robert Donovan, a journalist who saw the Miami police report, which is now missing, wrote in 1954 that the police doubted Mrs Cross's story, reasoning "that if Zangara's arm had been forced up even an inch or two, he could never have hit five people standing below him on the ground."

There were several eyewitnesses who agreed with Zangara that no one had touched him until after the shooting. Ann McNamara of Miami, who, with her sister, was only four feet from Zangara when he began shooting, wrote U.S. Senator Duncan U. Fletcher that Mrs

Cross "positively did not touch Zangara's arm until after the last shot was fired, if she touched him at all. . . . All the world loves a hero," she wrote, "and I hesitate even now to disillusion anyone in this case. The spotlight is pleasing to most people and Mrs Cross seems to have basked in it. I do, however, believe that it would be wrong for me to remain silent and allow Congress to be taken in and the Congressional Medal degraded and cheapened."

Armour's son recalls that a "greasy northern" man approached his father that night, offering to agent his story of the shooting. The senior Armour summarily rejected this offer, but his son could not say whether this same man had made this offer to Mrs Cross. Dr Armour does remember Mrs McCrary prodding a reluctant Lillian Cross to step forward and tell her story. "I don't know why, but I remember I didn't like them," he says. "It seemed like she [Mrs McCrary] wanted Mrs Cross to do something she shouldn't."

Although the national media apparently wanted to credit the little housewife with saving the President's life, locally it was Thomas Armour who was considered the hero. He was the only involved bystander called to testify at Zangara's sentencing and was honored several years later at a banquet given at the Biltmore Hotel, where he was given a commendation from the Miami City Commission.

At first Thomas Armour behaved like the stalwart, modest hero who wished no recognition for his deed. But after a few years of reading and hearing that Lillian Cross was basking in what he had reason to believe was undeserved fame, he began to lobby Congress for a Medal of Honor for himself. He sent affidavits, testimonials and the city's commendation to senators and congressmen. When in 1939 he heard that Mrs Cross was to be a guest on "We The People," a national radio show hosted by broadcast icon Gabriel Heatter, Armour bombarded network executives with the testimonials and affidavits. He traveled to New York, after writing the networks that "I believe that I am entitled to a hearing prior to the broadcasting which you have already designated for Mrs Cross and

I believe that you will desire that I be afforded at least the same publicity that is being given her in order that the public may have the statement of facts from my own viewpoint."

But it was too late for the reluctant hero to attain glory and his subsequent behavior did not help his cause. The president, the press and the public continued to credit the housewife who had apparently lost her balance and shaken the chair she shared with Zangara, while the man who said he had grabbed Zangara's arm and thrust it upward, receded into obscurity. Lillian Cross's death in the 1950s was reported nationally, but only family and friends noticed Thomas Armour's passing in 1973.

What actually saved Franklin Roosevelt's life was probably the fact that Giuseppe Zangara stood only five feet, one inch tall. He could not see over the heads of the crowd, although his first shot, at least, was unimpeded. The same thing, he wrote later, had happened when he had tried to kill King Victor Emmanuel III of Italy some ten years earlier. Zangara says he was at the depot with a gun when the king arrived there, but he could not even see the king, whose guards were over six feet tall.

As an added bizarre note, Joseph Tomaszewski, the man with the big box camera, was arrested that night when he tried to tell detectives that he had saved FDR's life by raising his camera directly behind him, thus deflecting the first shot. The police were arresting anyone who seemed the least bit suspicious—or who had a foreign name. Tomaszewski was imprisoned for twenty hours but wrote to the President that he did not resent it, because he was proud of the service he, Tomaszewski, had rendered the nation.

4

ROAD TO RECOVERY

Anton J. Cermak was a Slovak who had emigrated to America as a child. Now fifty-nine years old, he was a successful businessman who had defeated the corrupt mayor of Chicago, William Hale "Big Bill" Thompson, two years earlier. He was a popular anti-Prohibition reformer and had made so many enemies fighting the Chicago underworld that he had to travel with bodyguards. He wanted to talk to Roosevelt and Jim Farley, the chairman of the Democratic Party, about Illinois patronage and, more especially, to ask for federal money to pay city employees. Because of the Depression, the city could not collect enough revenue to pay salaries for basic city services. Cermak had intended to have this discussion in Jacksonville before Roosevelt departed on the *Nourmahal*, but was not able to arrange it; he waited in Miami with his friend Chicago Alderman James Bowler for FDR's return. He had had to turn down an invitation by a prominent industrialist to go on a yacht trip to Cuba because the yacht was scheduled to leave two days before FDR's arrival.

Cermak had been staying with two bodyguards at a house on Miami Beach which he had bought eight years earlier. The modest two-story, three-bedroom cottage was used often by his three daughters and their families; the mayor himself had been too busy to spend more than a few days a year there.

Cermak was x-rayed the night of the shooting by Dr Gerald Raap, the radiologist on duty. This technology was an advantage that the assassinated president James Garfield had not had. That president had lingered for ten weeks before dying from a chest wound. His doctors tried to find the bullet through a magnetic induction device which located metal in the body by detecting minute changes in electric current. They thought the bullet was within an inch of the surface of the groin and treated him accordingly. To their dismay, an autopsy was to reveal that the bullet was actually lodged directly behind Garfield's heart. At the time doctors attributed the fact that the victim survived for two-and-a-half months to "good nursing."

Dr Raap noted in his report that the bullet had entered Cermak's right side "below the tip of the scapula and traveled downward toward the middle line and lies at the anterior margin of the eleventh dorsal vertebra." In other words, the doctor was saying the bullet entered through the lower rib cage just below the ninth rib. It had clipped the lower lobe of the right lung, causing it to collapse, traversed the diaphragm and the margin of the liver before lodging against the spinal column. The doctors concluded that the bullet would do no harm where it rested and decided therefore not to remove it—if at all—until after the patient had recovered. Unfortunately for Cermak, this analysis of the damage done by the bullet was incorrect, and the decision not to perform an exploratory operation was a fatal one. At the time his condition was listed as serious but not critical.

The morning after the shooting—Thursday, February 16—FDR came to Jackson Memorial Hospital in a motorcade protected by motorcycle police and Secret Service agents riding the running boards of the presidential vehicle. Crowds lined the route. At the hospital he was greeted by Superintendent Woodard, lifted from the car into a wheelchair and wheeled to Cermak's room in the east wing. Interns, doctors and nurses, including many from an adjacent nursing school, lined the corridors to watch Roosevelt go by.

"Tony, I hope you'll be up and around soon," FDR said to Cermak, who was awake and alert. "We'll need you at the inauguration."

Cermak said he too hoped to be at the inauguration, but he felt "pretty bad now." He advised Roosevelt to be more careful in public, and then went on to talk about the reason he had come to Miami in the first place. "He told me about the failure to collect taxes in Chicago for two years," Roosevelt said later. "The predicament of the teachers seemed to be the one thing that was troubling him." Roosevelt promised that he would attend to this matter soon after he was inaugurated. When word of this conversation got out, two hundred Chicago teachers met and passed a resolution praising the mayor for his action from his hospital bed on their behalf. And this was a promise that Roosevelt kept.

It was during this conversation that Cermak is supposed to have said to FDR, "I'm glad it was me instead of you." According to A.A. Dornfeld of the Chicago City News Bureau, these immortal words were put into Cermak's mouth by Chicago reporter John Dienhart who happened to be present at the shooting because he was a friend of Cermak's. (Since Cermak's bodyguards were all Chicago detectives who quickly phoned their headquarters with the bad news, it was Chicago police reporters who first put together the most comprehensive eyewitness accounts of the shooting.) In any case, it is probably safe to say that Cermak would certainly have said those words if he had thought of them.

Roosevelt visited all the wounded except Mabel Gill, who had undergone surgery the night before. (Most of the newspapers referred to her as "Mrs Joseph Gill.") Despite her critical condition, she allegedly sent a message to the president-elect: "Tell him that from my stretcher I salute him." Doctors had removed the bullet from the forehead of Bill Sinnott, the beefy New York policeman, whom Roosevelt knew from the New York governor's mansion. FDR told Sinnott that he was sure that no bullet could penetrate his thick skull, and that he had instructed the hospital staff to starve the policeman until he lost twenty pounds.

Roosevelt left the hospital to be driven to the Florida East Coast Railway station in downtown Miami, from which his private train was scheduled to leave at ten A.M. His departure had been delayed for exactly twelve hours because of the shooting. The station, a rambling, open structure, had been built in 1912, and was torn down in 1963. Although its middle section was two stories high, it consisted primarily of a platform set under an overhang next to the track. There was also a small waiting room. People had gathered all around the station and on the steps and veranda of the Dade County courthouse, one block north, when Roosevelt arrived shortly before ten o'clock: the Associated Press estimated the crowd at two thousand. As Roosevelt was helped from his car to the special railcar attached to the Havana Special, even the prisoners in the jail twenty-four floors above the courthouse cheered, if the *Miami Herald* is to be believed. Roosevelt doffed his hat and waved it over his head as an acknowledgment to the crowd before he entered his railway car.

Before the train left the station, FDR sent a telegram to President Hoover updating him on the condition of the victims: "THE MAYOR HAD A FAIR NIGHT AS DID MRS GILL STOP THE OTHER THREE ARE ON RAPID ROAD TO RECOVERY FRANKLIN D ROOSEVELT"

En route to New York, Roosevelt talked to the press about the shooting. When they had been driving for three blocks, he said, he actually thought Cermak's heart had stopped beating. "It seemed like twenty-five miles to the hospital. I talked to him all the way. I remember I said, 'Tony, don't move—keep quiet—it won't hurt if you keep quiet and remain perfectly still . . .'" He didn't actually see the shooter, he said: "The second time the car moved forward I saw a melee down on the ground and I assumed he was in that. The police did one quick and clever thing. When they got him up from the ground they saw the car in which Kermit, Vincent and Moley were riding, two cars behind mine, they threw the Italian on the trunk rack and three policemen sat on him all the way to the hospital. . . . As we started out, there was a great deal of shouting and pressing from every direction. By the time we got to the gate seventy-five feet away, the crowd there didn't know anything had happened. It was providential that my car went about thirty feet ahead before the crowd closed in. It would have been difficult to get the car out if we had not reached the corner of the bandstand."

The president-elect's train stopped in Palm Beach to pick up Joseph P. Kennedy who was courting Roosevelt for a position in the new administration. (He was later to head the Securities and Exchange Commission and then was appointed ambassador to Great Britain until his pro-Hitler attitudes ended his political career.) John McCooey, a Brooklyn politico, also boarded the train at Palm Beach to pay his respects. He remarked that he did not see why anyone would shoot at Roosevelt at that point; he could understand it, he said rather tactlessly, if Roosevelt had been in office for some time and had "displeased some of the people." "Oh, I'll do that all right," Roosevelt replied, with a wry smile.

The train stopped again at Jacksonville to pick up the governor of Florida, Dave Sholtz, and the state agricultural commissioner, Nathan Mayo, who accompanied FDR to New York. Both men were to play a prominent part in the aftermath of the Zangara incident: Mayo was the elected official in charge of the state prison system and was in charge of executions, while Governor Sholtz signed the death warrants.

At four P.M. the next day, Roosevelt was met at the Baltimore & Ohio depot in Jersey City by one thousand Secret Service agents and local policemen, an unprecedented security force. He was whisked in a closed car, part of a sixteen-car motorcade escorted by fourteen motorcycle police, from the Jersey City station to his home on East 65th Street in Manhattan. The route was lined with cheering crowds. He arrived to be greeted by his wife on the steps of their house with a simple hello, and then he left to attend the induction of one of his sons into the Masons. He rode in the same motorcade: eight Secret Service agents stood on the running boards with drawn pistols. The doors of the Masonic hall were bolted behind him, and those inside were permitted to get no closer to him than twenty-five feet.

Eleanor Roosevelt remained calm throughout this experience: the *Miami News* described her as "unflappable." "I never let anything worry me," she said. "I do not believe in advising what precautions are necessary for my husband. This incident has undoubtedly not disturbed him, except for his anxiety for those who were injured. As far as I am concerned, I cannot imagine living in fear of possible death. This is all I have to say on the subject." She refused extra security protection for herself as she carried on her usual schedule, giving speeches in upstate New York and at Cornell, and travelling by taxi in the city only a day or so after the shooting. But the country was awakened to the dangers facing the president. During the thirteen years that Roosevelt occupied the White House—years of intense economic turmoil and war—no one would ever come as close to killing him as Giuseppe Zangara had done in Bayfront Park.

News of the Wednesday night shooting made headlines around the world. In Rome, Benito Mussolini immediately ordered a police investigation of Zangara's past, while the Pope expressed his happiness at the president-elect's escape from injury. Telegrams of congratulation arrived from Madrid, Brussels, London, Budapest, Copenhagen, Bucharest, Mexico City, Paris and Dublin. In Vienna, the story covered the front pages of the newspapers, while in Prague large crowds milled in front of newspaper offices awaiting the posting of bulletins on Cermak's condition. The Stockholm paper *Social Demokraten* summed up the general feeling in the world: "The bullets aimed at Roosevelt carried the possibility of more serious consequences than those aimed at Lincoln and McKinley. Roosevelt today carries international as well as national hopes."

Friday morning, February 17, a one-and-a-half-inch headline informed readers of the *Chicago Tribune* that "Past Crisis; Cermak Rests." One of the initial attending physicians, Dr T.W. Hutson, reported that he was encouraged by Cermak's condition. Dr John W. Snyder, the surgeon in charge, put Cermak's chances of survival at fifty percent. Surgery, he said, was not indicated and, barring complications in the next three to four days, the mayor was expected to recover fully. "His chances for recovery," Dr Snyder announced, "improve hourly."

Both doctors—Hutson and Snyder—believed, along with Dr E. Sterling Nichol, that Cermak might die if the bullet were removed. He had no fever, his pulse was good and he had had a good night on Thursday. The doctors were awaiting the arrival of Chicago specialists for consultation. Snyder, who had been trained at the Mayo Clinic, was Miami's leading surgeon, a taciturn man who did not like to admit error. Hutson was also a respected surgeon and the son-in-law of Dr James M. Jackson, after whom Jackson Memorial Hospital was named. Soon after evaluating Cermak, Dr Hutson turned his attention to Mabel Gill, who was not expected to live; he was later credited with saving her life.

On Thursday, the day after the shooting, Cermak's relatives and friends, as well as politicians, detectives and reporters, were converging on Miami by rail and air. Five U.S. Army observation planes carrying two of Cermak's sons-in-law, two doctors and a Chicago detective, were forced down at Jacksonville by bad weather; the passengers completed their trip by rail. One Cermak daughter, Helen Cermak Kenlay, arrived by chartered plane at the airport and received a motorcycle escort into Miami. Dr Frank Jirka, who was Cermak's son-in-law and who would later head the Illinois Department of Health and the American Medical Association, was on his way, along with Dr Karl Meyer, superintendant of Chicago's Cook County Hospital. Governor Henry Horner of Illinois and his wife were due to arrive on Friday, bringing Cermak's two-year-old granddaughter, Mary Alyce. More than 2500 telegrams poured into the hospital from around the world and a virtual avalanche of flowers flooded its corridors.

"Tell Chicago I'll pull through," the mayor instructed reporters on Friday. "This is a tough old body of mine and a mere bullet isn't going to pull me down." But on Saturday Dr Walter W. Hamburger, a prominent heart specialist and Governor Horner's personal physician, had arrived from Chicago and examined Cermak's charts. "He still has a 50-50 chance to live," Dr Hamburger said. "Each day he lives means another day without a complication setting in and a resultant crisis. But he is still a very sick man. I don't like his heart action. The heart muscle is not good. His breathing is irregular, his sleep is fitful and his kidneys are not functioning normally, but they are better than they were." He remarked that the mayor was not as robust as he appeared to be.

Cermak had supposedly suffered a heart attack a year earlier, which had weakened his heart. But the amount of strain Cermak's heart was to withstand in the weeks to come has raised a question among experts today about whether the mayor's heart was as weak as it was thought to be in 1933.

The hospital issued a bulletin on Saturday night, February 13: "Mayor Cermak is steadily improving. The possibility of complications appears remote. His general condition is satisfactory." But one of the doctors complained that the mayor had spent a restless Saturday night because of "too many visitors." Nevertheless, Cermak received Governor Horner on Sunday morning.

By Monday, Mrs Gill's condition had improved, but Cermak had a fever and the doctors said he appeared to be suffering from colitis; Jim Bowler, a friend of his, had told them that was a chronic condition. The doctors informed the family, gathered at the mayor's bedside, that he was "steadily progressing toward recovery."

On Tuesday Dr Karl Meyer, who had treated Cermak in the past, announced that the lung wound had healed and the lung had expanded to a normal size. The liver was also functioning normally and there was no sign of pneumonia. The press called Meyer "a noted specialist in gunshot wounds." "I am convinced," the doctor said, "the crisis definitely passed. Of course," he added, "we cannot foresee what might develop." Cermak's severe intestinal pain was still thought to be colitis or possibly enteritis.

Also on Tuesday, Cermak held a full-blown press conference from his hospital bed. His voice weak, the mayor announced that he was more concerned with problems in Chicago than with his own recovery. He signed some legislation; his signature was a feeble scrawl. The *Chicago Tribune* published copies of the mayor's signature before and after the shooting for purposes of contrast.

By Wednesday, February 22, a week after the shooting, Cermak's temperature was over 101 and his intestinal pain was severe. The doctors prescribed painkillers and sleeping pills and remained optimistic.

So it went. During the following week Cermak's doctors noted improvements and setbacks, but predicted recovery, "barring unforeseen circumstances." By February 24, the mayor was given an 80-20 chance for recovery. At that time, before the use of antibiotics, the body fought off infection with its natural defenses and with the help of "good nursing."

5

"TYPICAL OF HIS BREED"

The Dade County courthouse, completed in 1928, was for decades the South's tallest building; it was called, in fact, "the skyscraper courthouse" before the age of the ubiquitous glass towers. It is a twenty-four story granite eclectic neoclassic structure with porticos, columns, rusticated walls, surrounded by a wide veranda and capped by a grey stepped pyramid in the ziggurat style that became popular after the opening of King Tut's tomb in the early twenties. A granite staircase leads to the veranda and to what in 1933 may have been the only revolving front doors in south Florida. High ceilings over the central lobby were set with mosaics depicting the Great Seal of Florida and the *Niña*, the *Pinta* and the *Santa Maria*. This building was the pride of Dade County and the site of county government.

Until 1960, the nineteenth to the twenty-fourth floors of the courthouse held the Dade County jail. Prisoners took exercise in a sort of walled walkway circling the outside of the twenty-fourth floor; the walkway was caged with curved iron bars to prevent suicides. Until other buildings obscured it in the 1970s, the view from this balcony, as indeed from the jail cells themselves, was the best in Miami.

The night of February 15, 1933, was an electric one in the "Magic City"; the air was charged with excitement as news of the assassination attempt was flashed around the globe. The courthouse, a beehive of activity, was surrounded by curious crowds. Since the train station from which FDR was to have left Miami that night was no more than two hundred yards north of the courthouse, there were already an estimated two thousand people waiting there to see him off. Bayfront Park was less than half a mile away, directly east of the courthouse at the end of Flagler Street; crowds from the park were moving to the building. In fact, the bands, honor guards and drum and bugle corps, unaware at first of what had happened, had begun their scheduled parade up Flagler Street to the depot as FDR was driven hurriedly from the park.

It was after ten o'clock that Wednesday night that Zangara was brought to the jail, amidst much confusion. Swarming through the halls of the courthouse were city officials, county and state prosecutors, court clerks and stenographers, all called to duty, along with a host of newspaper reporters, cameramen, dozens of policemen, sheriff's deputies, FBI agents and at least three Secret Service agents. In addition, New York and Chicago detectives were in the building, along with some members of Roosevelt's entourage. Most of the national newspeople had missed the shooting because they were waiting at the train station; now they had rushed to the courthouse to cover the story. In those days the public learned about fast-breaking stories through "extra" editions of newspapers. A *Miami Herald* "extra" hit the streets twenty minutes after the shooting because a *Herald* reporter who had seen the shooting ran four blocks to a hotel pay phone to file his story.

Outside the courthouse and in the park, police were arresting anyone who looked suspicious, bringing them to the courthouse or to the police station across the street. The Chicago police reacted to news of the shooting by asking the local police to arrest some Chicago mobsters who were known to be in Miami, a request the Miami police refused to honor. But they did take many people into custody that night: all were interrogated and released, including several of Zangara's acquaintances.

Zangara was driven down a sloping driveway that ran through the courthouse and led directly to the basement—a rarity in Miami where water lies only a few feet under the city's limestone base—where elevators to the jail tower were located. Zangara describes his reception at the jail:

> When we arrived at the jail he [one of the policemen] threw me on the stone pavement like a dog. After a while they took all of my clothes away and left me nude. A little while after, they gave me a shirt and pants. A girl came to visit me and she had to write down everything I had to say. After she left, they took my shirt and pants away again and left me nude. They kept me nude until the next day. The county police then took me to a room that was just like a hotel room. While I was kept in this room people were coming to see me day and night, and would take pictures of me.

He was bruised and bleeding. Much of his clothing had been torn off at the park; the police stripped him of the rest and kept him naked, giving him a towel to wrap around his torso so that pictures could be taken. He was a gnome-like figure with the body of a twelve-year-old. The *Miami Herald* described him as "a swarthy Italian, typical of his breed."

His English was very poor, and he did not always understand the questions, but Zangara was eager to answer questions and remained cheerful, calm and cooperative. The *Herald* emphasized his accent and bad grammar through misspelling and rearrangement of his words when they quoted him. He was asked whether he liked Roosevelt, and the *Herald* quoted him: "As a man I like Meester Roosevelt, but as a president I want to keel him."

45

Some newspapers, far from attempting to mimic Zangara's English, gave him a facility with the language which he did not possess.

It was not clear to the people in the jail that night whether Zangara understood the gravity of his actions. He could speak comprehensible English, but he did not always grasp what was said to him. Among other bizarre events, there was the *Herald*'s statement that Sheriff Hardie spoke "Italian" to the prisoner. When Hardie attempted to introduce the mayor of Miami, it did not appear that Zangara understood what the sheriff was saying. So, according to the *Herald*, Hardie repeated the introduction in Italian. The paper reported that Zangara's face lit up. "Ah, yes," Zangara reportedly said, "*el mayor*, how do you do." Since the Italian for "the mayor" is *il sindaco*, one wonders what kind of Italian the sheriff, to say nothing of the reporter, spoke.

That night, a young New York *Mirror* gossip columnist got the first interview with Zangara, but was subsequently cheated out of his scoop. Walter Winchell, who happened to be in Miami, was in the Western Union office filing his column when news of the shooting came in, he immediately rushed to the police station across the street from the county courthouse and asked the desk sergeant where where the gunman could be found. "You might try the jail," the officer said. Winchell ran to the courthouse basement, where he bribed the elevator operator with a dollar to take him to the nineteenth floor. There he encountered the police chief who, on the strength of Winchell's promise to spread his name across the front pages of the world press, allowed the columnist to interview Zangara in his cell, even before the official interrogation began. After that, Winchell hurried back to the telegraph office and typed out the story and handed it to the teletype operator for transmission to New York. Then he went back to his hotel room, feeling good about himself, a gossip columnist who had scooped the nation's veteran reporters.

What he did not know was that his column had been added to a pile awaiting its turn for transmission. The city's publicity director saw it in the pile and lifted quotes out of it to give to the Associated Press and various other reporters. By the time Winchell's interview got to New York, his editor at the *Mirror* had already read the quotes in the extras which were on the street. So he killed it.

As if that were not bad enough, the editor sent Winchell a bill for eleven dollars for the telegraph costs. Winchell was so enraged that he complained directly to the *Mirror*'s publisher, William Randolph Hearst, who simply advised him that he had to "get along" with his co-workers. Years later, when Winchell was so popular, and it was estimated that one-fifth to one-third of the *Mirror*'s readers bought the tabloid just because of his column, Hearst paid a rare visit to the paper and, according to Winchell, walked into his office to introduce himself and handed the columnist eleven dollars, saying, "This is long overdue."

Jack Bell, a popular *Herald* columnist, gave the first description of the would-be assassin. "The little Italian, defiant at first, sat quiet and almost courteous as they questioned him. . . . His bulging eyes dilate in the dim light as he speaks. His hair, dark and curly, is awry. He sits on a narrow bench, nude after the officers have removed his clothing to search for other messengers of death. . . . His bone-like arms are taut, his fingers are clasped around two slender, brown knees. His face is dark, the heavy growth of beard common to his race showing prominently."

Zangara talked quietly and openly. He was bitter only when he spoke of rich men and the oppression of working people. He said that he stood for the working man and against presidents and kings and all rich people "who tread the poorer people under their feet." He would have been glad if he had killed the president, he said; "rich men send their children to school and when I was a young man, rich men's sons went to school while I worked in a brick factory in Italy and burned myself." He pointed to a six-inch scar across the right side of his abdomen. He said it was the result of a "stomach operation" connected with his injury.

He was, he said, thirty-three years old, an unemployed brick-layer who had come to Hackensack, New Jersey, nine years earlier from Calabria. He had become a U.S. citizen in 1929 and had never been in jail before. His only relative in America was an uncle who lived in Paterson, New Jersey. Between 1918 and 1923 he had served twice in the Italian army, the first time probably as a conscripted laborer digging trenches at the front line and after the war as an infantryman assigned to an officer as his valet. He was, he said, neither a Communist nor an anarchist and belonged to no organizations except the bricklayers' union, a part of the American Federation of Labor. He was an atheist. No one, he said, had encouraged him to make the attack, nor had he discussed his plans with anyone. He said that he had no friends.

The central fact of his life was the chronic abdominal pain which tormented him. "Sometimes I get a beeg pain in my stomach," the *Herald* quoted him as saying, "and then I want to keel these presidents who oppress the working man." His father, he said, had forced him to work when he was six years old. His stomach problems began then. He writes later:

> I remember my father not having much money in those days to buy animals. At one time he bought one cow and rented another one for three years from a man by the name of Antonio Romeo. During the next three years I worked for that man. He worked with the livestock and I had to do the hoeing. This work was too heavy for me at that age [between five and seven years]. One day we lost one of the cows. When my father found out about it he beat me and kicked me like a dog, and told me I was not working hard enough. From that day on he worked me so hard I became sick. I was beaten and starved and overworked when I should have been going to school, and eat and sleep like other children. That was when my stomach trouble started.

As the years passed, the pain had become so severe that it frequently drove him to distraction. He could not work; he could not eat. He had come to Miami because the warm weather alleviated the problem, which was worse in cold weather. The pain dominated his life: he was not interested in people, male or female. If it had not been for capitalism and greedy rich men, he said, he would never have had to work as a child and thus would not have received the injury that caused his unrelenting agony. If it were not for kings and presidents, he would have been able to go to school. Since his life was not worth living, he said, he was going to get even with the world by killing a president.

That night the county doctor, E.C. Thomas, gave Zangara a superficial examination, concluding that the prisoner was "normal in every respect" and even went so far as to say that the man was sane, suffering only from "nervous gastritis induced by fright." Everyone else who was there agreed that Zangara appeared to be rather bewildered, but not frightened: he seemed pleasant, cooperative and even cheerful. It is possible that if the doctor had ascribed the gastritis to stress or anxiety instead of fear, he might have been more accurate. It is certainly impossible to diagnose Zangara from this distance, but it is clear that he was a disturbed person and that he was in real pain. No one cared much about the cause of his pain, either before or after his execution, but his autopsy was to reveal that he had a diseased gall bladder. It is possible that a recent onset of gall bladder pain made his chronic agony unbearable and drove him to behave irrationally. This is, of course, mere speculation.

He never expressed any remorse for his actions. He would say in Italian, "*Ho ragione io . . .* I am right!" He would go to his death infuriating the authorities by steadfastly maintaining that he was certainly sorry—sorry that he had missed Roosevelt. On rare occasions he would express some regret that he had hit bystanders. The key to his actions may lie in his matter-of-fact statement, "My life is ended."

It is difficult to analyze the depth of conviction Zangara possessed for his political beliefs, such as they were. Wracked by what he believed to be an incurable abdominal condition—which may have been psychologically induced—abused as a child by his father, painfully diminutive in stature and having no moral compass, Zangara hated authority figures with deadly fury. Perhaps he saw in them his father's brutality and neglect, although he did not openly blame his father. He responded to life's cruelties by inventing his own political theory. He repeatedly claimed that it was his "own idea." "My idea," he would say. In the murky explanations of how his "idea" worked, he would mix philosophical anarchism with socialism. In the end, only hours before his execution, he would advocate the formation of a "civil society of Communism." Clearly, he was unread in any political theory; he freely admitted that. He did not read books, he said. What he knew about politics is what he may have picked up from other men while sipping *vino* in the cafes of Naples and Rome, or while playing checkers in Paterson and Hackensack. To add to the confusion, there is the fact that Zangara was a registered Republican who voted in the off-year elections in New Jersey in 1930 and reregistered as a Republican in California in 1931. Whatever his political beliefs, there is no doubt he at least gave the appearance of self-assurance to the bitter end. While his "idea" seemed improvised, whatever it actually was, he was willing to die for it.

6

THE BILINGUAL SHERIFF

It was after midnight on Thursday, February 16, but the day was not yet over for Giuseppe Zangara. After his harrowing ride on the trunk rack of Roosevelt's car, he had been stripped, searched, photographed, examined by the county physician and informally questioned by the sheriff, presidential advisors, Secret Service agents and reporters. He had met the mayor of Miami. Now he was in a jail cell in the southeast corner of the twenty-first floor of the county courthouse with Sheriff Hardie, Vernon Hawthorne the state attorney, Charles Morehead the county solicitor, two Secret Service agents, a stenographer and Roosevelt's private secretary, Marvin McIntyre. Hardie questioned Zangara for nearly an hour, and the interrogation was transcribed.

Dixie Herlong was the stenographer. She was a twenty-four-year-old lawyer who had been unable to make a living at that male-dominated profession in those Depression years. Since her mother had insisted on her learning shorthand in case she could not succeed at what was thought of as a man's profession, she had been able to find employment as a stenographer for Justice of the Peace Thomas Ferguson. As she and her mother were walking toward the courthouse about nine-thirty that evening on their way to the station to see FDR off, they heard about the shooting. Since her office was across the street from the courthouse, Dixie Herlong went there and phoned the sheriff's office; she was told that she was needed.

With the exception of one question asked by George Broadnax, the Secret Service agent, and several by prosecutor Vernon Hawthorne, the interrogation was conducted by Hardie, the newly elected (and soon to be removed) county sheriff. The newspapers called Hardie "something of a linguist"; what they found impressive, apparently, was that Hardie was speaking to Zangara in the same broken English that Zangara was speaking to Hardie. The only foreign words Hardie used were Spanish: *hombre* and *amigos*.

The transcript is a study in the provincialism of early twentieth-century southern towns, reflecting their prejudices and patronization of races considered to be "inferior." Sheriff Hardie was an obviously inexperienced interrogator who jumped erratically from topic to topic, leaving a subject and returning to it, often asking the same question again and again.

Zangara was uneducated, but he was not stupid. He answered each question promptly and without raising his voice. Raymond Moley found him intelligent and was impressed by the fact that Zangara had passed all the tests required for naturalization and had been naturalized only six years after his arrival in the United States. In those days a great deal more was required of applicants for naturalization than is required now. Two levels of testing in English proficiency, U.S. history and government had to be completed in a satisfactory manner.

The interview began with Sheriff Hardie informing Zangara of his rights. In 1933, the police were required to inform a defendant of his rights before obtaining a confession. But the accused was not entitled to a free lawyer, either before or after questioning. The methods of obtaining confessions were not carefully proscribed: this was the era of the third degree and the rubber hose.

Dixie Herlong recalls that Zangara's English was poor, but she has said that she customarily improved the grammar of people whose statements she transcribed. In those days, before radio had begun to homogenize American speech, there were regional accents and dialects which often made these statements difficult to understand; thus Dixie Herlong had fallen into the habit of "translating" this kind of speech, and consequently it appears from her transcript that Zangara had a better command of English than he actually did. This is obvious when one reads the transcript of Zangara's testimony at his second sentencing several weeks later. In parts of that testimony, transcribed by a court reporter who made no attempt to improve it, Zangara's English is often virtually incomprehensible.

"Joe," the sheriff began, "you understand that when you talk to me and you tell me about yourself that maybe I will go into court and the big judge, he ask me what Joe said and I tell him Joe said, 'I want to kill the president. I shoot the pistol. Yes, I kill president—I tried. I want to kill him because I hate government. If he didn't [die] I am sorry, sorry I didn't kill him. So if I kill him I am glad.' Then I say to you, if you tell me that, maybe I have to go in court and remember what you say. You say, 'I don't care'—"

Zangara interrupted. "No, I don't care. I'm half dead now because the capitalists, they make me this way."

This theme recurred when Hardie asked whether Zangara was "scared" that night. He replied that he was not. What, Hardie asked, was he going to do? Walk away? No, Zangara said, he wasn't going to walk away.

"You wasn't scared of all those people?"

"No," Zangara replied, "Why? I'm half dead now. What's the use of living? I'm half dead from capitalists."

He would not, he said, shoot the police or the sheriff to get away. He would not, he replied in response to more of Hardie's questions, shoot Henry Ford either, or governors or rich bankers or a "a rich man's baby" or the president's children. "Why kill them?" he asked. He just wanted to kill the president. "He's a good man but he is president."

"You like the president's children to see their papa dead?" Hardie asked, "Their papa?"

"I don't want to, no. But they wouldn't care for me. Capitalists wouldn't care for me."

"Joe, I ask you questions," the sheriff said. "Before you tell me—see, if this man die—if somebody die you shoot, I hang you. That will be too bad for you. If you like me all right you tell me the truth."

"I tell you the truth."

Hardie pointed to State Attorney Hawthorne, saying, "This big man is big lawyer—*grande* lawyer."

"I understand," Zangara said. "Speak in English."

But Hardie continued to refer to Hawthorne as the "*grande* lawyer" and to the judge as "the big judge." After Zangara was sworn in, Hardie asked him, "When did you want to kill president—how long ago?"

Zangara replied that he "got this idea when I was seventeen years."

"Seventeen years ago?" Hardie asked.

"No, seventeen years—I was sixteen."

Hardie then turned to the question of when and where Zangara purchased the gun and how he knew the time of Roosevelt's arrival. Zangara responded that he had bought the gun at a pawn shop on North Miami Avenue; he was not sure of the exact day. He said he had read about Roosevelt's arrival in the newspaper the day before. Hardie asked him whether he could read English; Zangara assured him that he could.

"The president came today," Hardie said. "You bought it [the gun] this morning?"

Zangara said he bought it "yesterday . . . or day before yester-day. Maybe day before yesterday."

"Joe, when you bought the pistol did you look in the paper to see president was coming and then you buy pistol?"

"I think that was about—before or after I don't remember."

"In the store where you bought the pistol—was he a Jew?"

"Yes."

"Did you tell him why you bought the pistol?"

"No."

"Did he ask you why you bought it?"

"No, he get the money. That's all he wanted."

It is significant that Zangara could not seem to remember *when* he bought the pistol. It would appear that he bought it *before* he knew that Roosevelt was coming to Miami.

The gun was a used, nickel-plated .32 calibre double action, top-breaking revolver with black checkered hard rubber grips. A flat metal strip holding a flute or groove ran the length of the barrel and ended the rounded front sight. The rear sight was a square notch. Zangara had bought ten bullets with the gun and had fired five of them. There was some confusion about what happened to the other five bullets: it was speculated that he might have used them for target practice before the actual shooting. One newspaper reported that the five bullets had been found in Zangara's pocket when he was arrested. Zangara said later that a "capitalist" had come to the jail and asked him for permission to sell the gun, but Zangara had told him he was not interested.

"Did you shoot the president when he stood up and make speech," Hardie said, "or when he sit down?"

"When he make speech I didn't have a chance . . . because there was people in front. I jumped on a chair. I thought he might speak a long time—about twenty minutes. He said just one second—just like that—ba-ba-ba—quick that way. When I see him speak in auto-mobile I don't get a chance."

"Was anybody with you? No friends?"

"No."

"No *amigos*?"

"No."

"Nobody in Miami?"

"No, no place."

Several witnesses in the park said that Zangara was with another man when he pushed his way to the front of the crowd. There were news reports the next day that three men, alleged associates of the shooter, were arrested that night. Their names were given only by the *New York Times* and the New York Italian daily, *Il Progresso Italo-Americano*: Steve Valenti, mistakenly identified as Zangara's cousin, and Andrea Valenti and Lorenzo Grandi, both described as acquaintances of Zangara. One—possibly Valenti—was reported to be a cigar maker who lived in or near Zangara's rooming house. These three men were released the following morning. The *Miami Herald* reported both the arrests and the releases that morning but only the *Il Progresso* did any follow-up when it published a letter, several days later, from Lorenzo Grandi denying that he was Zangara's friend. Police reports of the arrests have been lost, and Sheriff Hardie did not pursue this point. He went on to ask about the shooting itself: "When you shot, Joe, how many times did you shoot?"

"Two or three times."

"Two or three times?"

"Yes, I told you."

"Did you want to kill other people too?"

"No, just him."

"Did you know you might shoot other people?"

"No, just him. Just president."

"Why do you want to kill president?"

"Because the president rich people—capitalists spoil me when I'm six years old."

"Do you hate President Roosevelt as a man?"

"As a man I like him all right."

"But as a president?"

"President," Zangara said. "Always the same bunch."

The sheriff attempted to probe his prisoner's political philosophy. "Do you like anarchism?" he asked.

"No," Zangara said, "Foolish."

What about socialism?

"No, more foolish."

Nor did Zangara like Communism. He had never been to Russia, he said. And he didn't like Fascism. He didn't like Mussolini, either.

"Joe," Hardie said, "would you kill the president now if you had a chance?"

"Sure," Zangara said.

At this point George Broadnax, the Secret Service agent, possibly projecting his own fantasy, interrupted to ask Zangara if he wanted to kill Sheriff Hardie. Zangara said he would not, because he did not care to kill workingmen like himself.

On the subject of religion, Zangara testified that he did not believe in God or Jesus Christ. Asked what he believed in, he responded, "The land, the sky, the moon—what I see."

"Who make the world?" Hardie inquired.

"Nobody knows," Zangara said. He didn't believe in God, he said, "because I see lots of things I see in my mind—everything wrong—somebody trying to kill and steal and everything wrong. I figure no God—no nothing. Only air and land. I feel to myself that. If there was a God here, why I suffer all the time? Everything wrong."

His father was a Catholic, he said, but he was not. "I wasn't in a church. I used to go some of the time. When I was young boy I go to church with my father. I go for fun."

Hardie attempted to probe Zangara's feelings toward his father.

"Joe," Hardie asked, "Do you like your father or do you hate him? You love your father?"

Zangara's reply was indistinct and confusing. He said "I don't know much" or perhaps "He don't know much."

"He make you work?"

"He didn't have brains—no—no—"

"No education? No school?"

"No education. No."

"How much you go to school?"

"I never been," Zangara said, and elaborated on this point. "I got started going to school and my father wasn't able and I had five years. My father was over here. I was two months in school. My father come and take me out like this (reportedly grabbing himself by the collar and say, 'You don't need no school. You need to work.' He take me out of school. Lawyers ought to punish him—that's the trouble—he send me to school and I don't have this trouble. Government."

A few days after his father pulled him out of school, he said, a carriage passed him as he was shovelling dirt beside the road. It was filled with children on their way to school and that bitter memory had stayed with him. The change he hoped to bring about when he shot at Roosevelt was "new government. No money so everybody is same like. Everybody just the same as the country. I have no sick stomach because I have the right to go to school same as everybody else. Then the children of the capitalists make no difference. All born equal. All people just the same. All people can read just the same."

"Joe," the sheriff asked, "if you kill a man you don't care if you die or where you go?"

"No," Zangara said; he had no soul. And heaven or hell? "No," he said. "I go in ground."

From religion, Hardie shifted to Zangara's employment and union connections, asking whether the prisoner worked. Yes, Zangara replied; he was a bricklayer and yes, he was a union man. He had been one since he had come to this country.

"Joe, you like the union?"

"No. What is the difference?"

"Why did you go into the union?"

"Because if I don't go into union I don't get no job."

"Do you belong to any associations?"

"No, I told you the truth. However I do I tell you."

"When did you lay bricks for the last time?"

"Two years now since I did."

"Why don't you work for two years?"

"Because I can't find no job."

In fact, Zangara had worked almost steadily from the time of his arrival in the United States in 1923 until perhaps the onset of the Depression in 1929 when he began to travel. He earned good money on some large projects in New Jersey and New York.

He had been in Miami for two or three months, he said, and had come by bus. He had been living in a third-floor attic of a two-dollar-a-week rooming house at 126 Northeast 5th Street near Bayfront Park. The police found a cheap suitcase holding all his possessions. Apart from clothing, there were newspaper clippings: several discussing Roosevelt's impending visit and one reporting that FDR had taken out a $500,000 life insurance policy with the Warm Springs spa as beneficiary. There was also a clipped article about Lincoln's assassination. In addition to citizenship papers and bank books, there were three grammar manuals.

"You have money?" Hardie asked. Zangara said he had none. "How much money you got?" Hardie persisted.

"A little in the post office."

"How much?"

"Two hundred dollars. More than that. I have forty-five dollars in my pocket when police took me." His savings, he said, were "two thousand and a half."

Zangara gave the impression that he was frugal and had been living on his savings. His relatives and friends in New Jersey called him "stingy." In his memoir he writes:

I never was able to save any money because I used to spend it as fast as I made it in order to forget my troubles. Whenever I went out with any girls, I used to buy them whatever they wanted. My friends believed that I had lots of money, but the truth is that I spent all the money just as fast as I made it because my money did me no good and I suffered all the time so I wanted to spend my money in order for me to forget my [sickness].

Toward the end of the interrogation, Hardie appeared to be trying to trap Zangara. "Joe, you say to one man that if you don't kill the president tonight, your friends kill you tomorrow. You say that?"

"What?"

"You say your friends kill you tomorrow? You think that?"

"No," Zangara said.

"You don't tell no man that?"

"No."

"Some more Italian friends that know you, kill the president?"

"You mean crowd of people in park?"

"No," Hardie said. "Your crowd."

"No," Zangara said. "I don't belong to them. No party."

State Attorney Hawthorne asked him how long he was going to stary in Miami.

"It won't be long," Zangara said, prophetically.

Since there was some problem with the address Zangara had given for his rooming house, Hardie asked if he would take him to the address.

"Yes," Zangara said. "I no go away. You no have to lock me. No use. I am safe. What's the use to go away? I no like to go away."

7

BACKGROUND

The day after the shooting, the *New York Times* reported that W.H. Moran, director of the Secret Service, following consultation with his agents on the scene, had come to the conclusion that Zangara was "not a maniac, but a member of a recognized anarchist group making its headquarters in Paterson, New Jersey." At that time, Paterson was known to have been a hotbed of anarchist groups. But the next day the *Times* said that "after a close investigation" the Service had discovered that Zangara "had no connection with any political group or organization." He was "a lonesome, morose character, sorely beset by a chronic stomach ailment since 1923, but with no particular grudge against the government."

President Herbert Hoover ordered the State and Justice Departments to examine Zangara's immigrant status: since he was a U.S. citizen, he could not be deported unless it could be shown that he had lied on his visa or citizenship applications or violated the citizenship oath to uphold and defend the Constitution. The Newark divisional director of the Naturalization Bureau, H.P. Woertendyke, announced that his office would investigate to determine if Zangara could be deported, saying, "If we can prove that he is a Communist or an anarchist, we can institute an equity suit in federal court here to cancel his citizenship." Speeches were given on the floors of both the House and Senate, expressing the hope that Zangara's citizenship could be revoked. Hoover, frustrated by the fact that shooting a president was not a federal crime, ordered federal authorities to assist local authorities with their investigation and prosecution of Zangara.

Inevitably, immediately after the shooting, there arose, especially in Chicago, speculation that the intended victim had actually been Anton Cermak, and not Roosevelt. The *New York Times* reported that the Chicago police wanted Florida authorities to arrest eighteen Chicagoans known to be in Miami, twelve of whom were associates of the imprisoned mob boss Al Capone. The Miami police refused to honor this request because there were no grounds for the arrests. Robert Donovan, who saw the police reports, says that the Miami police never "put any stock" in the theory that Chicago gangsters had hired Zangara to kill Cermak. The Cook County State Attorney said, "My only official interest was to learn whether there were any Chicago gangsters involved. Evidently there was none." In Hackensack and Paterson, police and Secret Service agents interviewed Zangara's uncle and all his known acquaintances, co-workers and landlords, while agents on the West Coast questioned acquaintances in Los Angeles and San Diego.

On Saturday, February 18, the *Chicago Tribune* reported that the FBI had received a copy of Zangara's fingerprints the day before and they had been "carefully checked against the 3,000,000 criminal prints on file"—a formidable task even in the age of the computer. The check failed to disclose any match for a criminal record in the United States. Federal authorities determined, in the few hours after the shooting, that there were eleven Joseph Zangaras living in the country and there were outstanding deportation warrants against two of them. Neither one was the Joseph Zangara in the Dade County jail. It was reported from Morristown, New Jersey, that a Joe Zangara had been arrested in 1931 for drunkenness, but no fingerprints or photographs had been taken, so it could not be known whether this was the Joe Zangara under suspicion. According to those who knew him, Zangara did not drink.

In Italy, responding to Zangara's claim that he had tried to kill King Victor Emmanuel III ten years earlier, authorities searched for evidence of such an attempt. The only attempts on the king's life which could be discovered had occurred in 1912 when Zangara was twelve years old, and again in 1928 when he was in the United States. The bizarre notion was briefly entertained that Zangara had been linked to the Serbian nationalist who had shot the Archduke Ferdinand in Sarajevo, sparking the World War, but since the Dade County Zangara would have been only thirteen years old in 1914, it was decided that it was undoubtedly another Zangara who was an associate of the Serb.

The Italians told American authorities that they could find no arrest record for Zangara. But later, just days before Zangara's execution in March, the State Department received information from Italy that an arrest record had been located. In a communique, the U.S. Consul General in Naples quoted the findings of the Royal Italian Inspector of Emigration in that city: Zangara had been "sentenced by the Praetor of Brancaleone, under date of October 24, 1921, to twelve days detention for carrying an illegal knife, which sentence was suspended for eighteen months, in accordance with law." The Royal Inspector added that his investigation revealed that "Zangara had a good moral and political record, and was never a member of any political party." It is not known whether the Italian authorities interviewed Zangara's family and friends in Calabria.

In the United States, the investigation into Zangara's past and character was conducted primarily by the Secret Service, since that branch of the Treasury Department has responsibility for the protection of the president's life. Secret Service agents fanned out across the country, from Newark to Los Angeles, to interview anyone who might have known Zangara. They compiled a three-volume file which probably contained interviews, depositions, local police reports, photographs and the results of any Italian investigation. In addition, agents must have contributed insights gained by them when they attended all court hearings and stayed close to the state penitentiary in north Florida where Zangara was transported. However, the file is not available. The Secret Service says that it was sent to the White House in August 1945, and is apparently lost. So most of what is known about Zangara's life in Italy comes from his death-house memoir.

In thirty-four "chapters," many no more than a single paragraph, Zangara tells his life story, and it is difficult to assess its accuracy. There are conflicts between the memoir and known facts about timespans and some details, but there appear to be no obvious lies or contradictions in the document. He leaves out a great deal and of course it is a self-serving work. But this biography can be used in combination with interviews and statements from those who knew him in America to create an outline of his life.

Calabria, the province of Italy comprising the toe of the boot, is hot, dry, rocky and hilly. It was populated in the first half of the century largely by poor farmers and fishermen, its principal products being fish and olives. On September 7, 1900, Giuseppe Zangara was born to Rose, née Cafaro, and her husband Salvatore, a farmer from the town of Ferruzzano, on the Mediterranean Sea. Shortly after his birth, doctors operated on the baby to correct a defect in one of his ears. His mother, Zangara writes, commented that because of this he was "bad luck." Two years later his mother died in childbirth. When he was three, he was injured falling down two flights of stairs and when he was four he fell into a fire and was burned. These things, he thought, bore out his mother's opinion of him as "bad luck."

When Giuseppe was a child, his father travelled frequently to the United States, apparently to earn money to improve his life at home. Salvatore had no use for education: whether his father was at home or in America, he instructed Giuseppe's caretakers that the boy was to work in the fields and tend the stock. He was not to go to school. According to Zangara, his father physically abused him, sometimes beating him into unconsciousness for minor transgressions. His abdominal pain Zangara attributed to this abuse, but as an adult he openly focused his hostility on remote authority figures, and not directly on Salvatore.

When Giuseppe was seventeen, he left home for the first time, doing some undescribed work in the town of Giamoto, Cotrona, a little to the north of Ferruzzano. From there he began to travel, working in various towns in Calabria. He always wanted to travel, he wrote, and was very restless. Later, travel was to be his one strong interest.

At the age of eighteen, during the first World War, Zangara says he was sent to the front lines to build trenches "near Monte Grappo, Dalmatia." He gives the impression that he was inducted into the army as a laborer rather than as a soldier. In any case, the war ended just nine weeks after his eighteenth birthday, and he remained in northern Italy for a short time helping, he says, to rebuild an unnamed city which had been bombarded by the Germans. By the time he returned home, he had "picked up some knowledge of the stonemason's trade." His father immediately put him to work building a house for him. After the house was built, Zangara sought work at his new trade elsewhere in the area, but everyone told him that he should be working for his father. "Thus," he writes, "my hard luck continued."

On October 24, 1921, three weeks after his twenty-first birthday, Zangara had his only known brush with the law. The twelve-day suspended sentence he received may have had something to do with his impending induction into the army, because he says that at age twenty-one he was drafted, this time as a soldier. At that time, military service was compulsory in Italy.

Zangara disliked army life. His stomach seemed to hurt most when he held a rifle. Assigned to the 70th Infantry Regiment, he received basic training at Arezzo, a camp in Tuscany in north central Italy. "We drilled and marched every morning. This was hard on me because I was always suffering from the stomachache." Army doctors told him that his condition was "chronic," and there was no cure. He says he was told that the problem had been caused by his working too hard when he was a child. Later, whenever he was asked about what doctors had told him, he quoted this diagnosis. After he completed his basic training, Zangara was sent to the Italian Military College in Rome, on the Tiber near Vatican City. He was assigned as orderly to a forty-five-year-old captain with, Zangara notes, a twenty-year-old wife. Zangara disliked this work too; he was, he says, "not suited" for it. The captain, in addition to being born into a privileged class, made his orderly work too hard.

The orderly had to look after the captain's clothes, shine his boots, do all the housework and serve the meals. He never, he says, had a minute's rest, although once, when he and the captain were at camp, his duties were lighter and he and the colonel's orderly were able to "pass away the time fooling with the loose women of the town." One of his few duties at the camp was to awaken the captain each morning. When Zangara overslept one morning, the captain had him thrown into the guardhouse without meals for twenty-four hours.

After he requested a transfer several times, Zangara was assigned a job as gardener for the military college because of his farm background. He was given his own quarters in a stone building on the college grounds and the commanding officer asked him to use his mason's skills to add a second story to that building. This might seem to have been a good arrangement, but for some reason Zangara requested another transfer after only three months. His captain assigned him to guard duty. He and two other privates, under a corporal's command, were assigned to guard the paymaster's office. He used to dream about stealing the payroll. "I needed it," he says, "for my suffering."

Zangara claims that it was during his military service that he tried to assassinate King Victor Emmanuel III. If this were true, it would probably have happened in late 1922 or early 1923. The king was due to arrive at a railroad depot on a visit to his son. Zangara says he was there with a pistol in his pocket but "the guards got in front of me and I could not get a shot at him because the guards are over six foot tall and I could not even see the king." It is impossible to know whether this story is true.

Nor can details of Zangara's army service be verified. Except for a brief abstract of dates of entrance, discharge and status, his military records appear to have been lost. Before the second World War, detailed service records were usually kept at the military base in the capital of the veteran's home province, which in this case would have been the city of Reggio di Calabria, on the Strait of Messina, directly across from Sicily. Apparently all these records were destroyed in heavy fighting there during World War II.

After Zangara left the army, he went home to Ferruzzano where he worked as a stonemason for three months before deciding to leave for America. He applied for a visa at the U.S. consulate in Messina, Sicily, on August 14, 1923, and sailed on August 16 from Naples on the Cosulich liner, *SS Martha Washington*. He arrived at the Philadelphia port on September 2, 1923, five days before his twenty-third birthday.

The only reference Zangara listed on his visa application was his maternal uncle, Vincent Carfaro, thirty-five years old, whose address in 1923 was 367 Bay Ridge Avenue, Brooklyn. Zangara and his uncle would share rooms in various places in New Jersey between 1923 and 1928. In 1923, the two men moved to Paterson, where Zangara found work as a bricklayer. It is not clear what Carfaro did for a living. When Zangara was hired to work on a project in Bayonne, he was told that he must join the bricklayers' union, and that he could not do that unless he was an American citizen. Early in 1923, he applied for citizenship and, accordingly, was sworn in on September 11, 1929, only six years after his arrival in the country. Although his only motivation was membership in the union, he had had to exercise some effort to attain his goal: as we have noted, aliens at that time had to pass examinations in American history and the English language, and to be able to communicate satisfactorily in English.

Zangara maintained his union membership as long as he was able to work at his trade. In 1931, his membership lapsed for failure to pay dues, but by then he could not find work because of the Depression. He had never said or done anything to offend his union, the Bricklayers, Masons and Plasterers, which was affiliated with the American Federation of Labor, a relatively conservative organization. In 1926, when he was twenty-five, Zangara was admitted to Barnert Memorial Hospital in Paterson, complaining of sharp shooting pains in his abdomen, as well as a loss of appetite. The doctor, a specialist, charged him twenty-five dollars for three visits, an amount he considered exorbitant. According to Zangara, the doctor told him he had chronic appendicitis and that an operation would cure him. But medical records indicate that the doctor could find nothing wrong on examination and suggested the operation to rule out a chronically infected appendix or abdominal adhesions. The appendix was found to be healthy; judging from the size of the incision it is probable that his gall bladder also was checked for inflammation or infection. After the operation, Zangara's appetite improved and he was considered an exemplary patient. He was released in two weeks, and his stomach pains began again.

Little is known about the cause of Zangara's abdominal affliction. He was undoubtedly suffering from something, but all he could say was that he had been to specialists who had diagnosed his condition as "chronic." As we have seen, he writes in his memoir that his pains had started when he was a small child because his father had made him work too hard on his farm. But shortly after his arrest, the federal authorities and the newspapers said that his ailment was the result of a specific injury in a brick factory: that as a child he had fallen into a fire and this had triggered his pain—although he had no noticeable burn scars on his body. Finally, he seemed at one point to connect his six-inch appendectomy scar with the pain. In any case, he did not seem to be on any special diet: during the five weeks of his imprisonment, he ate little, but he ate whatever he was given. It was mentioned by two desk clerks at the Colonial Hotel on Miami Beach that Zangara had received packages from Chicago, which he told them contained stomach medicine. The police found no medication in his room.

Between 1923 and 1931, Zangara lived in a number of rooming houses in Paterson, East Paterson, Passaic and Hackensack. During the first five years he shared the rooms with his uncle, occasionally coming back for short stays after Carfaro was married, although his wife, Giuseppa, did not like Zangara. The two men lived in Jersey Street in East Paterson, then Market Street in Paterson before moving in 1925 to a boarding house at 428 River Street. In 1929 he moved to a rooming house on Summit Street in East Paterson, owned by his uncle's brother-in-law, Joseph Pitea. At least by 1929 Zangara had begun to travel, returning for several months at a time to stay with his uncle or in a rented room in New Jersey. His last address in New Jersey was in 1931, at 100 Green Street, Hackensack. Frank Yanni lived there with his family, operating a downstairs grocery store and renting rooms on the upper floors.

There was a booming economy in the 1920s and bricklayers were in demand at high wages. Zangara had steady work at his trade; the only exception was a job in a silk factory soon after his arrival in the country. He worked on the Fabian Theater and a new federal building in Newark, and on the Alexander Hamilton Hotel in Paterson. He even acted as contractor for several small houses, hiring his own employees. He was considered a competent bricklayer and a reliable worker.

He had a reputation for frugality, saving his money and spending it sparingly. Cafaro called him stingy, During his best years, Zangara was earning between twelve and fourteen dollars a day, which was good money at that time. He put most of it into several savings banks, and reportedly sent money each week to his father in Italy. At a court hearing, Zangara told the judge he had saved $2,500 and his uncle told investigators that Zangara told him he had saved $3,000. Zangara gives the impression that he spent his money freely.

8

"I WASN'T WELL"

In February 1933, a newspaper reporter called on Vincent Carfaro at 78 Lewis Place in Totowa, New Jersey, a hamlet near Paterson, to tell him that his nephew had tried to kill Franklin Roosevelt. This was the morning after the shooting; the township was abuzz with the news of the attempt and Carfaro, an ardent supporter of Roosevelt, had been discussing the shooting with a neighbor when the reporter arrived. Carfaro appeared genuinely stunned and bewildered; he knew his nephew better than anyone else in the country knew him, and he told the *Newark Evening News* that in nine years he had never heard Zangara say anything "against the government or capitalism." His continual complaint was of stomach pains, which were aggravated by cold weather and at times seemed to drive the young man "almost to madness."

His uncle had never heard Zangara express a desire to shoot government leaders. "Truly," Carfaro said, "I cannot understand what drove him to do such a thing unless he was driven to it by his pain. He never talked to me or my family about politics. . . . He had no interest in anything except to eat and sleep when he was with us. He wanted to be left alone to suffer with his stomach." On rare occasions he would rouse himself from his depression and go to the home of a neighbor, John Yearah, for an evening of checkers. Yearah, Carfaro said, was Zangara's only friend. And Zangara was a very private man: Carfaro never knew where his nephew went on his trips or when he would return. He once asked Zangara about these trips and where the money for them came from, and Zangara replied, "It's none of your business what I am doing."

Carfaro's brother-in-law, Joseph Pitea, a tailor from East Paterson who had been Zangara's landlord on Summit Street, told reporters that he too was shocked to hear that in the few months since he had last seen him, Zangara had become "a hater of all presidents." He said he "could hardly believe that the man who boarded with me for ten months and went to bed almost every night at nine is the same Joe who tried to kill Mr Roosevelt. . . . He was always quiet and I never heard him say anything against the government." He was "a very peaceful man."

Frank Yanni, the grocer who owned the rooming house in Hackensack, called Zangara a loner who "liked his solitude." Yanni was one of the few people who thought Zangara had "a radical streak." He was a model boarder, "a clean-cut young fellow . . . he was quiet, at times a bit radical, but not a mixer." The only odd thing about him, Yanni said, was that Zangara rented two rooms, but lived in only one, explaining that he did not want anyone living near him because another boarder had once stolen money from him and he wanted to prevent this from happening again. This does not fit with what is known about Zangara, who wrote that in Hackensack he roomed with a friend named Dominic Palafrone. He seemed always to have roommates.

Of all the people who claimed to have known Zangara in the nine years he was in America, only Rosario Candrilli, a Hackensack contractor, called Zangara a political agitator. Candrilli told both the *Newark Star-Eagle* and the *Newark Evening News* on the day after the shooting, that he had employed Zangara on several projects and that he was "an anarchist, socialist and Communist . . . an inflammatory character" and "lunch-hour orator" who would harangue audiences of fellow workers whenever a president was elected or took office or a king ascended a throne. "With accompanying gestures," Candrilli said, Zangara "would denounce governments and men in power, preach radical doctrines and advocate the killing of government leaders." He would "talk and talk and talk" about his beliefs.

The day after this interview was published, the *Star-Eagle* quoted Secret Service agents as saying that their investigation revealed Zangara to be "a very quiet man whose only pastime was an occasional game of checkers," who "had not harangued fellow bricklayers on the need for a change in America's social order, as reported." The Hackensack police agreed with this view, telling reporters that Zangara was "a quiet man who rarely went out at night."

Zangara says that he traveled around the country to try to relieve his pain, but it would seem from his descriptions of his travels that he simply enjoyed them. He says that he took his first trip to Tampa, Florida, in late 1929 when he had saved $2,500 in various banks and postal savings accounts in New Jersey. He went to Tampa, he says, because he had heard that it was warm there. On the train he met a girl who was going to Jacksonville, and he seemed to have had a good time chatting and playing cards until they reached Jacksonville. "There she left the train after thanking me for helping her pass the time on the trip," Zangara writes. In Tampa, he rented a hotel room and, walking about the city, came upon an Italian clubhouse. This was probably *L'Unione Italiana*, called "The Italian Club" in Ybor City, then a working class section of Tampa populated by Italians and Cubans. Someone at the club suggested that Zangara would like New Orleans, and the next day he was on the train to Louisiana.

In New Orleans, he checked into a hotel and began to take long walks through the city. There appeared to be plenty of construction work available there, but Zangara says he decided against working, preferring to enjoy his stay. He met a seventeen-year-old Spanish girl who told him she needed five dollars for her rent. Zangara offered to let her live with him in his hotel room, and she accepted. They lived together for three weeks, at which time Zangara decided his money was running low and he needed to return to Paterson. "The girl did not seem to mind my leaving and we parted like ordinary friends." He bought a steamship ticket and sailed from New Orleans to New York. It was a five-day trip and he called it "very nice."

When he returned from New Orleans, probably in the summer of 1930, Zangara bought a small used Chevrolet coupe. "I used to go riding on Sundays and visit my friends," he wrote. "I used to ride around all day long looking for work and my friends used to think that I didn't need to work because I had a car. But I could not make enough to pay for my expenses. I had heard that conditions in California were better, so I decided to leave for that part of the country." Having enjoyed the sea trip from New Orleans, Zangara booked passage on a steamship sailing from New York to Los Angeles via the Panama Canal. This was probably in the late summer of 1931. On board ship he made friends with a woman who was traveling with her daughter and sister and the four became traveling companions, sightseeing together at the various port stops. Zangara contributed to a car rental so that they could all sightsee in Havana together. He sent his uncle a postcard from Panama.

When Carfaro later told the police that he had received a postcard from Zangara in 1931 postmarked from Panama, the investigators scoured passport records and State Department files trying to find out when Zangara had left the country. At first the authorities decided the postcard story could not have been true, but eventually the Secret Service verified that Zangara had traveled to California through the Panama Canal, which explained the postcard. Prior to making the trip, the Service said, Zangara had consulted a doctor who had told him that a steamship trip might help his stomach condition. The Service added that the suspect did not stay in California because of dwindling finances.

At Los Angeles, his travelling companions directed Zangara to a boardinghouse owned by a friend of theirs. Zangara writes that he stayed there a week and then left for San Diego, where he caught a bad cold, going to a doctor for medicine, but getting worse. He then decided to go to Miami because he had heard that "the weather was always good there." This is all he says about his stay in California. When Secret Service agents in New Jersey discovered a cancelled bank book from a Los Angeles bank among Zangara's possessions, and when they heard reports that a street preacher was saying that he had been heckled by Zangara during one of his sermons, they began to investigate Zangara's California trip. They discovered that he had registered to vote as a Republican in Los Angeles on October 1, 1931. The bank book showed that he had opened a savings account at the Security-First National Bank of Los Angeles in late summer of 1931; by September 8 he had $150 in the account which he withdrew on October 22.

The Secret Service interviewed Paul Cenci, a tailor, who had roomed with Zangara in Los Angeles. Cenci's description of the shooter was much like others': "He seemed to have no friends and he kept to himself most of the time." But he also said that Zangara sometimes "talked wild about governments, but I paid no attention." Cenci said that Zangara had applied for a job with the Los Angeles Fire Department and that he had gone to night school. Zangara complained of chest pains and said he needed a warmer climate, so Cenci suggested he go to Bakersfield. He saw Zangara for the last time on December 15, 1931. Zangara was carrying a suitcase when he bade Cenci goodbye, and Cenci thought he was going to Bakersfield. In fact, he was probably headed for San Diego.

Three days after the shooting, the wire services reported that Rev. R.B. Griffith of Los Angeles, a "religious lecturer," had identified Zangara from newspaper photographs as the man who had threatened him sometime in August 1931, while he was delivering a sermon in an empty lot at Towne Avenue near 5th Street. Rev. Griffith said that when he told his audience "not to blame Hoover for everything," Zangara began to heckle him as he had done on several other occasions. This time Zangara appeared to be reaching for something in his pocket, but walked away when several bystanders moved toward him. A policeman, C.O. Walker, was summoned; he approached the heckler, searched him and found no weapon. "I think it was the same man," Walker told the press. "His pictures look like that fellow we had around here. He didn't have a gun so I didn't arrest him. But I told him to leave Griffith alone. I've never seen him since."

No one else came forward to identify Zangara with this incident. It seems doubtful that Zangara, a militant atheist with a poor grasp of English, would listen to an evangelist like Griffith; conceivably praise of President Hoover could move him to protest, but Griffith would have us believe that Zangara threatened to shoot him, which would not fit with Zangara's insistence that he was interested in killing only heads of state.

Another point that calls Griffith's story into question is that it came to the press through Captain William F. Hynes, chief of the Los Angeles Red Squad. In the early '20s, shortly after the Russian Revolution, the U.S. government began a systematic identification and prosecution of persons believed to be Communists or Communist sympathizers. This policy was carried out by Attorney General Mitchell Palmer. To monitor and control political dissidents of all sorts, who were generally assumed to be Communists, police forces across the country organized Red or Radical Squads whose duties were to ferret out and harass subversives and, if possible, prosecute them. The tactics of the Los Angeles Red Squad had recently come under intense public scrutiny, which made it necessary for Hynes to justify its activities. On the day of the Zangara shooting, there had been an ugly confrontation at City Hall in Los Angeles. An angry crowd of people, many of them targets of Hynes, had gathered at a city council meeting to protest against the squad and demand an investigation of its activities. Fights broke out and a number of people were injured. Fifty policemen battled more than sixty demonstrators in the council chambers and corridors and out into the street. Clubs swung, cuspidors were hurled, two city councilmen joined the fray and there were several arrests.

Several days after this, Hynes reported that his squad had investigated Zangara when he was in Los Angeles. On Sunday, February 19, the *Los Angeles Times* reported that the captain had made public the details of "many months'" investigation. The Red Squad, he asserted, had "almost trapped" a group of bomb-making anarchists "fostered and founded by Zangara." This group had averted arrest when "the culprits got wind of the police and escaped." Zangara had fled to the east and was next heard from when he fired on FDR in Bayfront Park. "When the activities of police became close," Hynes said, "Zangara abandoned his efforts and left." This revelation was considerably undercut by the fact that two days earlier, on February 17, Hynes had told the Associated Press that he "had no records of local activities by anyone named Zangara."

This inconsistency did not prevent Hynes from elaborating on his February 19 remarks: he had thought that Zangara intended to assassinate Mussolini and that a man had already been assigned to kill *il Duce* with a bomb. Later Hynes said that Zangara was an organizer for *L'Era Nuova* (The New Age), an Italian anarchist organization which had not been in Los Angeles for years. Zangara's assignment, Hynes said, was to recruit and reactivate a cell in the city so that the anarchists could assassinate President Hoover when he came to Los Angeles to open the 1932 Olympics. Zangara was foiled when Hoover sent Vice President Charles Curtis in his stead. *L'Era Nuova*, according to Hynes, was a particularly vicious organization of Italian anarchists that had been broken up by federal agents in 1922, during "a nationwide drive." Since then, they had been meeting covertly. "We have established pretty definitely," Hynes announced, "that Zangara contacted at least two of the anarchist leaders and we are searching for them to question them about his activities here."

These charges did not generate headlines, but were included in the *Los Angeles Times* as a few paragraphs in a general story about Zangara, and in the east were reported briefly or not at all. There were no follow-up stories.

The psychological profile of Zangara that emerges from people who knew him is of a lonely, morose and taciturn man who rarely expressed political opinions. He seems an unlikely choice as a recruiter and organizer of a group of international terrorists. Hynes's claims are brought into question further by the existence of red squads in both Newark and Paterson; for a time during the teens and twenties the latter city had been a center of anarchist organizations. These police groups had never heard of Joe Zangara.

The San Diego newspapers quoted interviews with several unnamed people who said they had been Zangara's friends when he lived there. Zangara had come to San Diego from Los Angeles in late fall, 1931, and had gone to work as a bootblack at the St. James Hotel barber shop. One person volunteered that Zangara had "received a check each month from an uncle in New York, but he wouldn't spend anything. He always talked about his stomach trouble and he ate nothing but onion soup." Like most others who had known him, these acquaintances said that Zangara had never talked about anarchy or any desire to kill presidents. One called him "a great admirer of Benito Mussolini."

Later Zangara told the prison warden that while he was staying in San Diego he crossed into Mexico each weekend to sightsee. His acquaintances said that he left San Diego to travel by bus to Florida in February 1932. Zangara gives no dates in his memoir, but he does say that he took a bus from San Diego to Miami. Between February 1932 and the shooting in Bayfront Park in February 1933, Zangara's activities are murky. Warden L.F. Chapman writes in his unpublished memoir that Zangara told him that he had gone to Washington to shoot President Hoover and had waited for his opportunity for ten days outside the White House gates but had had to abandon the plan. Zangara never mentioned this to anyone else nor does he write about it in his own memoir, even though he describes his aborted attempt on the life of Victor Emmanuel III. It is highly unlikely that Zangara had a gun in Washington, because he bought one just before the shooting in Miami. The frugal Zangara would not have bought two guns, nor did he need two. Immediately after the shooting, he told police and the press that he had originally bought the gun in Miami to take to Washington to shoot Hoover, but because he heard that the president-elect was coming to Miami, and because it was chilly in Washington in February, he decided to shoot Roosevelt instead. Thus, it is most unlikely that he had been in Washington trying to kill Hoover before he shot Cermak in Bayfront Park.

The weather, Zangara says, was the reason he left San Diego: the weather, he had heard, was always good in Miami. Once there, he writes that he boarded at the home of "an American family . . . fine people," at 20 Northeast 17th Street. That is the address to which the Paterson post office sent Zangara $100 from his postal savings account. The 1932 Miami city directory lists a Patrick H. Larkin and his family living at that address. There is no mention of the Larkins in any surviving record of the Zangara investigation. In any case he could not have stayed at 17th Street for more than six weeks because on April 7, 1932, he registered at the Colonial Hotel at 719 First Street in Miami Beach. He moved there, he said, so he "could be near the water all the time." The desk clerks identified him from a photograph, and said that he had stayed there for eight weeks before moving to another hotel. On August 23, 1932, $200 was mailed to the Colonial from his postal savings account. Zangara himself writes that his stay at the Colonial made him feel better and he stayed there "a long time." He left, he says, to return to Paterson.

This agrees with the recollection of Carfaro, who confirmed that his nephew spent several months with him in the summer of 1932 at Lewis Street in Totowa Borough and left in August. Zangara renewed his New Jersey drivers license on June 2, 1932. Carfaro told the FBI that over the years Zangara had sent nearly $3,000 to his father in Italy. Since he was out of work and needed money in the summer of 1932, he had asked Carfaro if he could stay with him until his father returned some of that money to him. The uncle agreed; bank records indicate that on July 1, 1932, Zangara deposited $700 into his Paterson account. This, his last deposit, brought his account balance to $1,200. Zangara had withdrawn fifty dollars from his postal savings account on May 6, and his last in-person withdrawal from that account was $100 on July 23, 1932. Zangara left New Jersey, telling his uncle that he was going to live in Florida for a while because his stomach felt better there. After he left New Jersey, Zangara continued to make withdrawals by mail.

Some time in 1932, Carfaro received several postcards from his nephew, with complaints about "gnawing pains" in his stomach and "heart attacks." Carfaro could not respond, because Zangara did not include a return address, but the uncle wanted to tell him that he had received a letter from Salvatore in Italy saying that Giuseppe had not sent him money for a long time and he had not had any news of his son for months. Zangara later said that he had mailed a book to his father in the weeks just before his arrest. Salvatore wrote back to him, but by the time the letter reached him, Zangara was in the Dade County jail.

During this last stay in New Jersey, Zangara may have been disappointed in love. Mary Yanni, the fifteen-year-old daughter of the grocer from whom Zangara had rented a room, told the *Newark Star-Eagle* that between March and September 1932, Zangara "repeatedly asked me to marry him and I told him certainly not. I told him I didn't love him and that he was much older than I." Zangara persisted, she said, and finally went to her parents, who said that it was their daughter's decision to make. Shortly after this, Frank Yanni said, Zangara left New Jersey for the last time. Witnesses claimed that he left abruptly, leaving his personal possessions behind and not even saying goodbye. The implication was that Zangara may have been pushed off balance by a broken heart.

Zangara writes about an affair of the heart, but this involved a different girl, and since he does not give dates in his memoir, one cannot know when this happened. But Mary Yanni's dates here are open to question. She said that he was in Paterson between March and September, but he seems to have gone to Paterson in early May and left by the end of July or early August. Zangara himself says that he wanted to marry the sixteen-year-old daughter of Pietro Galanto, with whom he had roomed in Paterson. "I admired her very much," he writes, "and had asked her father for her hand in marriage. He was willing and so was she." But one day he over-heard some friends talking about this girl. "I heard one of them say that she ought to get married right away because she was in a bad way. They did not know that I was engaged to this girl." His inten-tion had been to put on an extravagant wedding, but after hearing this gossip, he broke the engagement. "I could not marry her in that condition as much as I felt sorry for her."

During the interrogation by Sheriff Hardie, Zangara remarked that he was not interested in women because he was too distracted by his stomach pains. "I like the wife but since all the time—there is suffer all the time. I wasn't well," he said.

According to a Secret Service report, Zangara arrived in Miami for his last visit there on August 6, 1932; he rented a safe deposit box and opened a savings account at the First National Bank of Miami. This is unquestionably correct, although the Secret Service records are not always reliable: one synopsis contains the informa-tion that during the summer of 1932, Zangara visited Chicago, De-troit, and other cities in the north, "but he gave cold weather no chance to catch up with him." It is true that Zangara hated cold weather, but he himself said that he had never been to Chicago. In any case, it is a fact that he checked back into the Colonial Hotel in Miami Beach in August of 1932; he says that he stayed there for a week, then moved back to Miami where he shared a small cottage with a man who washed dishes in an Italian restaurant. After that he rented his last room, a dingy two-dollar-a-week attic with a dormer ceiling in a home at 126 Northeast 5th Street in downtown Miami.

He lived there for six months, according to his memoir, and spent over six hundred dollars. "I was living good," he writes, "and did not deny myself anything." Indeed, that was a lot of money to spend in the Depression years, especially for a man who had always been frugal, to say the least. At the time of his arrest, Zangara had only forty-three dollars and $250 in savings. He had had about $100 in a postal savings account in Miami, but had withdrawn half of it the day before the shooting.

According to the Secret Service files that are still available, in January of 1933, just a month before the shooting, Zangara began to run low on funds. He gave up his safe deposit box and closed his account at the First National Bank. Then, the report says, Zangara "made a fool's effort to recoup the money he spent. He tried the horse races a couple of times, but switched his efforts to dog racing and lost about $200 of his steadily shrinking savings. He became depressed and told an acquaintance that when his money was gone he would commit suicide, either by jumping off a high bridge or by injecting himself with poison."

In November 1932, Zangara moved into his last lodgings in the attic room on 5th Street. The Secret Service synopsis says that after he moved there, Zangara had no visitors but took his meals with the owner of a little cigar shop that he visited regularly. This was probably the "cigar maker" with whom, according to newspaper reports, Zangara had dinner on the evening of the shooting. These same reports mentioned that Zangara spent time watching the arrival of yachts and fishing boats at the municipal docks on the northern boundary of Bayfront Park. It was there, Zangara said, that he first heard that Roosevelt would be visiting Miami. Newspapers said, too, that Zangara sometimes guided visitors around Miami. There is some evidence that he traveled around south Florida, visiting Key West and Palm Beach. Gordon Davis, the Miami pawnbroker who sold Zangara the five-shot revolver and ten bullets, told police that he had known the shooter "for a long time."

Zangara did not talk about what he did in Miami in 1932 and the first six weeks of 1933. Robert J. Donovan, who saw the police file, now lost, wrote in 1954 that Zangara "became an out-and-out loafer and even something of a playboy, idling about the wharves, playing shuffleboard in Lummus Park, betting, with no success, on the horses, and losing $200 at the dog races."

Some caution should be exercised in considering Donovan's judgement in this *New Yorker* article. When discussing Zangara's behavior he picks up as a given Rosario Candrilli's statement to the Newark newspapers that "Zangara had something of a reputation as a lunch-hour orator on the privileges of the rich and the hard lot of the working man . . . ," ignoring the remarks to the contrary of Vincent Carfaro, Joseph Pitea and Frank Yanni, and the findings in this matter of both the Secret Service and the Hackensack police.

When the police searched Zangara's attic room, they found all of his possessions packed in a small, cheap suitcase; his clothing, they said, was rather expensive. The three books the police found were *Wehman Bros.' Easy Method for Learning Spanish Quickly*, *Italian Self-Taught* and an Italian-English grammar. The police also found several newspaper clippings which would figure into the court cases against him.

9

ALLEGATIONS

After the shooting, many stories were told about Zangara. The owner of the cigar shop that Zangara frequented was arrested the morning after the shooting, but undoubtedly released, since the *Miami Herald* never mentioned him again. He was described as an Italian "cigar maker and companion of the would-be assassin" who had met with him frequently since December 1932. This man told the police that Zangara had said he was a building contractor, that he had dined with Zangara at about seven o'clock on the evening of the shooting, and that Zangara had never mentioned plans to shoot FDR or anyone else.

In early March 1933, a woman named May Bostick, who, with her husband, operated the Bostick Hotel at 217 South Miami Avenue downtown, told the *Miami Herald* that Zangara had spent the day of the shooting at the hotel. He had, she said, arrived at about nine-thirty in the morning with a small black package under his arm, and had said, "Someone sent me here and I am looking for a room. Are you the manager?" He wanted a room until six that evening, he said, and just wanted "to be quiet." She took him to a room and asked him if he was in Miami to see the president; to which he replied, "No." He paid her $1.50 in advance. In the afternoon the Bosticks went out, and when they came back, the tenant was gone. He had apparently spent the day sitting on the bed smoking "half a hundred" cigarettes. Mrs Bostick said that she and her husband had been friends with Anton Cermak for more than eighteen years and that he had visited them at their hotel. She speculated that Zangara had intended to kill Cermak, and that he needed the hotel room in order to "load his pistol."

The *Herald* left the impression that the Bostick story had been corroborated by the police: "The investigations into the life of Zangara and his activities immediately preceding the shooting showed that he spent a good part of the day of the outrage in a room in the Bostick Hotel." No other newspaper seems to have carried this story and the *Herald* did not follow up on it. Anton Cermak's grandson, Robert Graham, who was only nine years old at the time of the shooting, said many years later that he had never heard of the Bosticks, or their hotel. In addition, neither Zangara's acquaintances and friends nor his jailers knew him to be a smoker, so it seems unlikely that he would smoke nearly three packs of cigarettes on the day of the shooting. And it is difficult to see why Zangara would rent a hotel room "to load his gun" when he had his own room on 5th Street, closer to the park than the Bostick Hotel.

Of all the apocryphal stories picked up by the media, the one most seriously investigated involved allegations that Zangara was a member of an anarchist group operating in Germantown, Pennsylvania and Newark, New Jersey. A year earlier, terrorists had blown up a Pennsylvania post office, causing some deaths. The FBI investigated that incident, trying to determine whether Zangara was linked to it. On December 31, 1931, this same organization mailed a bomb that prematurely blew up in the Easton, Pennsylvania, post office, injuring three people and killing three others. On January 28, 1933, just two weeks before Zangara's attempt on Roosevelt, the same group allegedly placed a ten-stick dynamite bomb under the front steps of the Philadelphia home of John DiSilvestro, Supreme Venerable of the Order Sons of Italy, killing his wife and injuring several of his children. These anarchists were believed to be responsible also for delivery of bombs in Chicago, Detroit, Youngstown and Cleveland as well as one in Vatican City in February 1932. They had supposedly threatened the life of Generoso Pope, a New York contractor and publisher of *Il Progresso Italo-Americano* (whose son Gene, incidentally, later founded the *National Enquirer*).

In connection with these bombings, the day after the shooting at Bayfront Park, J. Edgar Hoover received a telegram in code from one of his agents in Houston, Texas:

POSTAL TELEGRAPH

HOUSTON TEXAS
FEBRUARY 16, 1933

J EDGAR HOOVER
DIRECTOR, UNITED STATES BUREAU OF
INVESTIGATION

RE ATTEMPTED ASSASSINATION OF ROOSEVELT DURING MY INVESTIGATION OF THE EASTON POST OFFICE BOMB CASE LAST YEAR GUISEPPE ZANGARA WAS WITH SEVERAL OTHERS MENTIONED BY GRAZZI ITALIAN CONSUL GENERAL AT NEW YORK AS BEING A MEMBER OF AN ITALIAN ANARCHISTIC TERRORIZING GROUP WITH HEADQUARTERS AT A FARM NEAR NEWARK NEW JERSEY WHERE THE BOMBS WERE MANUFACTURED STOP CAPTAIN MCDERMOTT NEW YORK RADICAL SQUAD AND I SUGGESTED TO RAID FARM BUT POST OFFICE INSPECTORS OPPOSED SAME AND WE LATER DISCONTINUED INVESTIGATION STOP SEE FILE.

TURROU

Hoover underlined the last words, "See file," and wrote next to them: "No record in file 2/17/33. I have phoned this to Mr Moran." Moran was director of the Secret Service.

Two weeks later John DiSilvestro, the head of the Sons of Italy whose home had been bombed, contacted the FBI with information from an informant that Zangara was one of the people who had blown up the Easton post office. The informant was a bricklayer who had been working for a building contractor in the Philadelphia suburb of Germantown. He told DiSilvestro that Zangara was one of three bricklayers who had come from New York and worked for the contractor between February 26 and March 1, 1932, and that Zangara had given speeches in Philadelphia denouncing DiSilvestro as well as Eugene Alessandroni, a municipal court judge in the city.

DiSilvestro examined the contractor's employment records but did not find Zangara's name there. There was a man named "Bruno" who roughly fit Zangara's description. Two other bricklayers who had worked on the job said they recognized Zangara's photograph from newspapers as one of the three New York bricklayers who had come to Philadelphia in 1932. DiSilvestro was told by other contacts that Zangara was a member of a Newark anarchist group and was unknown in Italy, which could mean, DiSilvestro said, that "Zangara" was a fictitious name.

FBI agents interviewed a parish priest in Germantown who knew the bricklayers involved, had talked to them and told the agents that they had now agreed that they were mistaken about recognizing Zangara; the priest himself knew Bruno, and was positive that he was not Zangara. Judge Alessandroni told the agents about a conversation overheard on the platform of the Newark railroad station. A young Italian named Maida was waiting for his train, drinking a soda, when two short men standing near him began to talk in a northern Italian dialect about something that sounded like criminal activity. One asked the other about his brother-in-law and received the response: "He's all right. I got the two thousand. I'm going to de-

liver it to him in Miami and then we'll all meet later in California."
The men mentioned both DiSilvestro and Alessandroni. Maida gathered that the brother-in-law was a waiter in Miami, but he said in
the deposition he gave the FBI that he had difficulty understanding
northern Italian. "Sometimes I don't understand these fellows very
well," he said. He was shown photographs, but he could not identify anyone.

Since bombings had also occurred in Italy, Mussolini's government was interested in this matter. John DiSilvestro was an outspoken Fascist and friend of Mussolini, and had not been at home when
his house was bombed because he had been at the U.S. Attorney's
office, supposedly imparting information about anti-Fascists in the
Philadelphia area. Several days earlier, he had been shot at in his
office. He was so distraught over all these things that he traveled to
Italy by steamship to confer with *il Duce* about the situation. The
upshot was that nearly two months after the bombing and days before Zangara was executed, Mussolini announced that Mrs
DiSilvestro was to be included in his "list of Fascist martyrs." At
about the same time, it was reported by the wire services that the
Italian government was preparing to ask the U.S. State Department
to obtain a stay of Zangara's execution until they had completed
their investigation. There is no record in State Department archives
of any such official request.

The FBI continued, until shortly before Zangara was executed,
to search out Miami barbers living in Philadelphia, to interview not
only hairdressers in Miami hotels but even Charles Curtis, vice president of the United States, about information he received from an
informant. None of this led anywhere. R.G. Harvey, the special agent
in charge of the FBI Philadelphia office, reported to J. Edgar Hoover
on March 18, 1933, two days before Zangara was executed, that
both the Philadelphia police and his own agents agreed that there
was nothing to the stories about the anarchist conspiracy. The superintendent of the Philadelphia police force believed that not only

was there no connection between Zangara and the DiSilvestro bombing, but the bombing was probably the result of a personal grudge again DiSilvestro and not part of a terrorist plot.

There were many other false leads and bogus stories. The *New York Enquirer*, published in Brooklyn, ran a story about three labor leaders from the Brooklyn Workers Union who had identified Zangara from his photograph as a member of a Communist group that had helped to foment labor unrest on Coney Island in January 1933. One of these men said that he was certain that Zangara was a paid assassin working for Communist Russia; Zangara, he said, had followed him for five days and once put his hand in his jacket as if he were going to shoot and then escape. "The identification of Zangara as a paid agent of the Reds," the *Enquirer* wrote, "would confirm the rumors that have reached government agents that he is one of a group sworn to kill Roosevelt. Inasmuch as he has failed, many others will attempt it." But these allegations were easily disproved. *Il Progresso* reported the story, pointing out that Zangara was supposed to have done these things in New York between the 15th and 20th of January, when the Miami police had conclusive proof that he was in Miami.

On Saturday, February 18, five unemployed bricklayers were arrested in Washington, D.C., accused of plotting against Roosevelt, Hoover and other government officials. One of them had apparently written to a friend in Paterson, New Jersey, saying, "With my most sincere regrets I am forced to tell you of my brother bricklayer's unsuccessful attempt on the life of our president-elect. If I were the one who had the honor of shooting at our present president, I assure you that I would take a week to practice and make a good job of it. It seems a shame to have in our midst a man with such poor aim. I do believe we should have a place where we could all go and practice up on our shooting as it looks like an open season on presidents and politicians." This seems to have been intended as a joke, but the Secret Service was not amused. After a "severe grilling," two of the five were released, but the other three were held for "further investigation"—one of them to be questioned by immigration authorities.

In late February, a forty-year-old Chicago chef named Ludwig Rahmer wrote Zangara a letter in code and mailed it to his jail cell in Miami. It was easily decoded; the Secret Service said it congratulated Zangara on his "good work" and mentioned Mayor Cermak and Herbert Hoover's home in Palo Alto, California. Rahmer was easily found because he had written his return address on the envelope and included a self-addressed postcard for a reply. Rahmer told the authorities that he knew Zangara but he didn't know anything about a letter. Specimens of his handwriting matched the writing in the letter. He was taken to a Chicago psychiatric hospital where doctors found Rahmer to be an "unbalanced personality." He thought that the hospital was trying to poison him with inedible food. He was detained for an indefinite period.

In the days after the shooting, someone mailed Roosevelt a crude letter bomb from the post office in Watertown, New York, where it was intercepted and defused. Two weeks later, the chief of Watertown police, Edward Singleton, received a letter signed "Paul Antoneli of Italy," age fifteen. "Chief Singleton," the letter read, "Sir: I am a friend of Zangara and I want to take up work that he fail to do. I kill all presidents, governors and millionaires. I am Calabrian same as Zangara, I hate policemen and kill all your officers who I see on street at midnight." Several weeks later another shell bomb addressed to "Franklin D. Roosevelt, The White House," was intercepted at the Watertown post office. The authorities were apparently unable to find "Paul Antoneli of Italy."

Many crank letters were received by the Secret Service and the FBI; the latter's collection survives. A number addressed to Roosevelt had been directed to the Justice Department. An anonymous employee of the Cuban government wrote in Spanish, asserting positively that Zangara was a paid assassin hired by the chief of police of Havana. A New Yorker wrote that Zangara looked like someone who used to attend *vetcherinkas*: these were, he said, dances held by a group of anarchists in New York City. A doctor who seemed to work in a psychiatric institution in St. Louis wrote that he had considerable experience in administering truth drugs: "little secrets often" leapt out as a result of these drugs, he said, and gave instructions on proper dosages and the conduct of the subsequent interrogation, which he said would be a "wise" method to get the facts before Zangara was executed.

One man wrote from Long Island to tell the Justice Department that while he was having his shoes shined in New York City several days after the shooting, he noticed two "brazen and obnoxious" cabdrivers. One was Italian, the other probably Jewish, and they spoke in loud voices and "their laughter was noisy and raucous." One of them picked up a newspaper with a picture of Zangara on the front page and said, "Damn fool, damn worthless shot, can't hit anything." The writer admitted that he would not be able to identify either of these men if he saw them again, but he was offering the information "for what it may be worth as indicating the mental attitude of the Italian and Jewish element in New York."

An anonymous writer in St. Paul, Minnesota, typed one paragraph giving the name of a man who was "an underworld character, racketeer, licker [sic] runner, etc." The man, the writer said, was in Florida at the time of the shooting: "If it was intended to kill Cermak for activities against the Chicago underworld, why not find out what he was doing in Florida." In this connection, Cermak's "personal and private investigator on gambling, syndicates, vice, booze and dope" wrote directly to Roosevelt, two days after the inauguration, that he had copies of more than eight hundred reports he had submitted to the mayor, and promising to prove within four weeks that "organized Chicago crime had Mayor Cermak killed . . . I guarantee, personally to you, Mr President, to obtain and submit evidence sufficient to warrant indictments and convictions of the guilty individuals and higher-ups now scot free and unworried in Chicago." He asked that Roosevelt send him instructions and authority to proceed. "I am so sure of delivering all claims that I will post my liberty and even my life as forfeit." An assistant U.S. attorney general replied, "I beg to advise you that the matter of the shooting of Mayor Cermak is one falling within the jurisdiction of the State of Florida and this Department has no jurisdiction in the premises."

Great pains were taken to follow many of these leads to their conclusion. It is apparent from the record that the investigative authorities wanted to uncover a conspiracy, and it is of course equally apparent that if they had been able to prosecute anyone for aiding Zangara, nothing could have stopped them. But there was never any real evidence of either a conspiracy or an accomplice. In his response to the Attorney General's query about the assassination theory on February 14, 1950, J. Edgar Hoover summed up the conclusions reached by both the Secret Service and the FBI: "There was no evidence that Zangara had even been in Chicago nor had any relatives or associates in that city. . . . The entire investigation pointed to the fact that Zangara intended only to assassinate the President and no evidence was ever uncovered indicating that the attempt was intended for Cermak."

Bayfront Park, looking north, with Biscayne Boulevard on the left, bandshell at bottom right and Municipal Docks, center right (The Romer Collection, courtesy Historical Association of South Florida).

Miami's amphitheater in 1933, built for a Shriner's convention several years earlier (The Romer Collection, courtesy Historical Association of South Florida).

(top left)
L.F. Chapman, Sr., Superintendent of Florida State Prison from 1931 to 1956. Photo taken about 1935 (courtesy Gen. Leonard F. Chapman, Jr., USMC, ret.).

(top right)
Nathan Mayo, Florida State Commissioner of Agriculture and head of the State Prison system, 1933 (from the Chapman manuscript).

(right)
Governor Dave Sholtz delivering a radio address in New York, 1935 (courtesy Florida State Photo Archives).

(above) FDR with Florida Governor Dave Sholtz (center) and Jacksonville Mayor John T. Alson, Jr., during Roosevelt's departure parade in Jacksonville, February 3, 1933 (courtesy Florida State Photo Archives).

(right) Sheriff Dan Hardie

(left) Thomas Armour, Sr., about 1935 (courtesy Dr Thomas Armour, Jr.).

Shortly after nine, Roosevelt's open touring car nosed its way slowly through the tightly-packed crowd waiting to greet him at Bayfront Park. Mayor Cermak is second from the lower left with his back turned (courtesy UPI/Roosevelt Library).

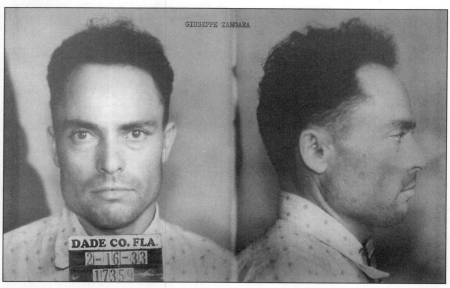

Dade County mug shots taken the morning after the shooting (courtesy United States Secret Service).

Anton Cermak, moments after being shot in Bayfront Park. Note bloodstain on his shirt above his belt and soiled trousers at knee where he fell (courtesy Florida State Photo Archives).

Jackson Memorial Hospital, 1925. Central administration building, later called "the Alamo" with east wing to the right and "colored" wing to the left. Cermak's room was in the East Wing (courtesy Dr William Straight).

(above) The main block house of the Florida State Prison at Raiford, 1933. Note the wood fence (from the Chapman manuscript).

Holding his chin in his hand with a sardonic smile on his face, Giuseppe Zangara faces Judge E.C. Collins who drops his gavel to open the trial (UPI/Corbis-Bettmann).

(above)
Zangara's death cell,
Florida State Prison at Raiford, 1933
(from the Chapman Manuscript).

(right)
Previously unpublished photo of "Old
Sparky," Florida's electric chair as it looked
in 1933 (from the Chapman manuscript).

(left)
Zangara and his court-appointed
counsel. (l. to r.) Lewis M. Twyman
Alfred E. Raia and James M.
McCaskill (photograph
by Herald Studio).

(right) Sheriff Dan Hardie (left) with one of the three City of Miami arresting officers holding Zangara's revolver. Taken the night of the shooting.

(below) Previously unpublished photo of Zangara taken in one of the two courtyards in the death house, March 12, 1933 (from the Chapman manuscript).

(above)
Zangara's grave, marked by a license plate, 1933 (courtesy Lt. Enoch Griffis, Union Correctional Institute).

10

THE FIRST ARRAIGNMENT

O n Thursday morning, less than twelve hours after the shooting, Sheriff Dan Hardie brought Zangara before Criminal Court Judge E.C. Collins for arraignment on four counts of attempted murder. It was in Judge Collins's sixth floor courtroom, Room 630, that Al Capone had been tried several years earlier on vagrancy and public nuisance charges and acquitted. In anticipation of Zangara's arrival, the corridors and large square waiting area outside the courtroom were filled with reporters, courthouse personnel and interested individuals who had not been able to get inside Room 630. Security was very tight: because newspapers and letters to the editor had demanded "swift justice," the sheriff was genuinely afraid of vigilante violence against his prisoner. Everyone who entered the courtroom was searched for weapons. When Zangara appeared, clad in a blue checked shirt and striped grey flannel trousers, he was flanked by large deputies who nearly lifted him off the floor as they rushed him through the crowd.

Courtroom 630 was large and rectangular in shape, entered through double doors which, like the four floor-to-ceiling windows opposite them, were set in fluted, carved Corinthian columns under ornate cornices. The judge's carved desk was mounted on a two-foot high marble dais, and lighted by two sizable shaded lamps beneath crystal chandeliers which matched several wall sconces. The wall behind the judge was covered by a large mosaic of Columbus landing in the New World; directly before the judge his clerk sat at an identical desk. Abutting the judge's bench, on his left, was the railed witness box and next to that was the jury box, also railed, with its twelve carved wooden chairs.

A curved balustrade separated the "well" or working area of the courtroom from the nine rows of spectators' pews.

This courtroom is now called Courtroom 6-1; its splendor is past. When the building was air conditioned, the tall windows were sealed and hidden behind off-white curtains. The walls, including the wall holding the Columbus mosaic, were covered from top to bottom with white acoustic tile. Many of these are now yellowed with age, dirty and broken. The chandeliers, wall sconces and even the lamps on the judge's bench have been replaced by fluorescent lights set in between the ceiling rafters. The carved wood is chipped, scratched, dirty and generally neglected. Exposed wires for speakers run along the walls; blue plastic signs glued to the balustrade read, "Reserved T.V. Cameras." Aside from the regulation flags and the clock, the room's single decoration is a sign on the wall behind the bench: "We Who Labor Here Seek Only Truth." No criminal case has been heard in this room since the 1960s when these cases were moved across town to the glass-and-concrete Metropolitan Justice Building. The room is now used only for civil cases. But on more than one occasion, the proceedings within it commanded the attention of the state and the nation, and, at least on one occasion, the world.

Zangara was brought into the courtroom and deposited in a large leather chair. Surrounded by the three hulking deputies, the diminutive prisoner looked childlike. While everyone waited for the judge, who was conferring with the prosecutor and other lawyers in his private chambers, Zangara seemed uninterested in the photographers with their flashbulbs and the newsreel men with their whirring cameras who swarmed around him.

When Judge E.C. Collins entered, pale from a recent illness, the bailiff called the court to order and Zangara was brought before the bench. The sheriff was standing next to him to act as his interpreter since, the *Herald* reported, Hardie could not only speak Italian, but could address Zangara in his Calabrian dialect. A formal reading of the charges was waived, but the sheriff explained them to Zangara, and when asked if the prisoner was going to plead guilty, Hardie responded, "He might."

The judge asked Zangara if he understood English, to which Zangara responded that he did, and if he wanted a lawyer, to which Zangara's response was a strong negative. But the judge declared that he would appoint one for him anyway. Zangara, apparently upset, said loudly—some reporters said he shouted—"You are the judge and you can do what you want." Appointment of the attorney was postponed until the next day, Friday, February 17, and the prisoner was taken from the courtroom and down the halls to the elevator serving the jail floors.

At this point rumors began to circulate that a lynch party was being put together. Hardie ordered special guards stationed at the basement elevator to screen all visitors to the jail. There was certainly strong feeling against Zangara in Miami, and obviously the Italian community was apprehensive that this could spill over into attacks upon them. On Thursday a delegation of five prominent citizens of Italian descent gave a statement to the *Herald* deploring Zangara's act: "All of Miami's Italian-Americans are honest and law abiding citizens . . . such persons as Zangara are to be considered without a country or a religion." One of the five signers was Caesar Lamonica, who later gained some renown as an orchestra leader.

On Friday morning when Zangara returned to the courtroom, it was cleared, as were the corridors he used. Judge Collins mounted the bench and announced that he had appointed three lawyers to represent Zangara: Lewis Twyman, James M. McCaskill and Alfred E. Raia. Zangara did not apparently understand this statement by the judge until Sheriff Hardie repeated it to him. Then, according to published reports, he became agitated, "snarling" that he had been appointed three lawyers when he did not want any. "All I want is the judge," he said.

The judge replied that he had to be sure that no one would think that Zangara was being "railroaded" by Dade County. Two of the lawyers were leaders of the Miami legal community. Iverson Lewis Twyman, a forty-four-year-old patrician from Fincastle, Virginia, was a graduate of Washington and Lee University in Lexington, Virginia. He was a general practitioner with trial experience and was president of the Dade County Bar Association. James M. McCaskill, a past president of the bar association, was also forty-four years old, had his law degree from the University of Florida at Gainesville and had some experience in criminal law as a prosecutor for the Judge Advocate General Corps of the Navy at Key West. Alfred E. Raia, who came from Rhode Island, was primarily a property lawyer. He did very little legal work during the trial; since he spoke fluent Italian, he seemed to have been included primarily to act as interpreter. The press referred to him as "the Italian-speaking lawyer."

It can be noted here that one of the five prominent Italian Americans who signed the statement deploring Zangara's actions was "Alfred E. Radia." This name is not listed in the 1933–34 Miami cross-directory of persons living or working in the city. The only similar name is Raia's.

These lawyers had obviously been appointed because of their positions in the community and not because they were skillful or effective criminal attorneys.

Immediately upon the lawyers' appointment, Twyman made a motion for the judge to appoint a "sanity commission" to determine his client's mental condition. The judge accepted the motion and at the same time set arraignment for the next morning, February 19, a Saturday: Courts normally did not hold sessions on Saturday. The judge asked Dr Gerald Raap, president of the County Medical Society—and one of Cermak's physicians—to choose two psychiatrists to examine Zangara. Dr Raap appointed I. Henry Agos, a respected psychiatrist, and Dr T. Earl Moore, a young practitioner. These doctors hurried to the jail on the day of their appointment and met with the prisoner some time before midnight on Friday. They said they would present their report the next morning. The Dade County judicial system was moving with uncharacteristic speed.

After this Friday morning session in which the judge appointed the psychiatric committee, Zangara's lawyers interviewed their client in the sheriff's office in the courthouse. When they emerged an hour and a half later, they held a news conference. James McCaskill announced that he believed that Zangara was "telling the truth and telling it with great sincerity," and was wholeheartedly cooperative and not hostile. "I actually believe," McCaskill said, "that he is one hundred percent honest in his conviction and one hundred percent courageous in his way, with absolutely no fear of death. He is decidedly a fatalist and an atheist, believing in no God." Alfred Raia, who had spoken to the prisoner in Italian, said that all their attempts to "catch him in a lie" had failed; "his story checks all the way through." Lewis Twyman said that his client "was friendly . . . not antagonistic . . . very willing to cooperate . . . had a very definite mind of his own."

On that same Friday, Circuit Court Judge H.P. Atkinson impaneled a grand jury so that it would be in place if one of Zangara's victims died. Under Florida law, only a grand jury could indict for a capital crime; lesser crimes could be charged by prosecutorial affidavit or "information." Judge Atkinson charged the grand jury with investigating conditions in the county which "came to their notice." The charge did not mention the shooting. The *Miami Herald* reported that Zangara's trial would be delayed until it was clear whether Mayor Cermak and Mrs Gill were going to live or die. If either or both died, the grand jury would indict Zangara for murder and the state attorney, N. Vernon Hawthorne, would prosecute. If they recovered, Zangara would be tried for assault with intent to kill and the case would be handled by the county solicitor, Charles A. Morehead.

Zangara was brought back to Room 630 on Saturday morning for the third attempt to arraign him. His lawyers and County Solicitor Morehead asked for a delay so that the sanity commission's report could be obtained before a plea was entered. Judge Collins granted the delay, but only until ten o'clock Monday morning. Zangara was returned to his cell where for the second time since his arrest he requested food: milk and soft-boiled eggs.

Governor David Sholtz did not feel that he needed the sanity commission report to help him formulate an opinion on this matter. The governor would become the motivating force behind the effort to expedite Zangara's case. Sholtz had been in office only a month and a half and was now basking in the national limelight because of the disaster in Bayfront Park. He had accompanied FDR on the train trip to New York; after his arrival there on Friday, February 17, the governor told the *New York Times* that Zangara could "be brought to trial within forty-eight hours. . . . Before I left Florida, I requested the [state] Attorney General to keep in close touch with the Zangara prosecution. I arranged, in the event of a death, that the grand jury should be called, or that there should be prompt filing of an Information . . ." That is, an indictment. The governor added, with apparent sincerity, "He will not be railroaded. Zangara will have a speedy but fair trial."

Sholtz was unquestionably influential as governor, but in actuality neither the governor nor the attorney general had any authority over criminal prosecution in Dade County. The attorney general is elected and answers only to the public; he is independent of the governor. The same is true of the county solicitor: Charles Morehead was elected and had to answer only to his own constituents or to a grand jury for nonfeasance or corruption in his office.

It was not only Sholtz who was demanding speedy action in this case. The day after the shooting, the *Miami Daily News* editorialized: "In this case, at least, there must be swift, decisive action. The facts seem plain, from Zangara's own statement, even though the full consequences of his act may not yet be realized. Let the law take its course, but make that course so speedy and sure as to emblazon a warning to the world against the toleration of a Zangara anywhere in the society of man." The Gainesville *Florida Sun*, three hundred miles to the north of Miami, said, "It is to be hoped that the laws . . . the ordinarily slow-grinding laws . . . will speed up to deal with him." According to the *Chicago Tribune*, Zangara's lawyers commented on February 17 that their client should be "shut away from society"; they were reported to have said that his "present views" made him a menace to public safety.

The *Miami Daily News* did urge caution on Saturday, February 19: "Surely a land which is gradually shaming out the disgrace of lynching can do something to check the murder mania that has destroyed one out of every five presidents since 1865." And on February 18, the Daytona Beach *News-Journal* said, "Nothing would be accomplished by the lynching of Zangara." But there were angry letters to the editor: one Edward Seifert of Miami told the *Daily News* that Zangara was "a canker on society"; that it was outrageous that taxpayers had to pay any lawyer for Zangara, let alone three lawyers; that it was "adding insult to injury" that Zangara should be housed in the county jail to eat up taxpayers' money, and expressed the hope that "the spirit of California's Forty-Niners will speed this farce of a trial to a finish without any plea of insanity . . . and make this beast harmless forever." This was a reference to a "vigilance committee" which lynched scores of criminals in San Francisco in 1849 when a corrupt justice system refused to indict them. It was in this atmosphere that south Florida's elected criminal public officials decided to reach a happy medium between the deliberate moverment of the law and the summary justice of the lynch mob.

The Jacksonville *Florida Times-Union* did not wait for the official conclusion of the "sanity commission," but reported on Saturday that two "psychiatrists" outside the commission had declared that Zangara was sane. These were County Physician E.C. Thomas, who had given Zangara a cursory physical examination on the night of his arrest and Dr Dan Hardie, Jr., the sheriff's son, who was an associate in the neurology department of Jackson Memorial Hospital. Neither of these men was a psychiatrist.

In any case, on Saturday morning the two court-appointed psychiatrists, Agos and Moore, delivered their report to the court. It consisted of eighty-three words and remains the only written psychiatric evaluation of Zangara during his lifetime:

> The examination of this individual reveals a perverse character, willfully wrong, remorseless and expressing contempt for the opinions of others. While his intelligence is not necessarily inferior, his distorted judgment and temperament is incapable of adjustment to the average social standards. He is inherently suspicious and anti-social. Such ill-balanced erratic types are classified as a psychopathic personality. From this class are recruited the criminals and "cranks" whose pet schemes and morbid emotions run in conflict with the established order of society.

The doctors had been asked to render an expert opinion on whether Zangara was legally insane; that is, whether he knew the difference between right and wrong. But they chose not to discuss this point; they maintained, and continued to maintain, that they had not been asked to reach this legal conclusion. The *Chicago Tribune,* on that same day, had reached a definite conclusion about Zangara's mental state: an editorial writer called him both "a mental defective" and "a maniac."

It looked at that time as though there would be no question of a death sentence: both Mayor Cermak and Mrs Gill were reported to be on the mend. So if Zangara pleaded guilty on Monday, the proceeding would end. But the press wondered whether he would plead guilty or not guilty by reason of insanity. Zangara's lawyers would not say; they suggested the press wait and see. Prosecutor Morehead said, "If he pleads guilty, we will not need witnesses, but if he pleads not guilty, we will not be able to have witnesses here by Monday." He added that he would have to bring in experts from outside to examine Zangara if he made an insanity plea.

While Zangara's lawyers kept their counsel, young Dr Moore of the sanity commission was in a mood to meet the press. On Sunday in an interview, he expanded upon his diagnosis, saying that Zangara's actions were "a product of very illogical reasoning. It points rather conclusively to an inherent inability to make a satisfactory social adjustment in even this broad-minded country . . . Dr Agos and I agree that this individual is not well fitted to take a place in the society of normal people. Such individuals are sent to the medical profession for an accurate diagnosis in legal terms, but in law there seems to be no terms or provision adequate to provide for the disposition of such cases . . . For such borderline cases there seems to be much quandary, at least over the legal terms involved . . . Zangara," he concluded, "may be considered by some people able to distinguish right from wrong, which constitutes sanity in legal terms." Thus he did not give his own opinion on that crucial point.

Twenty years later, in a *New Yorker* interview, Dr Moore expressed a more definite point of view. "I consider him a paranoiac character, if not a true paranoiac," he said. "Medically, he was *not* sane. Legally, he was considered sane in that he could recite the rules of behavior and knew when he was acting contrary to those rules. I am sure if he were alive today and we had the modern facilities for examining him psychiatrically, he would be adjudicated as a very insane person and probably hopelessly insane." He added in what he called "an offhand opinion" that if Zangara had lived, within five years he might have lapsed into "little more than a vegetative existence."

On Monday, February 20, four days after the shooting, Zangara was brought once more into Room 630 for arraignment and trial. As he entered the courtroom in the custody of chief sheriff's deputy Guy C. Reeve, the crowd stood up, photographers scurried about and movie cameras hummed. The prisoner, wearing beltless trousers and a blue dotted shirt open at the neck, was seated in the leather chair he had used before. Plainclothes deputies stood behind him, facing the audience to ensure against any attack. That morning's *Miami Herald*, in a particularly vitriolic editorial, had announced a "campaign against the Zangara class," those who come "to a great extent from southern Europe," and urged that "the United States round up such foreigners and ship them back home when possible. For those of the Guissepi [*sic*] Zangara type there should be no room. Any with radical opinions must be barred."

While they waited for the judge, the lawyers conferred with Zangara, who smiled, rubbed his chin frequently, wet his lips and gesticulated freely, talking in a low voice, his eyes roving about the room. He writes about this in his memoir:

> The day I went to court, I remember there was not enough room for the people to get in to the courtroom. I was in court for three days and the court was crowded all the time. The people could not understand how I could take things so calm and contented. They marveled at the way I took it. I was not worried. There were many people that took photographs of me while I was in court. They also took motion pictures of me.

At three minutes after ten that morning, Judge Collins entered the room, the bailiff called for order and the clerk called the jury venire, the group of qualified electors from whom the six-person jury is chosen. (In Florida, twelve-person juries hear only capital crimes and real estate condemnations.) The clerk, George F. McCall, called out the names of about twenty men, who took seats in the front of the courtroom. They took the venireman's oath in unison and Jo▓ ▓ V. Dillon an assistant prosecutor, questioned them collectively on their general qualifications to serve. All were found qualified and none asked to be excused. At this point the judge said he would consider motions.

Lewis Twyman moved for a dismissal of the three charges of attempted murder because Zangara was trying to kill Roosevelt and not the three bystanders whom he hit by accident. The charge of attempting to murder Roosevelt was justified, Zangara's lawyer said. The judge's response was simply, "Denied."

The defendant's lawyers had a problem with the kind of plea Zangara would make, since it was not yet known whether his victims would survive. Twyman therefore asked for a continuance until their fates were evident. He argued that there was no difference at law between those slightly wounded and those who might die. The intention of the perpetrator would be the same in either instance. If Zangara were found guilty of, or if he pleaded guilty to, attempting to murder FDR, Bill Sinnott, Russell Caldwell and Margaret Kruis, and then Mayor Cermak or Mrs Gill died, Zangara would, in effect, have already been found guilty of murder. "We will prejudice this man's fate if we move today." Twyman said. "The man doesn't care what happens—he'll tell Your Honor that— but we who represent this poor boy, in the interest of fairness and justice to him—ask that this case be postponed until the condition of the other two people becomes known . . . Lest we watch carefully our actions in this case, we may prejudice ourselves if the other cases arise. We are hurrying this trial—I don't think anyone is trying to do wrong, however—when we don't know, in fact, what he has done. We don't know yet whether he has killed or wounded two persons." He urged the court to proceed "with calmness," implying that it ought not to be influenced by public outrage.

Charles Morehead, responding for the state, said, "If there has ever been a case where calm prevailed in the court's proceeding, it is this one." Just the other day, he argued, the defendant himself had told the court that he wanted to proceed without delay; he did not even want to be represented by counsel. And "Your Honor, in the greatest of calm and fairness, delayed the proceedings until counsel among the most able at the bar was appointed."

However, the day before, Morehead had told the press that if the accused pleaded not guilty, the prosecution would have to ask for a postponement to get their witnesses to court and bring in out-of-state psychiatrists to examine the prisoner. This would have taken weeks. Thus Morehead could not have argued against a continuance if he believed that Zangara was going to enter a not-guilty plea. The prosecutor would have looked foolish if he had been forced to ask for a continuance moments after having argued against the defence's request for a continuance.

Twyman was correct here from the viewpoint of both fairness and practicality. The judge should have postponed the trial until the fate of the two severely injured victims was known. But publicity and politics added pressure in the case.

Judge Collins denied Twyman's motion to delay and Zangara was called to the bench to hear the charges read and to enter his plea. He seemed disinterested as Morehead began to chant the charges in the style of the time, using precise legal phrasing. But when he intoned, ". . . it is charged that on the fifteenth day of February 1933, the said Giuseppe Zangara, alias Joe Zangara, did then and there—"

"That means same thing," Zangara interrupted. "Joe and Giuseppe mean same thing. You call me Joe and Giuseppe. You make people think I'm fool." He added that the prosecutor had misspelled his first name, It was G-i-u, he said, not G-u-i.

When the time came for Zangara to enter his plea, Twyman said that despite the fact that the sanity commission had found that Zangara was a social misfit and "a psychopathic personality," his client did not wish to plead guilty by reason of insanity. His attorneys chose to leave it to their client to decide whether he was sane. Twyman pleaded Zangara guilty on each of the four counts. Having accepted the guilty plea, the judge would then be expected to listen to the defense argument for leniency, perhaps to listen to a few words from the defendant himself and then to pronounce sentence. But Zangara's lawyers were not finished.

"Your Honor," Twyman said, "my client has insisted on his guilt. He has one gruesome regret. He is sorry he did not succeed in his attempt on the life of President-elect Roosevelt. He scoffs at the idea he may be insane. After talking with the doctors and Zangara, we came to the conclusion he could be nothing but sane."

Alfred Raia, expressed some reservations. "We are fully determined that this plea we have entered for our client is correct," he said. "But this man's mental state presents a puzzle." James McCaskill, the third defense lawyer, asked the court to ignore "the cries from every city and crossroads in the nation for the blood of this man." He thus reminded the judge—if he needed reminding—of the public pressure against Zangara. According to the *Herald*, none of the three lawyers made a definite request for leniency. Twyman asked the judge to interrogate Zangara, although the defense lawyer had to know that Zangara could only harm himself on the witness stand. But this would be the first time the public would hear Zangara and the lawyers may well have wanted to show everyone what a difficult client they had.

"The court has no desire to interrogate him," the judge said. But on Twyman's insistence, Judge Collins agreed to hear Zangara's story and question him about his life. Zangara was led to the witness box on the judge's left; photographers, their big cameras flashing, pushed past the railing gate; newsreel cameras outside the balustrade were propped on tripods in front of the defendant. Collins gaveled for order while the bailiff shouted, "Everybody be quiet!"

When the room had settled down, Collins turned to the little man sitting in the witness box to his left.

"Zangara," the judge began, "how old are you?"

Zangara responded as usual that he was thirty-three (although he was thirty-two).

Collins asked him then where he was born, whether he had been married and whether his parents were living. His father, Zangara said, was living. Since he had been in America, he had been working as a bricklayer. The judge asked him if he had lived in New Jersey.

"A lot of time in New Jersey. I was go out sometime because I suffer with the stomach all the time, to change the air."

"How long have you been in Miami?"

"In the last year, three months, come back to New York, then here. Now been two or three months."

"What have you been doing since you have been down here?"

"Nothing. I have little money to live because when I work I keep."

"Do you engage in sports—games of any kind?"

"No, just shuffleboard in the park."

"Have you ever been in trouble before?"

"No, no trouble, no, no. I not been in any jail. This is first time."

"How long did you plan this shooting, or did you plan the shooting before it took place in the park?"

"No."

"When did it first come to your mind to do that?"

"All the time my stomach is in my mind."

"When did it first come to your mind?"

"When I get trouble in the stomach, when it come, my head look like I am gone. You see, I suffer all the time, and I suffer because my father send me to work when I was little boy. Spoil my life. If I no suffer, I no have trouble I no kill president. If I nice, well, I no bother the president. It got in my mind because capitalists make trouble to the poor people. Spoil my life. Everybody in school and no have this kind sickness. If I was well, I no bother the president."

He made good money as a bricklayer, he said in response to the judge's question about that, and when the judge asked him whether he felt he had been allowed a fair chance to make a living, he responded, "Yeah, all the trouble is here," rubbing his stomach. "What's the use of living? I was better dead. Suffer all the time. Suffer all the time."

"Has anybody in this country ever tried to harm you?"

"No, nobody. No."

"Why did you wait until after [Roosevelt] got through speaking?"

"No have chance because lot of people in front. No have no chance. Try to pass, chair move. When I try to kill Roosevelt somebody move chair and I miss."

"Did you know Mayor Cermak?"

"No. I didn't know him. I just want to kill the president and was too many people. I do not know nobody. Just know the president because I see picture in paper."

"You didn't know Mayor Cermak at all?"

"No, no, no," Zangara answered emphatically. "I want just the president. Do not want nobody else. I am sorry I shot somebody else. I want to shoot the president because capitalists is because I am sick. I am ready for die. No use living. When I am living I try to kill president because capitalists kill me. Take all my life away. I am no good. Stomach like drunk man. Can't walk on street, people think I am drunk. I make fifty-fifty."

At that point Twyman interrupted to explain to the judge what Zangara meant by "fifty-fifty." Zangara wanted to get even with society for his ill health, which he blamed on capitalism. "Yeah, yeah," Zangara agreed, nodding his head in affirmation. "I think the capitalists kill me and nobody can take my mind away [change my mind]. So long as I got the trouble nobody take my mind away. As I am well, I am good."

"Don't you want to live? Don't you enjoy living?" Judge Collins asked in a puzzled tone.

"No, because I sick all the time. I don't care whether I live or die. I don't care for that." He told the judge that his mother was dead, but that he had a stepmother and six sisters in Italy. At that point, Twyman suggested to the judge that Raia be allowed to ask some questions in Italian.

Raia then questioned Zangara in Italian, translating their dialogue. Had there been any insanity in Zangara's family? "Anybody crazy on your mother's side of the family? Anybody crazy on your father's side?" The answer to these questions was "No." But Raia persisted: was there anybody in Zangara's family that ever went to the "crazyhouse"? At this point, Zangara seemed to lose patience. "No!" he said, "I no crazy! No use asking same question. My stomach make me suffer all time. I suffer too much fire. Get in here like burn. I get mad. Like I mad. All fire in here. Fire in my head and I turn round like I am drunk man. I feel like I shoot myself sometimes, and I figure, 'Why shoot myself? I am going to shoot president and make it fifty-fifty.' I just think maybe cops kill me if I kill president."

Raia asked him if he drank; the reply was that with his stomach, alcohol would kill him. He had been to doctors in Miami, he said: "Miami, I have all specialists and nobody can know the trouble." Raia then began to cross-examine his client, creating a record of premeditated intent and unmitigated guilt. Did Zangara remember swearing an oath to this country when he was naturalized? Zangara said no. Did he know what he was doing when he shot at Roosevelt on Wednesday night? "I want to kill the president, that's all," Zangara said impatiently.

"You knew it, didn't you?" Raia asked accusingly. Zangara did not answer.

Probably even Twyman thought Raia was going too far. At this pause he interrupted his colleague's examination to ask whether Zangara had ever been to school and how old he was when he started to work. Then the tone of his interrogation began to resemble Raia's. "When you were down at the park that night, did you have—"

"I have trouble in my stomach."

"Did you have a picture of the president?"

"Yes, in my pocket."

"What did you have that for?"

"To see him."

"You didn't know him, did you?"

Zangara responded that he had taken the picture and accompanying article from the paper to read and had forgotten it in his pocket.

Twyman was insistent. "So you could tell who the president-elect was?"

"No," Zangara said. "Just to read."

Twyman appeared to be trying to establish that his client brought the picture in order to identify his target. "When you saw the president-elect, did you recognize him from this picture you were carrying?"

No, Zangara said, he just happened to have it in his pocket because he had been reading it.

"You took that picture down—" Twyman persisted.

Zangara interrupted impatiently. "That night, that same day I was shoot. Same day. Because I got a chance, I go to kill. That's all. Because I suffer all the time."

The judge asked, "Could you tell from the picture which man it was?"

"Yeah, yeah. Sure, I shoot straight to him. Somebody move my hand. Too many people across. Not my fault. People are fool to move." The judge asked why the defendant did not shoot when FDR was standing up to speak. Zangara replied that he did not get the chance; there were too many people in front of him while Roosevelt spoke and people standing on all the chairs around him so he could not get up high enough during the speech. As soon as there was room on one of the chairs, he jumped up and shot, but someone moved the chair just as he was shooting and spoiled his aim. "They fools!" he exclaimed. "They should let me kill him." He had climbed onto a small iron chair, he said, not a bench.

Judge Collins was interested in the way Zangara had been treated in the United States over the nine years he had been here. "Haven't the American people been kind to you since you have been over here?"

"No, nobody, no."

"Have they mistreated you in any way?"

"No, I don't bother nobody. Pay my board, that's all."

"Don't people treat you fairly?"

"No. Nobody treat me nothing. I don't treat for nobody. I suffer all the time. I stay to myself. I don't like no peoples."

Twyman asked if Zangara belonged to any church or organizations.

"No, nothing. Don't belong to nothing," Zangara said. "All I did was in my mind, because I suffer with the stomach."

Raia asked, "Do you regret it now, are you sorry that it happened?"

"I no regret much, because I no kill."

"What do you mean, you don't regret much because you didn't kill?" Raia asked. "Aren't you a little bit sorry now because you did that?"

"No. I no sorry," Zangara said with some anger. "You can put the electric chair on me, that's all." He made a backhanded diagonal slice through the air with the edge of his hand.

At this point the judge called a halt, saying that the interrogation was "sufficient." The prosecutor did not question the defendant; the defense lawyers had really done his job for him. The questions posed by Zangara's lawyers were sufficiently damning to ensure as maximum sentence and to foreclose any hope of a defense if Cermak or Gill died. Now the time had come for Judge Collins to pass sentence. Zangara was escorted from the witness box to stand in front of the clerk's desk before and below the judge's bench. The accused had pleaded guilty to four counts of attempted murder, each count punishable by up to twenty years in the state penitentiary. The maximum possible sentence for Zangara was thus eighty years. The judge had the power to sentence him to any number of years up to eighty.

He could, for instance, sentence him to twenty years on all four counts to run concurrently.

Zangara stood before the bench, his hands clasped in front of him, his legs trembling slightly as he swayed back and forth. Photographers scrambled to get their pictures; the room burst into laughter as one photographer's flashbulb popped prematurely while he was leaping onto a table.

After thanking the three defense lawyers for their good work, Judge Collins announced: "It is the sentence at law and the judgment of this court that you, Giuseppe Zangara, be adjudicated guilty of each count of attempted murder and that for each count you are hereby sentenced to serve a term of twenty years at hard labor, to be served consecutively with each other."

As he was being led away, Zangara turned to one of his lawyers and asked what the judge had said. Then he turned to the judge and, quizzically, held up eight fingers. The judge nodded. Zangara, smiling, called out loudly, "Oh, judge, don't be stingy. Give me hundred years!"

"Maybe there will be more later," the judge said. Zangara laughed as he was led from the room.

As Judge Collins rose from his chair, a reporter asked him what he thought of Zangara's mental state. "The man is unquestionably sane," the judge said, as he stepped down from the dais. In the corridor, reporters asked for Zangara's reaction. "It's fair, it's right. I am satisfied," he reportedly said as he was hustled to the jail elevator. Later, in an interview in his cell, he said, "Eighty years or one hundred years—make no difference. I die in two, three years." He writes in his memoir:

> I remember the judge giving me the sentence of eighty years. I asked the judge, why are you so stingy? Why don't you give me a hundred years. And I told him I would die in two years anyhow, and go to my rest.
>
> I was then taken back to the same cell in the jail. I had eighty years but it did not worry me at all. I was contented.

Asked about the possibility of an appeal, the defense lawyers issued a written statement saying that they had asked Zangara if he wanted them to take further action and he had told them "he was satisfied with the sentence and wanted no appeal."

Eighteen months later, Judge E.C. Collins was indicted for embezzlement, jury rigging and public corruption. He received the news while he was singing psalms at a Baptist convention in Deland, Florida. He was allowed to resign from the bench and was never prosecuted, but the charges were later substantiated by a local newspaper.

The court could easily have appointed a competent criminal defense attorney who might have attempted to soften the blow which Zangara would inevitably receive; there were competent attorneys in Miami. The *Washington Post* in an editorial suggested, "Send for Darrow!" and commented sarcastically, "This was an ideal case for Clarence Darrow, the eloquent legal defender of assassins. Here is an opportunity for Darrow to arraign society for its brutal attitude toward Zangara." Indeed, sarcasm aside, this was the kind of case which might have interested Clarence Darrow. Zangara's lawyers did more damage to their client than if he had represented himself. And the worst was yet to come.

11

THE MAYOR

Anton Joseph Cermak was born May 2, 1873, in the village of Kladno, fifty miles from Prague, then the capital of Bohemia, a part of the Austro-Hungarian Empire. It was a land of impressive forests, majestic castles and open coal pits. The senior Anton Cermak was a coal miner who yearned for a better life for himself and his wife Catherine. In the 1870s, America had few immigrant restrictions: in fact, some railway companies advertised in northern European cities, sometimes offering free passage and free land to people willing to settle in the many towns springing up along the ever-expanding railroad tracks.

The Cermak family arrived in Chicago in 1874, but stayed only a few days before moving to Braidwood in Will County, south of the city, where there were coal mines, and where the family remained while they brought four more children into the world. At school in Braidwood, the young Cermak's teacher was George E. Brennan, who had lost a leg in the mines before becoming a schoolmaster. Brennan taught Cermak for six years, but he was his mentor for the rest of his life. Brennan was the bridge for Cermak between the old world and the new, helping him meld his Czech constituency into the Chicago Irish political powerbase. Brennan was destined to become the Democratic Party boss in the city.

At sixteen, Cermak needed at full-time job, but he was too young to work in the mines, so he walked to Chicago to find work in a mill at two dollars a week. He stayed there through the winter of 1886, and returned to Braidwood in the spring. Then he followed his father into the mines, helping to drive the mules which carried the coals to the surface. The miners were earning a dollar ten cents a day and chose the young Cermak to ask the pit boss for a raise, which he did, at the bottom of the pit. The boss, John Cherry, told the boy to step into the elevator and ride with him to the surface. When they reached it, Cherry told him to step out of the lift. "There," the boss said, "you've had your raise. Now you're fired."

This incident caused Cermak to be blacklisted in the Braidwood area; he had no choice but to seek work elsewhere. He walked once again to Chicago, following a drainage ditch which ended in the Lawndale district near 26th Street. He would be identified with that district, eventually building a home at 2143 South Millard Avenue. He got a job driving horses and had a reputation as a labor agitator who helped organize workers in the Gary, Indiana, steel mills and who was often jailed for fighting when he had a drink too many. By the time he was nineteen, he had enough money to buy waste wood at the nearby International Harvester plant and peddle it as firewood door to door. At this time he met seventeen-year-old Mary Horeja, a waitress at his favorite restaurant; they married within the year and settled into their own home. He began to take night classes in business and law.

A few years later, Cermak had forty employees selling wood and coal and hauling freight. He was soon on the board of directors of a local bank and parlayed that banking knowledge into establishing his own building-and-loan association, and later his own real estate company. His ambition led him inevitably to politics. He began as a Democratic precinct captain, was elected ward secretary and then became chairman of the ward. His mentor George Brennan, now a power in Irish politics, brought Cermak to the attention of the party boss, Roger C. Sullivan, and at thirty Cermak was elected to the state legislature from the Lawndale district. He served four terms, ending as the Democratic floor leader.

He joined the United Societies for Local Self Government, a liberal group working against drinking laws and Sunday closings, fighting the prohibition organizations. Cermak became the United Societies spokesman, earning the title of "Champion of Personal Liberty." He became an alderman, a post he held until 1912, and was later elected municipal court bailiff, whose office served municipal court orders, writs and summonses and was responsible for order and security in courtrooms. The bailiff augmented the powers of the city police department and had arrest powers to enforce the law. At that time, judges customarily appointed political cronies to serve as their personal bailiffs, and these cronies were deputies to the elected municipal bailiff. Cermak provoked a storm of outrage from the judges by firing sixty-seven deputy bailiffs and other workers and replacing them with his own people. The judges claimed it was their right to hire and fire court personnel. But they lost this fight.

Next, Cermak announced that although he personally opposed the Sunday Blue Laws, which prohibited drinking and commercial activity on the Sabbath, he would enforce them—in an equal fashion. The police chief was a Republican who enforced these laws only against Democrats. Cermak sent his bailiffs out on Sundays to close down Republican enterprises. The judges, meanwhile, launched an investigation of Cermak's office, charging graft and corruption. Cermak had created the Bailiffs' Benevolent Association to assist poor families whom his deputies had to evict from their homes for nonpayment of rent. The bailiffs took up collections for these people; the judges charged that these collections involved the requirement that "tips" be paid to get papers served. Hearings were held, but the investigation came to nothing, while the judges cried "whitewash."

Tiring of his chores as bailiff, Cermak got the support of the Municipal Voters League and was elected once more to the city council. The League did not like his anti-Blue Laws stance, but applauded his fiscal conservatism. He wanted to trim government operations and balance the city budget. He taxed doctors to help pay for basic municipal services; they protested, but they had to pay. He had become the consummate politician, joining the Masons, the Elks, the Moose, Kiwanis, the Irish Fellowship League, and the Izaak Walton League, among other organizations. Nevertheless, he was defeated in a bid to become county sheriff. Undeterred, he ran for president of the Cook County Board, and won. The county's finances were in a shambles when he took office; he was the Democratic president of a Republican body with a two-million-dollar deficit. But he was able to bring the finances into line and balance the budget.

Over the complaints of various civic organizations that he was wasting taxpayers' money, Cermak embarked on an ambitious development program for recreational facilities in Cook County. Before he left the Board, miles of highway were paved and 34,000 acres of parks, golf courses, forest preserves, bridal paths, baseball diamonds, swimming pools, playgrounds, tourist camps and toboggan runs were built. He began what was to become Midway Airport, and oversaw modernization of Cook County Hospital, the county jail, the Criminal Courts Building, the Oak Forest Children's Infirmary and Tuberculosis Hospital, as well as the Juvenile Court Detention Home. He also established the office of public defender, an almost unheard-of institution in the 1920s. And he would later boast that during the ten years he served as president of the County Board, while every other government entity raised taxes, he was able to cut spending by a million and a half dollars a year and avoid any increase in county taxes.

His personal fortune from his banking and real estate interests was growing along with his political reputation. By 1928 he was wealthy, and his family of three daughters was growing. His daughter Lillian married Richey V. Graham, who would serve as president pro tem of the Illinois state senate from 1933 to 1939; his daughter Ella married Dr Frank Jirka, who was to be Illinois Director of Health for seven years, and Helen married Floyd Kenlay, a Chicago lawyer whom she would soon divorce to marry Otto Kerner, Jr., later a two-term governor of Illinois. In 1928 Cermak's wife Mary died of cancer. But that did not deter him from running for the U.S. Senate that year, on an anti-Prohibition platform, handing out bottle openers as campaign souvenirs and describing himself as "the wettest of the dripping wets." But 1928 was a landslide Republican year: Cermak's opponent, the incumbent Otis Glenn, rode to reelection victory on Herbert Hoover's coattails. Even so, Cermak got more votes in Illinois than Al Smith, the Democratic presidential candidate.

Despite this loss, many of his supporters suggested Cermak run for governor of Illinois; they believed he could win easily. But he told his son-in-law, Richey V. Graham, that Cook County was his power base and was a more potent springboard to national politics than the governorship.

When George Brennan died, Cermak became the Chicago Democratic Party boss, and decided to run for mayor. The Republican incumbent, Big Bill Thompson, had had three terms, running what was considered to be one of the most corrupt and crime-ridden city governments of the twentieth century. In Thompson's Chicago, Al Capone and Frank Nitti flourished: Capone pocketed $100,000 a week from rackets; there were over six hundred unsolved murders, and booze, prostitutes and numbers games were omnipresent. This situation could not have existed without the connivance of the police, and the mayor controlled the police department. Gang wars, drive-by machine-gunnings were a common occurrence in Chicago, which had become an international symbol of American crime. Chicagoans were sick of it.

Cermak decided to take on Thompson. Together with an old ally, Moe Rosenberg, and Rosenberg's protege Jake Arvey, Cermak combined his Slavic power base with the strong Irish and Jewish constituencies in the city. Thompson fought back by accusing Cermak and Rosenberg of charging huge fees on foreclosures in their receivership business and of vote fraud through registration of drunks and corpses. Thompson tried also to explore ethnic prejudice against Czechs. Despite this, Cermak was elected by the greatest mayoral landslide in the city's history. The *Chicago Tribune*, the *Daily News* and the *American* had endorsed him, heaping praise on him as a public servant of the highest order, a forceful fighter, industrious, patient, sensible and a master of detail. His first act as mayor was to fire three thousand of Thompson's patronage workers, slash the city budget by millions and organize police squads to attack the mob.

Nineteen thirty-two was a busy year for Anton Cermak. The city was preparing for the 1933 World's Fair, and it was also hosting both the Republican and Democratic national conventions. The mayor was chairman of the Illinois delegation to the Democratic convention, which delivered its votes to Roosevelt. Shortly after the convention, Cermak suffered a heart attack and went on vacation to the town of Kladno, Czechoslovakia, where he had been born, and where he spoke of a new Chicago, reclaimed from the gangsters and racketeers who had dominated it even in European headlines.

Cermak has had his detractors. Carl Sifakis, in *Encyclopedia of Assassins*, maintains that Cermak was not really a reformer, and that he simply set out to replace the Capone mob, then headed by Frank Nitti, with mobster Teddy Newberry, whom Sifakis calls one of Cermak's friends. After Cermak's election Nitti engineered Newberry's murder. Cermak, Sifakis says, was known as "Ten Percent Tony" because that was his standard kickback. And Nitti sent Zangara to kill Cermak in revenge for a near-fatal attack upon Nitti by a Chicago detective in December 19, 1932, just two months before Cermak was shot in Bayfront Park.

John H. Lyle, Cermak's Republican opponent in the 1930 mayoral election, did not believe that Cermak was corrupt, but he, like

Sifakis, believed that Cermak's murder was a mob hit. In 1957, Lyle said that in 1930 Cermak told him about his plans to oppose the mob once he was in office. After he was elected, Cermak carried out his plans. Lyle writes that Cermak said:

> John, I am against this Mafia business just as much as you are, but they don't know it. And I won't tell them now. If I am elected mayor in April, though, that is the time to speak up.
>
> I will have special policemen with instructions to waste no time with those people. No political organizations can control them or get along with them.
>
> As soon as I am elected, I am going to call in the leaders, and I know who they are, and I will tell them to fold up their tents. I will assign some tough coppers . . . and I will get rid of them. You remember what I'm telling you.

The attack upon Nitti occurred during a public raid when Detective Harry Lang shot the mobster three times, without provocation: another detective testified at Lang's trial that he had searched Nitti, whom he said was unarmed, and was holding his wrists for handcuffs when Lang aimed his pistol at Nitti and fired. Afterward Lang deliberately shot himself in the finger so that he could claim that Nitti had resisted arrest. Nitti survived and Lang was found guilty; it was revealed that the detective had gone to that raid directly from a conference with Cermak.

Lyle was not alone in his conviction that Nitti had hired Zangara to kill Cermak as an act of vengeance for Lang's attack. Walter Winchell believed it too, and it is always a question that is on the table whenever the story of the Bayfront Park shooting comes up. Federal agents conducted an exhaustive investigation of the shooting and could find no link between Zangara and the Chicago mob.

12

DEATH WATCH

Two weeks after the shooting—and five days before his death—the *Miami Herald* ran a headline: "Mayor Cermak Definitely Is On Upgrade," over a story reporting that the mayor's doctors were "confidently predicting he would overcome his wound." His heart action had improved and he was on a soft diet. X-rays showed that neither the right lung, which had been pierced by the bullet, nor the left, showed any sign of abscess—no congestion or pus. It was Dr Frederick Tice who told the *Herald* that Cermak was "on the upgrade" and that "barring unforeseen circumstances, we now can say he will recover." Another doctor, Sterling Nichol, said "he has a reasonably good chance to live." But Karl Meyer, the noted Chicago specialist in gunshot wounds, did not seem to share the other doctors' optimism. Now he would say only that he hoped the mayor's increasing irritability was a sign of returning strength.

The family had bought a specially constructed apparatus, a Barach-Thurston oxygen chamber, and had had it flown to Miami, where it was set up on the sun porch outside Cermak's hospital room.

The chamber contained fifty percent oxygen. One nurse remembered that it was so cold inside the chamber that she had to wear an overcoat. In that chamber, Cermak received the last two of his three blood transfusions. He was to remain there until his death.

There were no blood banks in 1933; transfusions were given either directly, with the donor on a cot next to the patient and his blood injected into the patient's arm one syringe at a time, or indirectly, pumped from a bottle filled with the donor's blood. Cermak received blood indirectly, to improve his general strength and heart function. He was asleep most of the time, drifting in and out of consciousness.

By the end of February, the once-robust, fifty-nine-year-old man was gaunt, his face drawn and pale from three weeks of agony. His hair was white, his abdomen swollen and his breathing labored. The bullet was still lodged near his spine.

The doctors had decided that his abdominal pain was the result of preexisting enteritis or colitis for which they prescribed painkillers. On Thursday, March 2, his diet consisted of soft-boiled eggs and tea and he was receiving glucose intravenously. In addition to the pain, he was now plagued by hiccoughs, which his physicians could not control. On Friday he had what was considered a mild heart attack: his lips were blue and he seemed to have no pulse. Digitalis revived him. But he had taken a crucial turn for the worse, and even his optimistic doctors now knew that their patient was dying.

Mabel Gill, although still on the critical list, was beginning to rally. The night of the shooting, the doctors had removed the bullet which had pierced her intestines, and had repaired internal damage. She was now apparently winning the fight against infection caused by the leakage of fecal fluid into the abdominal cavity. She was conscious and eating solid food; her doctors were optimistic for the first time.

On Saturday, March 4, Franklin Roosevelt took the oath of office in Washington, before a battery of microphones. Bareheaded, under a sullen sky, with the sound of flags flapping in the cold breeze, the thirty-second president told a distressed nation that all it had to fear was fear itself. At the same time, Anton Cermak lay in his hospital bed, asleep for the most part: he woke once and asked what day it was. On being told it was Saturday, he murmured, "Oh. It must be Inauguration Day," and dozed off again. Down the hall, in an unused sun porch, a group of reporters were holding what they called "a death watch." Among them was Damon Runyon, who wrote, "The greatest single contributing factor in Mayor Cermak's favor is his indomitable courage, his will to live. He has rare gameness."

Cermak's condition puzzled his doctors. On that Saturday they decided to perform an exploratory puncture of his wounded right lung and abdomen in the region of the liver. The mayor's chest and upper abdomen were now tender, which could mean that there was a buildup of pus there. A needle attached to a tube was inserted into the abdomen near the liver as well as into the cavity of his right lung to locate and drain any abscesses. The needle in the chest cavity yielded first a bloody fluid and, when pressed harder, an effluvium which indicated that the lung, declared healed a week before, was gangrenous. The end was now certain. He was given twenty-four to forty-eight hours to live. The physicians issued a bulletin:

> Mayor Cermak, last evening, developed pain in the right shoulder, together with tenderness over the right lower chest and liver. This together with his general septic appearance, caused us to suspect the presence of either a subphrenic abscess or pleural empyrema.
>
> For this reason the space between the liver and the diaphragm was aspirated with negative results. The pleural cavity yielded old bloody serous fluid.
>
> The lung itself, on aspiration yielded a very foul, fetid air, but no pus, giving evidence that a gangrenous process was occurring in the lung.

The family was called to the hospital. A week earlier they had been prevented from coming because too many visitors had exhausted the mayor. Now his three daughters were allowed to look at their father through a window in the door to his porch. He spent a fitful Saturday night and on Sunday the family was called to his bedside. He was not aware that they were there. He died at 6:57 on Monday morning, March 6, 1933, nineteen days after the shooting. An autopsy was performed at the hospital, attended by most of the mayor's doctors, and the body was taken to the Philbrick Funeral Home in Miami to be prepared for the train trip to Chicago.

The doctors spoke to the press after the autopsy, but they did not actually reveal its results. Instead, they gave reporters the diagnosis they had made while Cermak was alive: that his strength had been sapped by a preexisting condition, an intestinal inflammation that had caused colitis, and that this had progressed so rapidly that it had become ulcerative. These ulcers, they said, had perforated the intestinal wall and caused peritonitis—an infection from leakage of fecal fluid into the body cavity—and ultimately gangrene of the abdominal tissue. And at the same time, they said, gangrene had developed in that portion of the lower right lung which had been pierced by the bullet. This report required the acceptance of the idea that ordinary colitis had progressed from inactive to ulcerative, then to perforation of the intestine, then to peritonitis, then to gangrene of the intestines and lung and had caused death—all in nineteen days. An internist has recently commented, "Bullets don't cause colitis."

The *Los Angeles Times* printed an interview with one of Cermak's doctors. The reporter had suggested that because "a great variety of maladies"—enteritis, colitis, diseases of the heart, lungs, kidneys, liver—had "invaded the frame of the unfortunate patient since he was wounded," it was possible that Zangara could present a defense that his bullet did not cause death. "That's poppycock," the doctor responded. "Every one of us can testify under oath that the bullet wound was the cause of death." And indeed three of them did so testify and nine of them signed a statement describing the cause of death; this was introduced into evidence at Zangara's sentencing.

But none of them, as far as we know, ever attempted to make a causative link between the bullet wound and death by ulcerative colitis.

The results of the autopsy were never released or even mentioned by these physicians. There may not even have been a written report. In 1933, Florida law required a post-mortem if a doctor testified at the coroner's inquest. E.C. Thomas, the county physician, testified at the inquest on the afternoon of the autopsy, saying only that he had attended the autopsy and that the bullet was the cause of death.

The doctors' signed statement is not a legal document, an official medical record, nor was it given under oath. It consists of three short paragraphs plotting the course of the patient's decline and ends:

> There is a definite continuity of the disease processes dating from the shooting and ending in death.
> First the bullet wound with immediate collapse of the lung and hemorrhage and profound shock. With the cardiac failure as a result of it, a disfunction of the digestive tract resulting in first a simple colitis which evolved into an ulcerative and then gangrenous colitis and a virtually simultaneous development of the gangrene at the site of the bullet wound in the right lung. Final perforation of the colon with peritonitis with death culminating as a result of the bullet wound, cardiac failure, gangrene of the lung and peritonitis.

At the sentencing hearing, the first to testify was R.S. Woodard, the hospital superintendent, who had not treated Cermak but had attended the autopsy. He said only that the bullet was the cause of death. Then Sterling Nichol, the local cardiologist, spoke for two minutes, saying that he had attended the mayor, who had died of a gunshot wound. The testimony of the general surgeon, John W. Snyder, was longer, but he said only that the autopsy was conducted to determine "the cause of death and the effect of the bullet wound in the internal part of the body." But he did not say what the autopsy revealed. He testified to what he believed Cermak's condition was during the course of treatment. Zangara's lawyers did not question this diagnosis, nor did they object to the admission of the doctors' statement into evidence.

The mayor's medical records were lost by the hospital decades ago. But newspaper accounts remain. The *Chicago Tribune* kept its readers informed about the mayor's condition and treatment on a daily basis, often using medical language. Cermak's doctors gave reporters a news bulletin every day, and individual doctors often gave interviews and answered questions. These accounts and the doctors' statement submitted to the court have been studied by Miami physician Dr William M Straight and several of his colleagues. Dr Straight, who knew most of the doctors involved in the Cermak case, concludes that the symptoms and treatment were consistent with a subphrenic abscess caused by perforation of the colon by a bullet—or possibly the grooving of the liver or gall bladder, and not with ulcerative colitis as Cermak's doctors had claimed. "Cermak died of septicemia caused by a subphrenic abscess," Dr Straight said. The abscess had contained itself in a pocket under the diaphragm and was draining into the bullet hole in the intestine. There was no colitis or gangrene. "In retrospect," Dr Straight comments, "it might have been wiser to open the abdomen to look for an intestinal perforation. I think it is likely the bullet penetrated the lower right lung, tore a hole in the right leaf of the diaphragm, perforated a loop of the transverse colon, and lodged in the body of the eleventh dorsal vertebra." Fecal fluid leaked into the abdominal cavity and caused an abscess between the liver and the right diaphragm.

During the nineteen days that Cermak was in the hospital, the perforation in the intestine could not heal because the infection killed tissue at the tear. This would explain why they were finding bloody stool, according to Dr Straight. What the doctors mistook for gangrene was the leakage of the abdominal abscess into the cavity through the tear the bullet had made in the diaphragm. This in turn infected the lung, causing more pus and dead tissue.

One doctor with whom Dr Straight consulted disagrees with the infected lung thesis. This retired general surgeon who has asked not to be "identified" does not believe that the mayor's lung was infected. He thinks that when Cermak's doctors aspirated the lung with a needle, searching for the subphrenic abscess, they accidentally pushed the needle through both lung and diaphragm and tapped into the abscess below the lung. They failed to realize that they had found not a gangrenous lung, but the subphrenic abscess they were looking for. He points out that the medical reports do not mention coughing and bringing up of fluid which would have occurred if this lung was infected and gangrenous.

Dr Straight believes that Cermak did not have a bad heart, and had never had a heart attack. Both tachycardia (speeding up and slowing down of heart action) and fever spikes are symptomatic of septicemia, which is what the mayor was suffering from. Finally, Dr Straight and his colleagues think that by the time Cermak died, his doctors must have known that they had made a fatal blunder in not opening him up immediately after the shooting. This exploratory operation had saved the life of Mrs Gill. And certainly, even if they had not operated immediately, as Cermak's condition worsened daily, they should have suspected enough to operate while the patient still had strength enough to survive the ordeal. There was a specific operation, the Oxner Resection, for classic subphrenic abscess, although this exploratory surgery was not often performed in 1933 in provincial hospitals like Jackson Memorial, without a strong suspicion of intestinal perforation. But it would have been routine even at that time in leading hospitals like Boston General.

Dr Straight and the others think that the doctors did not mention the autopsy in their written statement because this acknowledgement of their error would certainly have hurt their careers. Possibly they had discovered their mistake when they performed the puncture procedure but had decided it was too late to save Cermak, and announced that they had discovered gangrene. There is a possibility that they could have been considered guilty of malpractice. It is certainly doubtful that the doctors' admission that Cermak's life could have been saved by proper medical action would have had any effect on the legal consequences for Zangara.

■ ■ ■

When Zangara was informed, in his jail cell, of Cermak's death, he said, "Not my fault. Woman move my hand." He was asked whether he was sorry that the mayor was dead. "Sure," he said, "I sorry, like when die bird, or horse, or cow, I sorry."

■ ■ ■

Cermak died on Monday morning, March 6; on that same day an autopsy was performed, an inquest was held and the grand jury, which had been assembled two weeks earlier in anticipation of this event, used the inquest verdict to indict Zangara for first degree murder. His arraignment was scheduled for the following morning.

While the coroner's jury and the grand jury were deliberating that Monday afternoon, hundreds of Miamians were filing past Cermak's ornate bronze coffin in the Philbrick Funeral Home on West Flagler Street. His grandson Robert Graham, who was nine years old at the time, still vividly remembers the glass window in the lid of his grandfather's casket. By 5:30 P.M. the funeral cortege was assembled and the casket was ceremoniously escorted from the mortuary to the railway station, where a special seven-car train was waiting. Thousands of spectators crowded both sides of Flagler street to watch the cortege pass, and many more were waiting to see it at the depot. Redmond Gautier, the mayor of Miami, led the procession with the funeral committee; the American Legion drum and bugle corps flanked the hearse, its drummers slowly beating the funeral march. Then came the Shriners and, following them, limousines carrying Cermak's family. Hundreds of people fell in behind the limousines and followed the procession to the station, where a band began to play "Nearer My God To Thee" as the distant bells of the Methodist White Temple tolled. Legionnaire pallbearers lifted the flag-draped coffin and carried it slowly to a baggage car where an honor guard of eight officers—four Chicago detectives and four Miami policemen—took their places around it. The Miami officers were Raymond Jackson, Lester Crews and N.B. Clark, who had arrested Zangara, and Fitzhugh Lee, FDR's driver on that fateful night.

The train, draped in black and purple, left the station at six P.M., and traveled all that night, and all day and night Tuesday, carrying friends and family, policemen, politicians and the press. At ten in the morning on Wednesday, it arrived at Chicago's 12th Street Station in a gentle rain. The city was preparing for three days of mourning; flags were at half staff and schools and public buildings were closed. The train was met by the city council, the mayor's cabinet, a military escort and a crowd estimated at ten thousand. The city flag was placed on the casket as it was carried from the baggage car, with hundreds of policemen clearing the way through the throng. The funeral procession marched on foot from the station to the Cermak house on Millard Avenue, before thousands lining the streets in the blustery spring day. The casket was placed on a bier in the bay window of the modest parlor; it was opened and there the mayor lay in state for twenty hours. All day and all that night forty to fifty thousand Chicagoans passed through to view the body, wearing a path from the kitchen through the parlor to the front door. The press reported that there was a line four blocks long waiting to enter the house.

The next morning the body was taken from the house through the crowded streets to city hall, which was draped in black and purple. The casket was placed on a catafalque under the central archway of the building; the body lay in state there for another twenty-four hours: the mourners passed between lines of five hundred policemen in full dress uniform, while a choir sang hymns.

Finally, at ten o'clock on Thursday morning, March 9, a procession extending for more than a mile, consisting of public officials, representatives of civic organizations, federal troops and the National Guard, escorted the casket west on Randolph Street, south on Canal and west again on Washington Boulevard, to the Stadium, where a Masonic service was conducted. Cermak did not belong to any church, but eulogies were delivered by a Catholic and an Episcopal priest, as well as by a rabbi. The main eulogy was delivered by Governor Henry Horner.

After the services, the procession formed once more and moved north on Sacramento Boulevard and Kedzie Avenue to the Bohemian National Cemetery on Crawford Avenue where the body was interred. At about the same time that Cermak was being lowered into his grave, Giuseppe Zangara sat in Room 630 of the Dade County courthouse, listening to Circuit Judge Uly O. Thompson pronounce the sentence of death.

13

THE LAST ARRAIGNMENT

More than two weeks after his eighty-year sentence, Zangara remained in jail awaiting the fate of his seriously wounded victims. On the afternoon of March 6, the day of Cermak's death, the grand jury presented its first degree murder indictment to Judge Thompson, who immediately scheduled an arraignment for the next morning. Zangara's case now moved from the Criminal Court of Record to the more senior Circuit Court.

On that same day, Dr Thomas W. Hutson, Mabel Gill's physician, issued a bulletin: "Mrs Gill is less critical than last week. She is slowly improving and is overcoming the infection. She is now having normal temperatures off and on and is taking nourishment regularly through mouth."

Just before 11:30 on Tuesday morning, March 7, Zangara, wearing a yellow print shirt and displaying his usual broad (and, to many, infuriating) smile, was escorted into Room 630. The sheriff's deputies, who had searched the male spectators for weapons (and would search the women's handbags as well), surrounded Zangara to protect him from the crowd.

As the sharp-faced middle-aged judge entered, the court rose and, after Thompson had settled into his chair, he asked the prisoner if he had counsel. With a casual gesture, Zangara pointed to his three attorneys, Lewis Twyman, James McCaskill and Alfred Raia, who were sitting in the well of the courtroom. "These ones take care of me," he said, and leaned back in his chair, smiling faintly. The three lawyers were reappointed to represent him on the new charges. Then State Attorney N. Vernon Hawthorne stood up and announced that the State of Florida was ready to proceed.

Lewis Twyman said that he and his associates wanted the arraignment and sentencing to take place that afternoon. But Judge Thompson had to preside over another trial and could not take the plea then. Twyman amended his request: in view of the international attention centered on this case, he said, he and his colleagues needed time to prepare their plans carefully. Thompson agreed to reschedule the arraignment for the day after next.

Under Florida law, if Zangara pleaded guilty to capital murder, he could be sentenced, after an evidentiary hearing to establish facts, to life imprisonment or electrocution. But if Zangara pled not guilty, he was entitled to trial by a twelve-man jury. If he was found guilty, he could be sentenced to death only if a majority of the jury refused a recommendation of mercy. Surely this jury panel would have been the best course of defense for Zangara's lawyers, who could have appealed to the members to spare the defendant's life. Even without a recommendation of mercy, the judge in a jury trial was not required to impose the death penalty. The lawyers could have an opportunity to convince the judge to show mercy. Zangara wanted, it is true, to plead guilty, but he was ignorant of legal procedures; even if he wanted to die, his lawyers could have convinced him that he would enjoy his notoriety a little longer if he entered a not guilty plea. There is no indication that his three lawyers ever attempted this course or even considered it.

Court was adjourned; reporters were able to interview the prisoner briefly as he was led through the corridors to the jail elevators.

Zangara appeared to be relishing the attention he was receiving. He had been photographed holding newspapers with his name in headlines and his picture on the front pages. He announced that he was going to write a "beega book" about himself and his views of life and politics. He was asked if he was going to write about Communism.

"No, no, no," he said. "Just about me—Zangara—what I do. So everybody read."

Did he hope to make a lot of money from this book?

"No. What good money do me? I be in electric chair."

Asked about how he felt about Cermak's death, he said, "Too bad," and added that it was the woman's fault. In an odd display of what could be called gallantry, he was saying that Mrs Cross had deflected his aim, but privately, his lawyers said later, he agreed with the police and Tom Armour that she had really done nothing.

On Thursday morning, March 9, three days after Cermak's death and twenty-three days after the shooting, Zangara appeared again before Judge Thompson, and again seemed to enjoy the attention he was getting. He rubbed his left cheek and chin constantly with his left hand.

At the outset of the proceedings, Twyman approached the bench and argued that the state should dismiss the second count of the indictment charging that Cermak was murdered by premeditated design. Count One of the indictment, that Zangara had killed Cermak because of a premeditated design to kill FDR, was, he said, sufficient. Zangara was going to plead guilty to the first count anyway. This was a meaningless technicality, which the state readily abandoned. This more or less completed the exercise of legal skill by Zangara's lawyers.

The arraignment then began. Zangara and his three lawyers rose and stood before the clerk's desk below the judge's bench. Hawthorne asked, "Is your name Joseph Zangara? . . . Also known as Giuseppe Zangara?"

"Joseph when I been in America—Joseph. It is the same thing. Means the same."

"You will please pay attention to the reading of this indictment," Hawthorne said. He then read the formal indictment and asked, "Do you, Joseph Zangara, to this charge of murder that I have just read, plead guilty or not guilty?"

"I want to kill the president because I no like the capitalists. I have the gun in my hand," Zangara said. "I kill kings and presidents first and next all capitalists."

Twyman pleaded his client guilty "with his full consent, knowledge and preference."

Next came the taking of testimony. The first witness was Tom Armour, who said that Zangara was the man he saw shooting a pistol at Roosevelt from thirty to thirty-five feet away. After Zangara, who was standing on a bench, had fired the first shot, Armour said he grasped the shooter's right arm and held on to it. He could remember feeling the recoil of four separate shots; there was a brief pause between the second and third shots.

Twyman's cross-examination, like his entire approach during the proceedings, did not seem to reflect any coherent defense strategy. He asked Armour to stand and demonstrate what had happened. "Well," the witness said, "he was standing on his tiptoes. He raised the gun over the heads of the crowd and shot, and by that time the heads parted, and by that time he had a clean channel or sight to the president-elect's head. He drew the pistol down, taking a more direct aim. I recall that because as I walked over to him I sighted over the barrel of the gun and it was directly aiming at Roosevelt's head. I don't say it was directly right on a level with my eye, but I could recognize that the revolver was aimed pretty near the president."

"Couldn't you pull his arm down?" Twyman asked.

"Down! If I had, it would have shot someone in front of us. I remember concluding to push [his arm] up in the air, thinking he would stop shooting when I got it up. That was where all the pushing was. From the second shot, I caught his arm and just shoved it up before the explosion of the second shot. He seemed to be undecided what to do, and he turned his wrist down. Of course his hand was free and he turned it down and shot; and I remember I looked up and seen the guy and thought, 'The son of a gun is going to shoot anyway.'"

"Why didn't you jump on him and stomp him down?"

"Well, maybe you would have done it if you were me," Armour said, annoyed. Twyman persisted, asking again, "Why didn't you do it?" but the judge interrupted, telling Armour to sit down. Twyman's last question was whether a woman had been there, holding onto Zangara's arm. Armour responded in the negative.

The next witness was Dixie Herlong, the stenographer for the justice of the peace, who had testified at the inquest two days before. She testified now that she had heard Zangara's confession the night of the shooting, that he was warned of his rights, and that he was not threatened and had no reason to fear for his safety. He told his story in a "reasonably calm way" and he admitted shooting at President-elect Roosevelt because "he didn't like presidents or capitalists."

Twyman asked what kind of language Zangara had used. She said that he had not cursed nor used any improper language in his statement the night of the shooting, but that he complained of a stomach ailment that bothered him all the time,

Hawthorne next called Sheriff Hardie, who said he was sitting on the bandstand stage when the firing began. He knew Anton Cermak, he said, so he recognized him in the crowd. When the shots were fired from about twenty to twenty-five feet away, Hardie leapt off the stage, passing Cermak, who still stood shakily on his feet, and attacked Zangara whom he took to jail where the defendant gave him a statement saying that he had planned the shooting; he had read the newspapers about Roosevelt's impending arrival and had decided to shoot him.

Hardie testified that his deputies had searched Zangara's room at 126 Northeast 5th Street and confiscated his effects. There were several newspaper articles among them, with pictures of Roosevelt and information about his Secret Service protection, the car he would be using and the times and routes of the motorcade. (Ironically, the same clipping contained an unrelated story about the recent discovery of a death threat which had been sent to Abraham Lincoln by John Wilkes Booth, promising "death in its most awful forms.")

On cross examination, Twyman asked the sheriff what kind of prisoner Zangara was; Hardie replied that he was a model prisoner, that a records check had been performed and no evidence of a prior criminal record had been found. He believed that Zangara had never associated with criminals, that the prisoner had a stomach complaint and apparently did not smoke, drink or curse.

Hawthorne next called H.L. Edmunds, winter visitor from Ottumwa, Iowa, who had been staying at the Park Hotel in Miami and had come to Bayfront Park to get a glimpse of FDR. All the seats had been taken approximately two hours before the speeches began, he said, but about an hour and a half before the ceremonies started, he saw the man he identified as Zangara moving toward him. "He came pushing in through the crowd until he came to where some ladies were standing right behind me," Edmunds said. "He started pushing them around and I turned and said, 'Where do you think you are going,' and he said, 'I am going right down in front.' 'Well, I'm sorry, but you cannot go down there, it is full' and he said, 'It don't look like to me it is full' and I said, 'There are many people sitting on the ground, it isn't proper, it isn't right for you to go and stand out and push yourself in front of someone else.' And from that he didn't push any more but stopped and didn't try to go any further." Zangara, the witness said, fired the shots from the place where he had stopped him, just two feet behind him. Twyman had no questions for this witness.

Next called were the three doctors: R.S. Woodard, Sterling Nichols and John W. Snyder. Each testified that Zangara's bullet had killed Cermak. "The death, I believe, was due to the gunshot wound in the right chest," Dr Snyder said.

"You have made reference to a colitis and to a pneumatic condition," Hawthorne noted. "Are you in a position to say they were accelerated by the gunshot wound?"

"I think they were the definite result of the gunshot wound," Snyder said, although, having helped perform the autopsy a few days earlier, he probably knew that there had never been any colitis or pneumonia. Asked whether he had participated in an autopsy, Snyder replied, "I did." Strangely, Twyman had no questions for this crucial witness. But Hawthorne said months later that he had some misgivings about the doctors' testimony. He asked a further question: "I might ask you this, doctor: was the autopsy performed for the purpose of definitely determining the cause of death and the effect of that wound in the internal part of his body?" Snyder answered, "It was."

The door had been opened for Twyman to ask the doctor about how the mayor had died of colitis caused by a bullet, and about what precisely had been discovered in the autopsy. A man's life hung in the balance here, and the doctor's response could have meant the difference between a sentence of death or life in prison, even for a man like Zangara. An argument could have been made that the judge could not in good conscience sentence the prisoner to death for a murder which—but for physicians' blunders—might not have happened at all.

Hawthorne offered the doctors' statement into evidence. This was actually an inadmissable document under the rules of evidence, but Twyman did not object. In his turn, Twyman submitted the report of psychiatrists Moore and Agos into evidence. This was the one-paragraph report that labeled Zangara a "crank" who was "perverse—willfully wrong, remorseless, and expressing contempt for the opinions of others." Apart from being damaging to the defense, this report, too, was inadmissable. Hawthorne gave a short speech in which he pointed out that the report was not only inadmissable as hearsay, but was also irrelevant, because sanity was not an issue in the case. But he did not argue against its admission: "I don't think it is necessary but [it] can do no harm."

Twyman said the report was being offered as a "contribution" so that the court would know "the real situation." He seemed simply to want the court—and the public—to know how difficult his client was.

The state's case rested and Twyman put Zangara on the stand. In response to the usual questions about his age, his place of birth and so on, Zangara said, as he always did, that he was thirty-three years old, although actually he would not be thirty-three for another six months. He had never been to school he said; when he was nineteen he attempted, out of embarrassment, to learn to write "a little bit." His father had refused to send him to school because he did not have the money; the capitalists had the money and his father worked for the capitalists. Zangara had had to work when he was six, and the work was hard enough to kill him : he had to shovel grain on the farm to feed the pigs, "things like that." His hard work and lack of schooling had caused his stomach condition, he believed.

"That way I make my idea to kill the president," he said. "Kill any president, king, and I have a machine gun in my hand—I will kill all president and king, and all capitalist and everything they take. Money I put in the fire and burn 'em up because the poor people need no money. Just bread. No money. Bread is good thing. Lot of people have millions and lot of people haven't a nickel and little kids hungry for bread." The audience found this remark amusing, and the judge rapped for order. How long, Twyman asked, had Zangara had this idea?

"I started when I was about fourteen up. Got this same thing in my mind all myself," he answered, with an air of pride.

Except for one maternal uncle—Vincent Carfaro—Zangara's family, he said, lived in Italy. His mother had died when he was two years old and his father had remarried; he had a stepmother and six half-sisters. He said again that his stomach ailment had begun when he was six years old. He had been to doctors, but they wanted to be paid and he had no money, even though his father made him work. He blamed the capitalists for that, too.

Twyman asked, "You are not mad at your father, are you?"

"I am mad at capitalists," Zangara said, "because capitalists boss to my father. I am mad at capitalist because capitalists have education and the money."

His stomach, he said, was hurting even as he spoke; it hurt all the time. "The doctor told me can't cure it out because I was worked when a little boy. Nobody can take it away. I hurt all the time. When a little boy, I hurt all the time." He could not smoke or drink; not only liquor, but he could not even drink hot or cold water; he could drink only water tepid from the tap.

Twyman asked him if he had ever been arrested before. Zangara avoided the question as he had with Hardie, by saying "No, this is the first time I been in jail."

Had he tried to get away after the shooting?

"No, I can't get away from there because there was twenty-five thousand people. I give the gun to the policeman."

No one, he said, had held his arm. A lady standing on the chair with him had shaken the chair and touched him as she tried to get away. His eyes flashed and he exhibited some signs of anger as he rebutted Tom Armour's testimony. "I no see a man," he said emphatically. "He told you I was in the bench. I wasn't on iron bench. I was on an iron chair. A little iron chair, you know, got bars on the back." Then, without being asked, he told how close he came to killing Roosevelt.

"When the president was talking, that little chair move. There was a lot of people standing up and I have no chance and when the people get down—give me a chance. I jump up then. After they down, I jump on the little chair to kill the president. The car was there and I tried to shoot straight to the head. I have a lot of people to cross and that time my little chair move, I think by a touch. I missed about a quarter of an inch here, and three feet there. That is why I missed Roosevelt and kill somebody else." He had no chance to shoot while Roosevelt was giving his speech. "I try to and have no chance. Lot of people was in my front. To my front was about twenty peoples standing on a chair and I was on the ground. Can't see him."

Did he think what he did was right or wrong?

"What I was think, I do right. I went to kill president. He was run the government. I think I was right to do it because I no think I was do wrong."

"You thought you were right?"

"Yeah, I think I have right to kill him."

This could have been used to raise the sanity issue; to raise the question of whether Zangara really knew the difference between right and wrong. It also raised the issue of "irresistible impulse," which the judge later attempted to develop further. This could have been used to convince the judge to show mercy. But Twyman persisted in showing the world how defiant his client was. "You knew it was against the law at the time you shot, didn't you?" he asked.

"Yes," Zangara said. "I know the law can put me in electric chair but I no care for that. I know that because I kill him I get electric chair. I am no scare electric chair."

"But you insist you are right?" Twyman persisted.

"Yes. Do right. I no care if they put me in electric chair."

"Nobody can change you in that feeling?"

"No. Nobody can change my idea."

Twyman's next question could have been a model of prosecutorial righteousness. It was surely incompetent defense work. "You would have tried to kill Mr Hoover just as quick as Mr Roosevelt?"

"I see Mr Hoover, I kill him first. Make no difference. President just same bunch. All same. No make no difference who go get that job. Run by big money. Make no difference who he is."

Would he have tried to kill Mussolini?

Sure, just as soon as he saw him, he would kill him.

"Joe, are you sorry you shot these other people?"

"Well, I sorry because Roosevelt still live. Ain't shot Roosevelt. I want to shoot Roosevelt."

"But you are sorry you shot these other four innocent people, are you not?"

"I sorry because I no aim for, because I try to kill Roosevelt. The people no ain't kill [*sic*], you see. You see the people don't give me no chance to. People in the front, so when pass in the front, I no kill Roosevelt."

Zangara seemed to be having difficulty making a distinction between what he intended to do and what he inadvertently did. Twyman asked him if he had wanted to hurt anyone else.

"No. I no went to kill anybody else. Went to kill the president first."

Here Twyman relinquished his witness to Hawthorne, who began to question Zangara in an angry tone while he was still walking toward him. "If Mr Roosevelt should come in this door now," he said, pointing to the double courtroom doors, his voice rising, "and you had a gun, would you kill him now?"

"Oh, yes," Zangara replied earnestly.

"Suppose Mr Hoover should come in, would you kill him too?"

There was a stir in the room. Zangara replied with his now-familiar half smile, "No use kill him because he ain't no president no more. Supposed to kill the chief. The chief is the boss."

A murmur rose in the room. The judge used his gavel. "I will have to insist that you people in the courtroom remain quiet," he said. "This is no spectacular performance and I want you to keep quiet in the courtroom or I will have to clear it."

Hawthorne softened his tone. "Joe, if the governor of the state of Florida should come in this door and you had a gun, would you kill him?"

"Governor?"

"Governor of the state of Florida."

"Oh, yes. No. I no kill him . . . because he no chief of whole United States. I want to kill chief of United States." He had seen Governor Sholtz at the park once when he came to make a speech, he said, and he did not want to kill him then, either. He only wanted to kill presidents.

In response to a question, he said he was sure the man he shot at was Roosevelt because he recognized him from the newspaper photograph he had been carrying in his pocket for two days; he did not have to look at it on the night of the shooting. When he saw Roosevelt, he recognized him immediately.

An odd interlude occurred when Hawthorne asked the witness about a newspaper clipping found in his room reporting that Roosevelt had recently taken out a $500,000 life insurance policy. Zangara appeared confused by this question. Hawthorne showed him the clipping and asked him if it had been in his suitcase. Zangara replied, "Well, I have a whole piece made by some people there." This was of course an incomprehensible response; it might have been taken to imply that someone else had given Zangara the clippings. But Hawthorne did not pursue it.

"Having looked at these pictures," the prosecutor said, pointing to the clippings on the clerk's desk, "when you saw him in the car, you knew at once he was the man you wanted?" Upon receiving an affirmative response, Hawthorne went on, "And you are sorry now you didn't kill him?"

"Yes. I am sorry because he is still living."

Would he like to kill Mussolini? He had said earlier that he would, but now he said he would not. The king of Italy, he said, was the chief of the Italian state and Mussolini was only his servant. Thus he displayed ignorance of the political situation in his native country.

"Did you talk this over with anybody else?"

"No, no bother anybody else. All my natural idea in my head," he said, tapping his right temple.

"When you heard Mayor Cermak was dead, did it worry you?"

Zangara did not appear to be a worrier. "What is the use to worry?" he replied.

Questioned about his religious beliefs, Zangara repeated his conviction that there was no God, no heaven and no hell. People are like animals: when they die they go in the ground. "I believe everything is here on this land."

Had he read these ideas somewhere? No, they were his own ideas. He did not read well.

Had he ever heard of Cermak before the shooting?

"Oh, no, no, no, no, no." He had never heard of him and did not know anything about him. His target was Roosevelt. He repeated that he was sorry that Roosevelt was still alive and that he would try again to kill him if he got the chance.

"Would you try again to kill him in a crowd?"

"Oh, that doesn't make no difference."

"Wouldn't you care if you shot anybody else?"

"I want to kill him. I try to kill him. You can't find a king or a president alone. Lots of people stick around him and you got to take chance to kill him. All the chiefs of people, never alone. The chief of government you no see alone. He go all the time with a bunch."

Hadn't he told the police that he had saved nearly $2600 by 1926? Was he mad at the capitalists when he was making all that money?

"Sure, I mad all the time. I no care for the money. After I work I have two thousand dollars. I spend the money. I no care for the money but mad I got this trouble with my stomach." He did not remember how long it had been since he had last worked, but he thought it was about two years. He had not looked for work in Miami: "no same trade and no look for job any more."

Hawthorne had completed his examination, and he offered Zangara to the judge: "Any questions, Your Honor?" Judge Uly O. Thompson, who had Zangara's life in his hands, addressed him by his first name in a kindly tone. He asked him when he had come to the United States, whether he had come alone and whether his father had ever been in trouble with the law (he hadn't). "Joe," the judge said, "you said you knew you were violating the law when you shot at the president?" Zangara agreed that he did. Could Zangara have avoided shooting at Roosevelt if he had tried? "What I mean is, [could you] have left the park without doing it after seeing him?"

Zangara could not understand the question. The judge put it differently, but still Zangara could not grasp it. "I want to shoot at him," he said, "I have no chance. People no leave me pass."

Had he told anyone what he was going to do with the gun?

"No. I tell nobody. Nobody know because I got my own idea and no talk with nobody what idea I have to do."

Did he know who Cermak was, had he ever heard of him before?

"Oh, no, no, no. Somebody ask me, who is the lawyer from there. I don't know nobody. I don't know nobody where he live. He was mayor of Chicago. I know nothing of that. I got interested in Roosevelt. How I know the mayor of Chicago?"

Had he bought the gun before or after he heard that Roosevelt was coming to Miami?

"No," Zangara said. "I think it was good buy it before, because I was going to kill Hoover before he get out.'

The judge registered surprise. "You were going to Washington?"

"Yes. And I see in the paper Roosevelt was coming here. I kill Roosevelt because it was just the same."

He had never before mentioned any intention to travel to Washington, especially in the middle of winter, since he had often said that cold weather aggravated his stomach problems. It seems odd that he would undertake such a trip to kill a president who he knew would be out of office in a few weeks. But he had had to admit that he had bought the gun *before* he learned of Roosevelt's visit.

When the judge had finished, Twyman rose once more, and asked, "Joe, you are not insane or crazy, are you?" Zangara responded once more that he was not. "You know what is going on all the time, don't you?" Twyman asked, making the point that Zangara was competent and thus eligible for execution. Zangara responded that he did. Then, in a display of ignorance (or in an attempt to complete the record), Twyman asked, "What kind of business are you in? I don't know whether you told us what you did in this country." After he received his answer, he embarked on a series of pointless questions about whether Zangara would prefer to kill Roosevelt when he was alone or in a crowd. Zangara said that he would shoot him when he was alone if he got the chance, but as he had said several times already, presidents do not walk down the street alone. "He never run on the street because he scared because he know he a wrong man. He is the chief of the government. He is scared to run himself on the street. All the time he got the bunch to watch."

Twyman asked his client what sort of change he would like to see in government.

"I think the change is, new government," Zangara said. "No money at all so everybody is same, alike. Everybody just the same the country. I have no sick stomach because I have the right to go to school same as somebody else. Then the children of the capitalist make no difference. All born equal. All people just the same. All people can read just the same. Because [capitalist] is a crook, steal and make a bunch of money. The other people have no money in pocket and go out on street. That is the way I think this government is run."

"Are you going to change your views?" Twyman asked.

"I no going to change," his client said. "My mind is like that."

When Twyman stopped, Alfred Raia entered the questioning for the first time. Addressing Zangara in Italian, Raia asked a question the judge had tried to ask, and which Zangara had not understood. "If you had changed your mind about killing the president in the park that night, would you have left the park?"

Zangara's eyes brightened and his tone became impassioned as he replied, "I could change my mind? I can't change my mind! I have my mind with that. Put me in electric chair. The electric chair no change my idea. The idea just the same." (Thus Zangara is quoted in the trial transcript. Several newspaper reports, perhaps wishing to give the impression that Zangara could be flexible, said that he shouted, "The electric chair—maybe it change my mind.")

Twyman introduced a scene that was bizarre even by the standards of this hearing. He asked Zangara whether he had sent or received any letters from his family while he was in jail. Zangara said he had not. Did he have any friends in the United States? "No," his client replied, "no friends. Everybody is a friend. I have no special friends. Everybody is a friend." At this point Twyman handed Zangara an unsealed envelope containing two three-page handwritten letters and two small photographs of two men. These letters, written in Italian, had been received at the jail but had not been given to the prisoner.

"I ask you to tell us what this is," Twyman said.

Clearly surprised, Zangara took them from him, asking, "Where that from?" He looked at them and said, "That is nothing. I think it is all right. Nothing here for me."

"Nothing there for you, Joe?" Twyman asked. Zangara said, "No." Twyman persisted. "Are you sure of that?"

"Sure it is so," Zangara said. He pointed to a place on the page. "Sign some name there," he said.

Twyman, whose client was on the stand in a sentencing hearing where it would be determined whether he lived or died, said, "We just got it and don't know who it is from."

"Show me the name," Zangara said. "Show me the name. Show me the last name. Who write that name?"

Raia rose and came to the witness stand to look at the letters. "What does it say there?" he asked. "Is that your cousin's signature?"

"No," Zangara said, "I have no cousin."

"Doesn't that word mean 'cousin'?" Raia asked him.

"No, I never have no cousin named Zangara in Italian town. Only one," Zangara said, still looking at the letters.

"That isn't your father's signature there?" Raia asked.

Zangara was becoming irritated. "No," he said. "My father is old. All a baloney story."

Twyman did not give up. He handed his client the two photographs. "I hand you two little pictures referred to, and ask you if you ever saw the people represented by those?"

Frowning, Zangara studied the photographs. "No, I never saw any," he said.

"What is your father's name?" Twyman asked. On being told that it was Salvatore Zangara, he demanded, "Look at that signature. Is that his signature?"

"That is the name," the prisoner said.

"Doesn't that appear to be the signature of your father?"

"The name is there," Zangara said. "But I think somebody else write this letter."

"Have you ever received a letter from your father since you have been in America?"

"Yes, all the time."

"Don't you recognize that as his signature?"

"No. I know nothing."

But Twyman refused to drop this line of questioning. "Joe," he said, "you have told some mighty straight stories. Now I want you to tell us that—tell us truthfully what that is." He handed the letters and the photographs back to Zangara.

Even the judge had had enough of this by now. "Let him look it over," he said to Twyman, and then to Zangara, "Joe, you will bring that back to court with you."

"Yes," Zangara said to the judge. "After I read it, I will see what it is."

The judge called the noon recess. He reminded the spectators that when they returned they would all be searched. "If I catch anyone in the crowd with a gun on them coming into the courtroom, or coming into the court building, I will put you in jail for contempt of court. So don't undertake to come up here armed in any way. I am sure there is no one in here who would do such a thing."

By two o'clock everyone had reassembled. Twyman told the judge he wanted to recall the defendant "for a little further examination." Zangara was escorted once more to the witness stand, and once more shown the letters and photographs and asked if he had had an opportunity to examine them during the break. He had, he said, and now everything was clear to him. One photograph was of his father, who had aged considerably in the ten years since he had last seen him, and the other was of a new brother-in-law whom he had never met. That was why he had not recognized them. Furthermore, the letter was not in his father's handwriting. He thought one of his sisters must have written it for him. When he first saw the letters, he said, he thought it was "a joke" [a trick?], but everything was clear to him now. The letter had been written in Italy the day before the shooting and sent to his Miami address. It had been written to acknowledge a package Zangara had sent to his father.

Twyman asked the judge, "Would Your Honor care to see the letter? We didn't know whether it had any bearing at the time, but we see it is just a family letter." The judge ignored this question, and asked if anyone had anything else to ask the accused. Twyman did. "Joe, did you attend or have you attended at any time any Bolshevistic [*sic*] meetings?"

"No, no, no," Zangara said impatiently.

"Joe, the court asked you whether you told anybody about or talked with anybody about this intention to kill?"

"No, I don't talk to nobody."

"Why didn't you tell somebody you bought the pistol?" Twyman asked.

"No, no. Why do I have to talk? I don't belong to any party. I belong in my own mind. That is why I no tell nobody because I hear a lot of stuff."

Twyman had no more questions, but the prosecutor had some. "Zangara, why did you want to become a citizen of the United States?"

"Well, because I have work. When I was union bricklayer and I have to have it because I no have it, I no get any work. Understand what I mean?"

"You became a citizen of the United States so that you could join the union."

"The union made me join up. I get the citizen's papers because I no have them."

"Before you became a citizen, before you came to this country, did you have the same idea you have now about presidents and kings?"

"Oh yes!" Zangara became animated. "I have this in my mind when I was eighteen years. I start in my mind to kill kings, capitalists and everything."

Hawthorne asked him if he remembered anything he swore to when he became a citizen. Zangara said he did not. "And if you said you would obey the laws of the country, you didn't mean it; but you would, if you got a chance, kill a president." The prosecutor seemed to have an idea that Zangara could be deported if he had lied when he took his oath of citizenship.

"No," Zangara replied, his voice rising, "I no told nothing. Nobody told me anything like that."

Hawthorne concluded, and the judge began to question the prisoner for the last time. "Joe, how long do you say it has been since you worked any?"

Zangara, misunderstanding, said he had started when he was six years old. After further misunderstanding, he finally said that he had last worked as a bricklayer a year and a half earlier. "I don't remember the day because after I was gone to California, and I come here to Miami, and I had to go back to Paterson again and go around." All his work was done in New York and New Jersey, he said; he did no work in California. He named some of the jobs he had worked on and the contractors.

"You say you don't belong to any Communistic clubs?" the judge asked. No, Zangara said, and he had not attended any gatherings, neither in this country nor in Italy, where there were several Communist groups when he lived there. He did not join them, he said, because he knew his "right idea." Their "idea was make a little reform, but my idea was more higher than 'give money' idea. The money, all we got, go up in fire. Nobody [should] have money. Everybody got to work just for eat. Just for bread . . . Everybody just the same. That is my idea . . . because you see for yourself now poor people. I see lot of poor people are hungry for a piece of bread. People want bread. Don't have bread to eat. Stay a couple of days without a piece of bread. Too bad! A lot of people have money. People have money and other people are poor . . . The rich man is crook man and steals and make money because he steals more. And the other man is not educated—like a jackass. The other man have no money to eat."

He summed up his theory: "In my mind, my idea is kill the president in one country. After he is killed, kill another, and then kill another. The people go to be scared and nobody take the job. And that is going to change us."

"Have you read any literature published by Communists?" Judge Thompson asked.

"No! No read nothing. No read nothing."

"That is all just your own idea?"

"Just all my own idea."

"You never talked over your idea with anyone?"

"Nobody know at all. Nobody. I no talk much. I can't talk much."

"You never have attended any meetings or made any speeches about your idea?"

"No. Just all my own idea."

It was now time for closing arguments. Twyman called his client "a sane man . . . a political zealot who had told the truth at every stage. . . . He knows that he is right, and at the same time he knows that he is sinning against the land of his adoption." Twyman himself was, he said, not opposed to capital punishment and his client was also "shockingly agreeable to the punishment which he knows he will receive." Thus, incredibly, Zangara's attorney was telling the judge that neither he nor his client objected to the imposition of the death sentence.

When Twyman concluded, Raia, whose daughter was later to characterize him as a deeply religious man, made a passionate plea for Zangara's life. He asked the judge to consider the circumstance of the prisoner's sad childhood: a boy who lost his mother when he was two and whose cold, ignorant father forced him to hard labor at the age of six. "The death sentence will not arrive at the root of this trouble," Raia said, and reminded the judge that had it not been for the stomach ailment Zangara had developed as a child and his life-long consequent suffering, he would never have committed the crime of which he was accused. Raia said that he personally opposed capital punishment; he pleaded with Thompson for a sentence of life in prison.

Hawthorne came next, speaking about Zangara's demeanor throughout the hearing. He mentioned the prisoner's smile as a defiant one, saying the man was "the most defiant man I have ever seen . . . He not only tried to kill the president-elect, but he boasts of it. He says he stands alone, but standing alone he would destroy the civilized world. He assumes the attitude of a martyr, if you please. He confesses with a smile of defiance a crime which shocked the world—not the death of Mayor Cermak, but an attack on the organization of society, the best society has perfected . . . I have complete confidence and abiding faith in Your Honor's judgment and keen insight into the problem before you, and as Mr Twyman says, each of us should ask Divine Guidance, and as Your Honor reaches

THE FIVE WEEKS OF GIUSEPPE ZANGARA

a conclusion, that the God of the nation and of men have mercy on this unfortunate man. I make no recommendation. I repeat, I am sure that the magnitude of this case is clear to Your Honor."

James McCaskill, who, like Alfred Raia, had barely spoken during the proceedings, concluded on Zangara's behalf. He appears to have made the most eloquent defense statement, but it was too late to save his client from the gallows. McCaskill pointed out that Hawthorne had not asked for the death penalty and reminded the judge that the law gave him the authority to spare the prisoner's life. Aside from his perverse determination to kill anyone who ruled a nation, his client had no offensive qualities. Even his tragic bent of mind could be explained by his background and upbringing. He had earned his living by the fruit of his own labor; and, despite his claim to have made an attempt on the life of the king of Italy—which Italian authorities denied—had always respected the rights of others.

"He has accepted the blame for his act and there is no evidence that he had any accomplice," McCaskill said, and, pointing to Zangara, concluded, "He is no more responsible for his 'idea' than he is for the color of his eyes."

Zangara sat smiling, undoubtedly unable to understand the formal English being spoken around him; he had never broken the law before. The judge thanked counsel, telling them he would take the matter under advisement. He set sentencing for ten o'clock the following morning, Friday, March 10. Cautioning the crowd once more to stay until the prisoner left the courtroom, he ordered Zangara removed, and then gaveled the court to adjournment.

14

"YOU GIVE ME ELECTRIC CHAIR?"

W hen Judge Uly O. Thompson reconvened his court the next
morning, he was well aware that he had, for a rare moment,
the attention of the nation. He thanked the spectators and the court
officers for their "splendid decorum" and "the dignified manner" in
which they "deported" themselves, and made special mention of
the sheriff, his deputies, the state attorney and "counsel for the defendant," singling out Alfred Raia by saying, "I am very much
pleased in this particular case that a reputable member of the bar
and a good lawyer happens to be of the same nationality as the defendant."

He then delivered a strong gun-control statement. "It is my firm
conviction," he said, "that the Congress of these United States should
immediately pass legislation, or an act, for the confiscation of all
firearms that may be carried and concealed about the person of anyone. It is a ridiculous state of society, in my opinion, that an assassin
may be permitted to arm himself and go at liberty throughout the
land killing whom he will kill. Out of every ten [presidents], one
had been killed, so far, by an assassin. This unfortunate defendant at

the bar undertook, I think through zealous effort on his part, though misguided, to assassinate the incoming president of the United States." All past assassinations of presidents had been accomplished or attempted by men with pistols, the judge said and the people of the United States continue to "steadfastly permit" the manufacture, sale and possession of these "useless" weapons. "I say 'useless' for this reason: a pistol in the hands of an assassin is sure death and murder, while a pistol in the hands of you good people, and the good people of this country, is about the most useless weapon of defense with which you can arm yourself."

No living person could foresee what might have happened if Zangara had killed Roosevelt, the judge went on. He drew a comparison between that act and the assassination of the Archduke Ferdinand, which precipitated the World War. "The Congress," he said, "will not be remiss in what, in my opinion, it ought to do. The Congress will be reminded that the assassination of President Roosevelt would have been a disaster well calculated to affect the peace of America, if not of the whole world." It should be the business of such lawmaking bodies, he said, to remove the possibility of such tragedies happening in the future.

Then he asked Zangara to stand; when the large lamp on the left side of the judge's desk partially obscured the prisoner's face as he stood before the bench, the judge asked him to move "a little to the right so I can see you." Lewis Twyman pulled Zangara slightly to the right, and the judge then offered the prisoner what is known as the right of elocution: "What have you, Giuseppe Zangara, now to say why sentence should not be imposed upon you?"

Zangara slouched forward, with his arms resting on some files on top of the clerk's desk. Twyman repeated the judge's question to him, in a low, almost reverent voice, asking, "Do you have any word you want to say to the judge?" Zangara straightened to his full five-foot, one-inch height. "To the judge?" he asked. He clearly had no idea what was happening; his lawyers had probably not explained to him that he could now plead for his life. "Well," he said, "I want to kill the president because I no like the government. Because I think it is run by the capitalists, all crooks, and a lot of people make a lot of money. Things run for the money."

He went on with his pathetic, simplistic beliefs, oblivious of the fact that he was about to hear his death sentence. "That is my idea. There was the boss. I have a gun in my hand. I have idea to kill all capitalists and until all money is burn up on a fire. I can't talk the American. My idea, it is for all of us. That is why I tell you I no understand." He became incoherent in his struggle to express himself and then concluded, "That is all my idea." There was no coughing or shuffling of feet as the packed courtroom listened in silence to the prisoner's thin, reedy voice.

The judge spoke as though Zangara had said nothing. "Whereupon you having said nothing that does or should influence the court in further delay of its sentence and judgment herein, it is, thereupon, the sentence of the law and the judgment of the court that you, Giuseppe Zangara, be remanded into the custody of the sheriff of Dade County, and be safely confined by the sheriff in the common jail of the County of Dade until such time as you, Giuseppe Zangara, shall be delivered to the superintendent of the state prison, at Raiford, Florida, and you shall there be securely kept and confined until such time as the governor of the state of Florida, by his warrant, shall appoint for your execution. And sentence of death shall be carried out and executed upon you on some weekday in the week fixed by the governor of the state of Florida, as the week of your execution. The time of carrying out such execution to be decided by the superintendent of the state prison.

"And at such time and place, punishment of death shall be inflicted upon you by causing to pass through your body a current of electricity sufficient in intensity to cause immediate death, and application of such current shall be continued until you shall be dead. . . . And may God have mercy on your soul.

"Done and ordered in open court at Miami, Florida, this tenth day of March 1933. Defendant being present in open court.

"Let the judgment be filed. Anything further, Mr Hawthorne?"

"That is all for today, Your Honor," Hawthorne said.

It was at this point that Zangara realized what had just happened.

"Judge," he said urgently, as he was about to be led away, "I say something—a couple of words. You give me electric chair?"

"Yes," Thompson replied. Now for the first time since all this began, Zangara lost his composure. He cried out, in what reporters would call a shriek, "Well, I no scared of electric chair because I am thinking I am right to kill the president. Because it is capitalists, for the crooked government. And you is a crook man, I think," he shouted over his shoulder at the judge as he was being pulled toward the door by the deputies, "because the crook man put me in the electric chair. Put me in electric chair, I no care. *You is a crook man!*" he cried again, as he was hustled from the courtroom.

It would seem that Zangara was genuinely surprised by the sentence; he may have thought that the judge was impressed by the sincerity and logic of his credo. He seemed to feel that the judge, an authority figure even more powerful than his father had been, had betrayed him. In his memoir, Zangara makes no mention of his outburst:

> I got up and said: "Judge you have sentenced me to the chair, however I am not afraid of the chair for trying to kill the President who was the head of a crooked government." I was then returned to the room where I had been kept. The lawyers came up there and told me they had done all they could to help me. Before the trial started, the judge asked me if I had a lawyer to defend me but I told him I did not need a lawyer.

Zangara's defense team seems to have received some public approval. In a letter to the *Tampa Tribune*, one K.A. Nisset said:

"The Miami attorneys appointed to represent Zangara showed their good sense and are thereby entitled to the gratitude of all good Americans, by not attempting to gain cheap publicity for themselves with a lot of 'fol de rol' practices all too common with some lawyers of mediocre caliber, resorting to technicalities to defeat or delay justice." The *Tribune* echoed this sentiment and pointed out that justice can move expeditiously when there are no appeals, petitions for rehearings, applications to the Pardon Board, "*etcetera, ad nauseam.*" The speedy execution of justice "is a matter for decision, not of the courts and juries, but of the defendant's attorneys." This case showed, the *Tribune* held, "that criminal justice can move swiftly if the lawyers for the defense are willing."

15

"A TOUCH OF THE SWEAT BOX"

In the late nineteenth century, Alfred P. Southwick, a Buffalo dentist, lobbied the New York legislature to use electricity, the new marvel of the age, as a means of conducting clean, quick and painless executions. The legislature eventually concurred: on August 6, 1890, William Kemmler, convicted of murdering his fiancée, was the first person to be electrocuted by the state. A witness, the inventor and industrialist George Westinghouse, said that he thought the job could have been "done better with an ax." Consequently, he invented an electrical switching device which bears his name: many a condemned person's last sight had been the name "Westinghouse" embossed on the electrical cabinet in the death chamber.

Until 1923, hanging was the statutory method of execution in Florida. Each county sheriff was responsible for conducting the execution, which took place in the county where conviction occurred. The execution statute, adopted shortly after the Civil War, allowed executions to be public, at the discretion of local authorities. Most sheriffs permitted the public to attend: Miami's last legal hanging took place in 1914, in the back courtyard of the two-story court-house which stood on the site of the present building. These grue-some events were subject to unpleasant accidents. Sometimes the prisoner's neck would not break and he would slowly strangle to death, kicking wildly at the end of the rope. In Pensacola in 1900, everything, according to the sheriff, went "nicely until after the drop." The prisoner was pronounced dead, cut down, and brought in a cof-fin to the jail, where he was found to be "breathing in spasmodic gasps and giving utterance to smothered groans."

The sheriff ordered the unfortunate man to be hanged again—to the apparent delight of the crowd: the presence of the morbidly cu-rious often made a mockery of this solemn punishment. By the end of the nineteenth century, public executions had fallen into disfa-vor. In 1923, in response to pressure from sheriffs, newspapers, ministers, educators, public officials and the Florida Federation of Women's Clubs, the Florida legislature made electrocution the pre-ferred method of execution, which would take place at a specifi-cally created "death chamber" from which the general public would be barred. Only "a jury of twelve respectable citizens," counsel and ministers for the condemned, prison officers, deputies and guards, would be admitted. The sheriff would still conduct the execution. No mention was made of the media.

On October 7, 1924, at the Florida State Prison Farm at Raiford, some forty miles southwest of Jacksonville, the first person to be electrocuted under the new law was Frank Johnson, a black citizen of Jacksonville, who killed a man during a burglary. Although Johnson confessed, entered a guilty plea and did not appeal the sen-tence, the state did not execute him for ten months. At that time executions took place in a back room of the decrepit, rambling, wood-frame prison hospital. In 1931 the legislature authorized construc-tion of a death chamber at the state prison farm; this was completed in early 1933. Giuseppe Zangara would be the first person to be executed in this chamber.

He was sentenced to death four days after Cermak's death; when the sentence was pronounced on Friday, March 10, Cermak had not yet been buried. Three days later, Governor Dave Sholtz signed the death warrant, specifying that the execution be carried out during the week of March 20. (The warden carried out the warrant on the morning of the first day on which he could legally do so.)

The meting out of such swift justice was not customary in Florida or anywhere else in the United States. In fact, it surprised even those who were crying loudest for a speedy disposition of the case. The week before the execution, the Tampa *Tribune* complained that while there had been more than four hundred murder convictions in the state during the past four years, only nine of the convicted killers had been executed in that timespan. And the murderers who were scheduled for electrocution after Zangara had spent nearly three years on death row. The day after Zangara's execution, the *Tribune* commented, "Never before, in all Florida court procedure, has punishment so quickly followed crime and conviction. . . . Justice in every other case in this state where there is no doubt of guilt should move with equal or approximate speed as it has in the case of Zangara, who had no funds to hire resourceful lawyers, no relatives, no influential friends."

The governor was required to receive, before he could sign the death warrant, a transcript of the sentencing hearing including testimony of all witnesses, along with the judge's written sentence. It would have taken at least a day for the record to be transcribed and certified, and another day for this material to be brought to Tallahassee over five hundred miles of bumpy, two-lane roads: at best a ten-to-twelve-hour trip. It could not have reached the governor's office before late afternoon or evening of Sunday, March 12. The governor was required to submit the record to his six-man cabinet; these men would have had to read the documents, presumably discuss them and then vote on whether the sentence should be carried out. Sholtz signed the death warrant the next morning—Monday,

March 13. In response to people who wrote letters pleading for clemency for Zangara, Sholtz asserted that the cabinet convened, considered the evidence and unanimously agreed to carry out the sentence. But there is no record in the state archives that the cabinet actually met or, if it did meet, that the transcript was physically in hand there at the time.

It was Governor Sholtz who would have expedited this execution. Just days after the shooting, the governor, who had travelled to New York with Roosevelt, told the *New York Times* that he wanted the matter to be brought to a swift conclusion. Later, when he learned about the sentence, Sholtz announced that he was gratified to know that Florida rendered "prompt and fair justice" to "men of that caliber."

Dave Sholtz had made Florida history when he won the 1932 Democratic gubernatorial nomination, which at that time was tantamount to winning the election. As a transplanted New Yorker, he was a 200 to 1 shot in the primary. In addition, his family was Jewish, although he himself had become an Episcopalian before he entered politics in 1916 at the age of twenty-five, when he was elected to the state house of representatives. He continued to practice law until he was elected governor, but he had little campaign money and was outspent by his opponents, so that he was reduced to soliciting donations door to door. Nevertheless, he came in second in a field of eight candidates, and ran in a run-off election against John Martin, the favorite, who had been governor of Florida from 1924 to 1928. Martin's campaign was scurrilous, and even anti-Semitic. In a stunning upset, Sholtz defeated Martin by 70,000 votes, earning the nickname of "Darkhorse Dave." Later he was called the "New Deal" governor.

Sholtz undoubtedly acted in response to what he perceived to be the popular will and certainly also the will of the White House, which were as that time one and the same. On Saturday, March 11, the *Miami Herald* editorial writer demanded an immediate execution. But not perhaps without a touch of sadism. "Possibly," the *Herald* said, "a touch of the sweat box might tone down his defiance before he dies." Raiford's "sweat box" had made national news a few years earlier when a New Jersey youth, serving time for a minor offense, had died in it and two guards were convicted of manslaughter in the case. Later, when Sholtz signed Zangara's death warrant, the *Herald* expressed pleasure, saying that Florida was showing "how swiftly justice can function." It urged immediate action: "Lose no time, for the sentimentalists are already beginning to speak."

And, indeed, in the short time between the sentencing and the execution, some opposition was forming. On Thursday, March 16, Harold S. Cohn, managing editor of the *Jacksonville Journal*, sent a telegram to Col. Louis Howe, FDR's secretary, at the White House, asking that the president intervene in the execution. Writing as "one journalist to another," he asked, "do you not think that our hysteria has gotten the better of us?" It was, he said, "almost" national policy not to execute the insane, and he was positive "that mature consideration will convince us that we have acted hastily and hysterically if this man is permitted to die contrary to custom. . . . Zangara could not and did not get a fair sanity test in Miami. I believe Governor Sholtz would not be willing to act alone due to the enormity of the crime, but I believe a suggestion of life imprisonment from President Roosevelt will be favorably received." He asked that this telegram be kept confidential. There is no record of a reply from the White House.

In the seven days between the signing of the death warrant and the execution, Sholtz received at least three letters pleading for clemency, all from out of state. A Methodist minister wrote from Lima, Ohio, protesting the execution on religious grounds. He prayed that Sholtz would see the "justice and sanity" of his plea "and not stand guilty before God for the life of this man." From Pennsylvania, Mrs J.H. Rodgers wrote pleading for mercy "as a mother" because

Zangara had "no mother or friends to defend him." He did not commit murder "and you men know it" because he did not intend to kill Mayor Cermak; the woman who seized Zangara's arm caused Cermak's death and the wounding of five others. Mrs Rodgers made clear that she was not "of Italian descent": she had "a true German Mother's heart" within her breast. Cora McConnell, a 64-year-old Southerner living in New York, wrote expressing gratitude that Zangara had not been lynched: "Knowing the temper of the average southern man, I would not have been surprised to have learned that swifter justice had been meted out to him and I am glad that the men of Florida were able to wait for the courts to settle the case." She mentioned recent examples of southern "justice": the Leo Franks case in Georgia, where the Jewish manager of a pencil factory, later proved innocent, was taken from prison and lynched after his death sentence had been commuted by the governor; the Raiford "sweat box" case, and the nine black youths on trial for rape in Scottsboro, Alabama. Mrs McConnell suggested that it was time for "a gesture from the higher-ups" in Florida to show that "the heart of the southern men is in the right place." She believed that an appeal was in order because Zangara's "expressions and acts do not bespeak thoughts and deeds of a sane man."

Although the governor did not respond to Mrs Rodgers, he thanked Mrs McConnell for her letter, assuring her that his cabinet had thoroughly considered the case. "It was unanimously agreed, however," he wrote her, "that there was not sufficient evidence submitted to warrant disturbance of the sentence of the court."

President Roosevelt, too, received letters asking for his intervention. John Fleming of Washington, D.C., wrote that he had "neither patience nor sympathy with anarchists and their kind" but that "it would be a serious miscarriage of justice and a ghastly error" to execute Zangara "when there is any doubt as to his sanity." Oscar Palmer wrote from Rawson, Ohio, four days before the execution, to comment that this "unusual speed . . . savors of revenge" and "most humbly" asked that the president recommend a commutation to life imprisonment. George Sladovich, a New Orleans lawyer, suggested that the execution "be continually set but always postponed" to break the prisoner's morale through "constant fear." In this way Zangara could be brought to confess who had paid him for the shooting. Mr Sladovich went on to offer advice on foreign policy and cabinet and ambassadorial appointments.

At about this time the Italian government was reportedly on the brink of asking for a stay of execution, so that they could have more time to investigate Zangara's possible anti-Fascist activities in Italy.

While the editor of the Jacksonville paper requested that his plea for a commutation or postponement of execution be kept confidential, a law student spoke openly in the *Florida Alligator*, the campus daily of the University of Florida at Gainesville, about 300 miles north of Miami. Melvin J. Richard, a 21-year-old law student at the university, became incensed at an editorial in the *Tampa Tribune* that called Zangara a "homicidal pervert" who must be punished "to the limit of the law" and punished promptly. Richard responded in his weekly column in the *Alligator* that Zangara had been diagnosed as a psychopathic personality, and that anyone who had done what Zangara had done for his stated reasons was sick and needed treatment and not "vicious torment." He did not write in approval of Zangara's actions, he said, but he wished to advocate "a humane attitude toward a victim of circumstance." Without naming the *Tampa Tribune*, Richard suggested that "the vicious attitude taken by some writers" might indicate that they too might be among "other psychopathic cases who also need treatment."

Before he submitted this column, Richard asked the chairman of the university psychology department to review it; the chairman approved it, so Richard added a sentence asserting that his column had been reviewed by an "eminent psychologist."

It evolved that the *Tribune* editorial had been written by Col. Edwin Dart Lambright, who was the newspaper's editor-in-chief, and also a member of the state board of control which supervised university operations statewide. Col. Lambright replied in another editorial, and with a threat: "If the *Florida Alligator* is devoted to the dissemination of that sort of rot, it should be suppressed." Lambright called Richard a "collegiate sympathizer with an assassin who would have Zangara placed in a luxurious hospital . . . comforted, coddled and regaled daily with flowers and dainty food at the expense of the taxpayers." Finally, he asked whether the "eminent psychologist" was a university professor "paid by the state to endorse such anarchistic propaganda."

A few days later, Richard was summoned out of class by the university president, John J. Tigert, who told him that Lambright had demanded his, Richard's, expulsion from the school. Tigert asked the student to apologize to Lambright and to name the "eminent psychologist." Richard refused.

The editors of the *Alligator* sought to distance the paper from Richard, explaining in a column that he was a contributor and not actually on staff. "We assure Mr Lambright that the article to which he refers . . . does not represent the view of this paper or of the student body," wrote student editor Bill Joubert, who pleaded that Lambright cease to seek the paper's suppression, since it played an important role in campus life. Lambright's response in the *Tampa Tribune* was that a university newspaper should not print opinions, no matter whose, of "an anarchistic character, calculated to inflame or improperly agitate public sentiment or to disturb law and order."

President Tigert empaneled a board of inquiry of fourteen professors to investigate Richard and several of his friends. They wanted to know his background and how he had come by the opinions he had expressed. The "eminent psychologist" and two other professors volunteered to testify for Richard, who demanded to know what charges had been leveled against him and by what authority the board acted. He had, he said, consulted an attorney and he gave his solemn assurance that if he were expelled, he would sue not only the university, but each member of the board as well.

Richard's case reached the national media. Columbia University in New York offered Richard a scholarship if Florida expelled him, and the Gannett newspaper chain offered him a job when he graduated. Some of Lambright's journalist colleagues began to cite the First Amendment to him. Possibly as a result of this pressure, the board decided not to expel Richard, but simply to chastise him. Calling his comments on the Zangara case imprudent and injudicious, the professors decreed that Richard could not write for any campus publication while he was a student. By this time, the student body had rallied; they promptly elected him summer editor of the *Alligator*. As would be expected, both Tigert and Lambright were infuriated by this: Tigert locked Richard and his staff out of the newspaper offices before the first issue could be printed. If Richard was editor, the president said, there would be no student paper in the summer of 1933. At this point, Richard was ready to give up, when help arrived: the editor of the *Gainesville Sun*, the city's principal newspaper, offered to print the *Alligator* and distribute it to the students along with free copies of the *Sun*. Richard himself delivered a copy of his first issue to President Tigert.

Melvin Richard's career did not suffer because of his opinion about the Zangara case. He practiced law, became a judge and eventually a city councilman and mayor of Miami Beach. In the early 1950s, he worked for the Kefauver Commission, helping to break south Florida gambling rackets.

16

"PUSHA DA BUTTON!"

Just after midnight on Saturday, March 11, Sheriff Dan Hardie and several heavily armed deputies, operating in secrecy, drove Zangara 400 miles upstate to the Florida Prison Farm at Raiford. This prison, now called Raiford State Penitentiary, is located on the west bank of the New River in Union County, a few miles from the Georgia state line. In 1933, this was an area of vast pine forests, earning the prison the courtroom soubriquet of "the piney woods."

The superintendent of the prison, Leonard Fielding Chapman, had held that position for only two years: he was to remain superintendent until 1956. He was born in 1884 in Phoenix, Arizona, where his father, "a wandering Methodist preacher," ministered to Apaches. Chapman himself, after earning a divinity degree from Vanderbilt University, tried his hand at various occupations before being elected to the Florida House of Representatives where he supported the governor, Doyle Carlton, in a protracted struggle against state-sponsored horse- and dog-racing. The governor's veto was overridden, but Chapman distinguished himself sufficiently so that a few months later Carlton, offered him the position of superintendent of the state prison farm; the incumbent, Clifford Blitch, had been shot by an escaped prisoner and was not expected to live. Chapman at first refused, but the governor was persistent and finally successful. "Okay," Chapman said, "I'll take over at the prison. Where is the blame place?"

Chapman found his first view of the prison to be a depressing experience. Prisoners wandered aimlessly about; three of the department heads were ex-convicts: one was actually a prisoner. "They were all," Chapman writes, "unkempt and shiftless looking." The physical condition of the place was equally depressing: except for one large concrete building and an automobile license plate plant, the entire facility consisted of "old wooden structures" surrounded by fences of "rusted wire on rotting wooden posts." The laundry was a large iron kettle in a yard, under which an open fire burned while the clothes were punched with a hoe handle. "Words," Chapman writes, "can never describe the wretched condition in which four hundred white prisoners, eight hundred negro prisoners, and one hundred and thirty-five women of both races, were compelled to live."

When Chapman retired in 1956, having served nine governors, he was considered an international authority on penology and crime prevention. He had converted an infamous southern chain-gang prison to a modern penal institution. By 1956, Raiford had built eleven new major prison buildings, including a chapel, modern kitchens, laundries, a hospital and a library, all managed by a professional staff. Chapman prided himself on the fact that his door was open to all prisoners every Sunday—no appointment necessary. He walked freely among them without a guard. No prisoner ever threatened him.

When Zangara arrived at the prison, most of Chapman's improvements had, of course, not yet been carried out. While Zangara was there, Chapman later said, the place was a "madhouse." FBI and Secret Service agents literally camped on the grounds, while Sholtz had activated the National Guard to maintain the perimeter, searching all vehicles entering the area. According to Chapman, some people in Washington believed that Mussolini's government was behind Zangara's action. Others thought that the Chicago mob was involved and that an attempt would be made to free Zangara. The Florida authorities, too, were nervous, not only about some action to free Zangara, but about an action to kill him. That was the reason that Sheriff Hardie had transported Zangara in secrecy to Raiford; the sheriff later told Chapman that he had offered Zangara the choice of being transported hidden in a large box, or disguised as a woman. Zangara, according to Chapman, refused both these suggestions, saying, "No! No dress, no box."

This nervousness may have been partly a response to an illiterate letter written to Governor Sholtz on March 13, the day he signed the death warrant. The letter was signed by one S.F. Brooks, from Eau Gallie, a tiny hamlet north of Palm Beach; it warned the governor that since the Zangara affair, Italians with submachine guns had been driving on the Florida byways in roadsters. "It may be wise to Notify Rayford to use every Precaution, as they may storm the Palace and try to free Zangara," the letter said. "I notice in this Morning's Times union where Zangara is writing a Diary in the Italian language and will ask for a Stay of Five Days Moore [sic] before he is Electrucuted. There should be no Time granted that Wap, as Florida is filled with Italians, and Greens so they will not stop at anything." "Green" meant someone holding a legal immigrant's green card.

Brooks added that he had written to the sheriff before the sentencing and issued the same warning, and that, as a result, the sheriff had "used every precaution during the tryal." The writer said that Hardie had stopped in Eau Gallie on the way back from Raiford to thank the citizen for his warning.

By March of 1933, both the main prison block and the death house had been built under Chapman's supervision, but there was no wall or fence around the compound. Chapman, in a reference unrelated to Zangara, complained that Sholtz, whom he referred to as "a sap-headed politician," wanted the legislature to appropriate

$400,000 to build a massive concrete wall around the prison, as was the case with large northern penitentiaries. Chapman wanted a chain-link fence, at a tenth the cost of Sholtz's wall, and the legislature followed the superintendent's advice. Perhaps it was this lack of a concrete wall, together with the threat of roving bands of armed Italians in roadsters, which caused the governor to activate the National Guard.

■ ■ ■

When Zangara was brought to Raiford, he was put into a cell in the death house next to the execution chamber. This death house was a single-story concrete building set within its own walled compound on the prison grounds. Inside the building were six steel cells, called "death cells." After Zangara was issued his striped prison uniform, he was taken to one of the building's two inner courtyards to have his picture taken. In one of the two photographs, Zangara stands in profile; in the other, he poses smiling with three unidentified men. Both photographs were pasted into the manuscript of Chapman's memoir. Zangara signed the back of the group photograph, and the back of the profile shot bears the inscription, possibly in Chapman's handwriting: "Like Mussolini."

Sholtz had given strict orders that Zangara could not be interviewed. Consequently the prisoner saw, during his ten days at Raiford, only Chapman, Chapman's secretary and Nathan Mayo, the Florida commissioner of agriculture, whose office supervised the prison system. Chapman had a procedure for dealing with men on death row: he was not interested in legal matters, he said, or in questions of guilt or innocence and would not discuss these matters with condemned men. "In two regards I always take a keen interest," he writes, "in religious preparation for the future and in the matter of sanity or insanity. I urge the man to consult the chaplain freely, and follow his admonitions, and I also study each man to determine for myself his sanity. I have a horror of standing in the presence of a fatal error."

Chapman says that he gave Zangara an unusual amount of attention. Indeed, in his twenty-five years as warden at Raiford, Chapman supervised more than 135 executions, but Zangara's is the only one he describes in his memoirs. He barely mentions the others. "I wanted to determine for my own satisfaction," he writes, "to say nothing for the several authorities, three different matters: First, whether he really was insane; second, whether he had confederates who had not been arrested or he was a 'lone wolf'; third, whether he was attempting to kill Roosevelt or Cermak." On each of the ten days, the warden spoke to Zangara at length in his cell, while his secretary Rose Dunbar "took down every word." In addition, he instructed the guards to report anything that Zangara said to them that could have a bearing on those three matters of interest.

The conclusion Chapman came to at the time was that Zangara was not insane; that he was a 'lone wolf' who had no confederates, and that he was attempting to kill only Roosevelt. Chapman saw clearly that Zangara liked him and the warden believed that the prisoner would not have concealed anything from him; he found Zangara to be without guile. When Chapman asked him the inevitable question, "Are you sorry you killed the mayor?" Zangara replied, "I sorry for him—what's his name?—Yes, I sorry. But he should not have been there with the president." The fact that Zangara did not know his victim's name helped to convince Chapman that the prisoner had no interest in Cermak.

But Chapman says he heard Zangara's last words at the execution—words that the warden believed the reporters missed: *"Viva Camorra!"* In the final version of his memoirs, written later in life, Chapman apparently came to believe that Zangara was a member of a secret Italian terrorist organization, although he may have acted alone in the final instance, and that he wanted to kill Cermak as well as Roosevelt. "Certainly," the revised manuscript says, "he aimed first at the President but doubtless he also intended to kill Mr Cermak also. He planned to be a double hero. . . ."

The contrast between Chapman's first draft and later revision is striking. "What," Chapman came to ask in his later version, "if this Italian order had seed planted in the darker sections of American cities? What if the presence of death brought forth the real Zangara— the Zangara of the Camorra? He kept his secrets well, but death is a great revealer as well as a great leveler. 'Viva Camorra!' . . . Zangara could well have been an emissary for such a cruel heritage of far lands. That he was such, I have no doubt."

So much for Chapman's earlier statement that "Zangara seemed to be an enigma to everyone except me. By the time he sat in the chair for his execution, I was satisfied that there was no mystery about him. Nothing to this day has changed my opinion. So far as I am concerned his life and action in attempting to kill the president-elect is an open book."

■ ■ ■

The *Miami Herald* reported that Zangara "simply sits or lies sullenly in his cell. . . . He speaks to no one but his guards who bring him his food." As when he was confined in the Dade County jail, Zangara ate standard prison fare and made no special requests because of his stomach pains. "He has not shown the slightest sign of remorse," the *Herald* noted, mentioning that he had refused to see a clergyman, which was undoubtedly true, and that he had done nothing toward writing the book he had promised in court that he would write. That was not true. The newspaper remarked that Zangara's guards had told the press that, far from being able to write a book, the prisoner could barely sign his name. It is difficult to see why the press would be told this, unless it was because Chapman did not want reporters to see the book Zangara was writing. Zangara was guarded twenty-four hours a day: the death cell was a metal cage;

the guard sat next to it in an adjacent cage. Zangara did almost nothing during his last ten days but write on notepads that Chapman had given him.

In an apparent attempt to explain the rapidity with which the case was being processed, the Associated Press published, on the day before the execution, a history of the manner in which previous presidential assassins were treated. It was pointed out that all, except Garfield's assassin Charles Guiteau, were swiftly executed. The four Lincoln conspirators were hanged three months after Lincoln's death, and the assassin of William McKinley, Leon Czolgosz, was executed seven weeks after he shot the president in 1901. Guiteau, the only exception, was put to death in 1882, nearly a year after the assassination.

As the day for the execution approached, Zangara wrote feverishly in his native language on the three steno pads given him by Chapman's secretary. Chapman never gave the name of the translator, but he said the manuscript was written in a low Calabrian dialect, in a cramped hand, without any punctuation. The translation seems amateurish, lacking as it does punctuation, and containing many misspelled common words. For example, the word "just" is always spelled "yust." According to R.P. McClendon, for many years the state prison inspector and a protégé and friend of Chapman, another Italian immigrant, in prison for a robbery committed in Miami, was asked to share the death cell with Zangara, not only to act as translator, but also to coax any new information from the condemned man. That would explain the poor quality of the translation.

Zangara, in his memoir, had only kind words for the warden and his secretary. "Let me tell you right here," he wrote, "they are two very gentle persons. Every day they would come to my cell and visit me. The Superintendent told me that if I wanted anything, to ask for it and he would see that I get it. One day the secretary brought me a bouquet of beautiful flowers. Another time she brought me a nice basket of fruits. I wish to thank them both for the kind treatment I received."

Meanwhile, as the statute required, a jury of "twelve respectable citizens" had been selected to observe the execution along with three reporters, a physician, the superintendent and the executioner, Sheriff Hardie. Scores of requests to witness the event were received and denied by the agriculture commissioner's office. One Baptist minister from Jacksonville wrote directly to the governor requesting permission to view the execution from the "angle" of a clergyman and a writer.

Shortly before the execution, Agriculture Commissioner Nathan Mayo paid a visit to Zangara's cell. Perhaps his visit was in response to newspaper stories just coming out of Philadelphia and Rome, discussing a possible link between Zangara and anti-Fascist terrorists sending letter bombs. As many had before him, Mayo asked the condemned man if he was a member of any gang or organization. Zangara repeated what he had said on many previous occasions: he had no friends and the whole affair was his own idea. Then, of course, Mayo asked Zangara if he was sorry. Perhaps he did not believe the newspaper stories that Zangara showed no remorse. Mayo asked if he was sorry at least for wounding Mrs Gill, who was still in the hospital, though recovering. "No," Zangara replied, "she had no business getting in the way of the bullet." Finally Mayo asked him the most inane of the repetitious and irrelevant questions: if he were free would he try again to kill the president? "At once," was Zangara's reply. Zangara would go to his grave giving no one any satisfaction. It was perhaps understandable that the public and officials were infuriated by his attitude. What good is the death penalty if its recipient willingly submits and shows no regret, remorse, or fear? In the final analysis, this execution took on the dimensions of a state-assisted suicide.

On Sunday, March 19, the day before his death, Zangara requested chicken for lunch. He ate it not knowing that it was his last midday meal. He had not been told that the execution was to take place the following morning. It was Chapman who decided that Zangara would die on Monday morning, the first day of the execution week. Under Florida law, the governor set the week of an execution, but it was the superintendent of the prison who determined the exact day and hour. Chapman had found that for at least a week before any scheduled execution, the entire prison population, himself included, would be upset. In the last few days, the tension within the prison would become palpable. Most wardens at that time, Chapman said, set the hour of execution at midnight, while the prison slept. "Actually," he wrote, "a prison never sleeps when an execution is about to be staged." So it was his policy to get the matter over with as soon as possible: he scheduled executions early on the Monday morning of the specified week. "It seemed to prove best for everyone concerned and the tension in the prison quickly and completely passed." But not for him: he said it always took him several days "to get back to normal."

A torrential rainstorm ushered in the morning of Monday, March 20: this is typical of spring in north Florida when the moist tropical Caribbean air meets the cold northern atmosphere. The skies were overcast and rain was drumming on the roofs and windows of the rural prison. Wearing slickers and squatting at their posts with machine guns, the national guardsmen who encircled the compound had to brave the downpour. It was just two days before spring began. It was the last morning of the five weeks of Giuseppe Zangara.

Just before 9 A.M., Chapman, Nathan Mayo, three wire service reporters and a complement of guards made their way to Zangara's cell to begin what the warden called the "death march" to the execution chamber. Chapman had asked the prison chaplain, Rev. L.O. Sheffield, to attend. The men found Zangara sitting on his cot, looking lonely and forlorn. They accompanied him to the preparation room, where the crown of the prisoner's head is shaved so that the electrode will make solid contact with the skull. Although he knew that Zangara was an atheist who disliked ministers, Chapman beckoned to the chaplain to follow. Zangara eyed him and snapped, "What's your business?" Chapman told him and wrote later that at that moment, "the Italian lost his loneliness" and began dancing about the room "at a lively rate, shouting with great clamor."

"I no believe in church. There is no God. It's all down below . . . Get out of here, you son-of-a-bitch. Get to hell out of here," he yelled, waving his arm. Rev. Sheffield ignored him and began to pray aloud; the guards restrained the prisoner and sat him down so that his head could be shaved. As the chaplain began to read the fourteenth chapter of John, Zangara snarled at him once more, but then quieted down. Sheffield continued to pray in a low voice as the group made its somber way into the death chamber. It was 9:11 when Zangara, wearing striped prison trousers and a faded tan shirt open at the neck, entered the death chamber. The diminutive prisoner was lost among the clutch of large men who filed into the chamber with him, but according to witnesses, he walked in front of his guards with his head held high and a look of defiance on his face. He glanced at the thirty spectators on the other side of the room and then at the ugly, straight wooden chair bolted to the middle of the floor. There was no sound except for the shuffle of feet, the rustle of paper, and the dreary sound of the rain on the roof and windowsills.

The death chamber was a single room bisected by a waist-high wooden partition, on the far side of which was the spectators' gallery, accessible by a separate door. Twelve highbacked wooden chairs stood there, for the execution jury. The high, arched backs of the chairs, made of solid wood painted white, resembled twelve tombstones in two rows of six. On the near side of the partition was the massive electric chair, said to have been fashioned by prison craftsmen from a single live oak taken from the banks of the Suwannee River. It was like no other chair anyone had ever seen: highbacked and angular, with a wide seat, it had leather straps on the arms and back, and a small V-shaped wooden headrest. On the floor beneath it was a square rubber mat. Six feet or so behind it, against the wall, was a set of plywood cabinets, seven feet high, containing the electrical apparatus which was fastened to the condemned man. In the cabinet closest to the door was the executioner's switch with three electrical gauges near its top. The chair itself did not administer the lethal shock; it was then, as now, only the seat in which the prisoner was secured.

Chapman was already in the room when Zangara entered ahead of his guards, barefoot and carrying the three notepads which Chapman's secretary had given him. He hurried to Chapman and, with what the warden described as a courtly bow, handed him the manuscript. "He handed me these books," Chapman writes, "making the calm and confident announcement, as if he were leaving for the ages a legacy of priceless value, 'This is the book.'" Chapman slipped them quickly into his coat pocket and later told the press who had seen this transfer, that they contained only personal requests and would not be made public. He intended, he said, to turn them over to federal authorities. But the warden eventually decided that they contained nothing of value and he did not allow their contents to be published.

Two guards attempted to take Zangara's arms to lead him to the chair, but he waved them off: "No, don't touch me. I go myself. I no 'fraid of 'lectric chair. I show you. I go sit down all by myself." With a slight smile, he walked quickly to the chair, turned to face the spectators, hesitated and then in a peculiar manner "plopped" himself into the chair without touching its arms. One reporter said that he "hopped" into the chair "as calmly as a man stepping into a barber's chair." Chapman was sure that Zangara believed the chair was charged with electricity and that he would die on the instant he sat down. "One can know something, I believe," Chapman writes, "of the steadfast nerve of this little man. It was a cool and determined act [in which] there was not much of the bravado."

Chapman was not alone in his admiration of Zangara's demeanor. Dr Ralph N. Greene, a Jacksonville neuro-psychiatrist, later wrote a friend, "I am not making a hero out of Zangara. I am admitting that he had the most wonderful bravery." He was the sort of man, Dr Greene said, who might, as he sat down in the electric chair, have been expected to have carefully extinguished his last cigarette so as not to cause a fire. Commissioner Nathan Mayo said that Zangara "had more nerve than any man I ever saw."

Chapman noted that after he sat in the chair, Zangara looked surprised to find himself still alive. He looked about the room and after a moment loudly exclaimed, "See, I no 'fraid of 'lectric chair." Chapman said that he was the smallest man ever to sit in that chair; his feet did not quite reach the floor. He stared boldly at the crowd as the guards strapped him in. The only sound was the rustle of the guards and the melancholy drumming of the rain beating on the gray windows of this grim room, filled with silent staring people. After a few moments, Zangara suddenly realized that there were no cameras present.

It was the only important request the condemned man had made. Zangara called out, "Where the picture man? No movies, hey? You going to take my picture?" Chapman replied that no pictures would be taken. Zangara's eyes flashed in anger and his face tightened. "Nobody here, hey?" he said in a low, bitter tone. "You no let them. You dirty capitalists! Lousy bunch of capitalist sons of bitches! All capitalists lousy bunch of crooks. No chance for nobody to come here and take my picture." Zangara was livid, Chapman says: "He evidently felt that he would remain in the memory of the world as a martyr for he showed deep and amazed wrath while he was being strapped in the chair by saying to me: 'Where the picture men?' 'No pictures,' I replied. His face flushed and his eyes blazed as he shouted, 'What! No take picture when the great Zangara die? Lousy capitalist son of bitches.'" Of all the reporters and witnesses at the execution, only Chapman said that Zangara called himself "the great Zangara."

Chapman began to read the death warrant, as he was required to do by law. Zangara, in a low voice, instructed the electrician about the placement and tightening of the straps. Because the condemned man was so small, they were having trouble fitting the cap, which serves as an electrode, on the back of his head. This "death cap," made out of Tarpon Springs sponge soaked in salt water, with copper wire woven into it, fits over the shaved spot on the back of the head and is tightly secured by a strap under the chin.

Lastly, the black hood was fastened over his head and the guards stepped away. Zangara leaned back to await the shock as Sheriff Hardie walked to the cabinet behind the chair where the switch was located. A motor on the back wall began to hum, red and white indicator lights flashed and a wheel as big as a dinner plate started to spin. Then, his voice muffled by the hood, Zangara spoke his last words strongly and dramatically: "*Viva Italia!* Goodbye to all poor people everywhere!" Then, after a moment, he said, "Pusha da button! Go ahead, pusha da button!"

"Just a minute, Joe," the sheriff said quietly, and then after a slight pause, "Goodbye, Joe." He turned the red-handled switch, sending 2,300 volts surging from the skullcap through Zangara's brain, down his torso and out to ground again through the electrode strapped to his right ankle. His hands clutching the chair arms, Zangara's head jerked, his body stiffened and heaved upward. It was exactly 9:17 A.M. Hardie let the current flow for a full three minutes. At 9:27 A.M., March 20, 1933, Giuseppe Zangara was pronounced dead. It had been thirty-three days since the shooting in Bayfront Park. The five weeks of Giuseppe Zangara had come to an end.

17

GOPHER HILL

A s many as forty people may have witnessed Zangara's execution. Wire service reporters were there, recording everything that happened. But only Warden Chapman heard Zangara say, "*Viva la Camorra!*" or refer to himself as "the great Zangara." Chapman considered this the most important statement Zangara had made during the entire five weeks; to the best of his knowledge, the warden writes, no one else caught the words, or, if they did, they did not understand their significance. The *Camorra* is a Neapolitan crime organization similar to the Sicilian Mafia.

One reporter, R.W. Simpson of the *Tampa Tribune*, sought a simple explanation for Zangara's behavior: "Looking at Zangara in the chair as they were putting on him the harness of death, I got the distinct impression that he had been doped. He had lost his defiant air. Judged by his former performances, he was too quiet, too silent during the six minutes he sat in the chair. A pig awaiting slaughter would have carried on more fiercely." Clearly Zangara's bravery in the face of death astonished and baffled many of the witnesses, some of whom at least remembered it for the rest of their lives.

The body was removed immediately to the prison hospital for an autopsy by a team consisting of, among others, a New York psychiatrist, the Jacksonville medical examiner and the prison doctor. Dr Greene was also present. The autopsy report has been lost; all that remains of it are what was quoted in newspapers and in a letter to President Roosevelt from Dr Greene, the Jacksonville psychiatrist.

Zangara's brain, which had been removed for examination, was found to be perfectly normal. Thus the doctors, who had never talked to Zangara, pronounced him sane, saying that he was "medically as well as criminally responsible for the crime for which he was executed. . . . [His] conduct during his last moments in the execution chamber indicated clearly he had a proper understanding of his surroundings and realized fully the nature of the punishment about to be meted out to him as evidenced by his verbal expression and demeanor." There may have been a note of defensiveness here, a response to the unexpressed fear that the state had executed an insane man.

Nothing remarkable was noted in Zangara's stomach and viscera, but there was evidence of disease in his gallbladder: "Zangara had a chronically diseased gallbladder which had adhesions and was therefore a victim of chronic indigestion. He was, however, a healthy, well-nourished individual." The adhesions referred to here are the filament-like scar tissue which forms between the pouch of the gallbladder and the liver upon which it rests, and which are caused by repeated infection and healing of the gallbladder. No other comment was made about the cause of the apparent lifelong abdominal affliction which may have driven Zangara to become a killer.

■ ■ ■

Shortly after the execution, a kind of mystique appeared to develop around Zangara. Chapman wrote that letters came "from everywhere" requesting a specimen of the dead man's handwriting, or asking that his handwriting be "psychoanalyzed." Some people wrote that they had had visions about him, while others, whom Chapman considered sadists, wanted "minute descriptions of his facial expression when the current hit him." There were those who asked for proof that Zangara was really dead; the belief existed that he had been revived after the execution. Chapman remarked grimly that they would have been convinced if they had seen the autopsy photographs of Zangara without the top of his head. One correspondent in New Jersey sent Zangara a note wrapped around a three-inch file "so he could escape." Chapman reported that T. Earl Moore, one of the Miami psychiatrists who had examined Zangara, claimed that he had the dead man's brain in a jar. An anonymous magazine article speculated that Florida had rushed Zangara to his death "in order to silence a voice which might talk out of turn."

Chapman attempted to put a stop to all this speculation by refusing to answer letters on the subject or to grant interviews, by prohibiting visits to the grave and denying the existence of Zangara's memoir. The *Tampa Tribune* conjectured that the contents of the notepads handed to Chapman in the death chamber "was supposed to be the story of [Zangara's] wretched life . . . [but] Chapman had wisely announced the document would not be available for publication, even if anybody wanted to publish it."

It was not Chapman alone who did not want Zangara's manuscript to see the light of day. The day after the execution, the president of the Texas Women's Democratic Association of Dallas wrote to FDR, saying that she had read that the "killer Zangara" had given Chapman his book, and that she felt "a movement should be put on at once by our womanhood to the effect that not one word of his story be published and not one moving picture be screened concerning that outlaw. It would without doubt be a crime breeder."

Years later Walter Winchell wrote several columns claiming that he had proof that Zangara was a Chicago mob hit man whose real target was Cermak. Chapman commented that "because of this glaring inaccuracy I have lost interest in Winchell's column."

■ ■ ■

Zangara characteristically had made no request for burial. His uncle Vincent Carfaro, who lived in New Jersey, refused to claim the body, saying that he was going to try to forget that he ever knew Joe. In the week before the execution, Governor Sholtz received requests from several clinics and medical schools for Zangara's body. However the body was unceremoniously buried in "Gopher Hill," the prison cemetery just outside the compound. Sixty years later, the small graveyard lies within the shadow of the massive modern penitentiary with its watchtowers and chainlink fence, now two rows deep, twelve feet high, sandwiching a jumble of razor-sharp concertina wire. Prisoners have been buried in groups, according to the date of death, from 1915 to the present. Zangara, for some reason, is buried with prisoners who died in 1926. As with the others, a license plate marks his grave, with his name, prisoner number and date of death. His last name is written first, in the Italian style, but it is misspelled, and the date of his death is wrong.

18

DEATH WISH

What was Giuseppe Zangara's real purpose when he shot Anton Cermak? Was he a mob hit man—or a terrorist? Was he legally—or, at least, clinically—insane? Why was he in almost constant abdominal pain? For three generations the man has been a mystery.

By February 1933, Zangara had not worked at his trade for at least three years. He had spent most of his savings, and his prospects for future work seemed as dismal as the nation's economic condition. In addition, his physical pain had intensified to the point where it was unbearable, possibly as a result of stress. If Zangara was really a political zealot, he had nothing to lose by killing the president. The question arises: to what extent could Zangara's actions be attributed to political convictions as opposed to an actual death wish? He had said that his life was not worth living because of the pain, and at one court hearing, he told the judge that he had expected the police to gun him down in the park that night. If he actually did expect that to happen, what does it say about his ultimate motive?

At the time there was a lot of discussion about whether he acted alone or whether he was a member of a secret political or criminal organization. And was he aiming at Roosevelt or did he hit his real target when he shot Cermak? However, authorities in both Miami and Washington D.C. decided that Zangara was what he appeared to be: a disturbed zealot, legally sane, acting alone, whose target was the president-elect. Nothing in the record supports any other conclusion. Law enforcement officers did in fact actively search for a more sinister motive and found none.

The question of a government conspiracy might arise, but there is no credible evidence to justify such a cover-up in 1933. The opposite seems to be true. If the Secret Service, the FBI or the Miami police had discovered that Zangara had links to organized crime, terrorist groups or foreign governments, it seems certain that these links would have been hotly pursued. Apparently this line of inquiry came to nothing.

Speculation about Zangara's true motive in the years following his summary execution may have arisen because his own explanation seemed so implausible. Those who came to know him during those five weeks concluded that he was not only sane but was an intelligent man. At first his "political theory" was accepted at face value. But later, after his execution, men like Walter Winchell and L.F. Chapman came to the conclusion, for different reasons, that a sane, intelligent person would not die for an ideology as ill-conceived, illogical and poorly articulated as Zangara's. They decided that he must have had a secret motive. Chapman believed him to be a loyal follower of *la Camorra*, the Neapolitan crime organization about which the warden knew very little. Winchell decided he had worked for the Chicago mob, a crime organization about which the columnist knew a great deal. These theories seemed to make more sense than Zangara's "kill-the-king" philosophy.

In retrospect one thing seems clear: Zangara wanted to die. This seems to have been something everyone overlooked at the time, possibly because to most Americans, suicide was an impulsive, desperate act, done perhaps from a kind of hysteria; not a calculated deed involving murder. It simply would not have occurred to them that suicide can also be an arcane act of exhibitionism. Public execution was considered to be the worst kind of punishment. Today, psychologists recognize a phenomenon known as "suicide by police," in which a person provokes the police into killing him.

It seems reasonable to believe that the last thing Giuseppe Zangara would want would be to spend the rest of his natural life in pain, caged with criminals in a southern American prison. It could be conjectured that when he found himself still alive and in custody after the shooting, he was genuinely frustrated, and fell back on a successful improvisation in which he manipulated his captors: outraging them, making himself so despicable in their eyes that they could not wait to kill him, bury him and forget him in the swiftest legal execution in twentieth-century U.S. history. This is a possible explanation of his behavior.

Clearly Zangara believed the political views he expressed. He was not an educated man. He did not read political tracts or manifestoes and had little or no understanding of government function, let alone such complex systems as Communism, capitalism or Fascism. At a time when the king of Italy was nothing more than a figurehead, Zangara apparently thought the monarch was ruling the nation.

The timing of his purchase of the gun may shed some light on Zangara's motives. When the pawnbroker testified that Zangara bought the gun before Roosevelt's visit had been announced, the defendant was asked the reason for the purchase. His explanation in court was that he bought the gun because he intended to go to Washington to assassinate Herbert Hoover. But during his interrogation on the night of the shooting, he was evasive about whether he had bought the gun before or after hearing of Roosevelt's impending visit; he said he could not remember.

It might seem implausible that anyone would attempt to assassinate a president three weeks before he was going to leave office;

but Zangara's foggy conception of the American political system and his implacable hatred of capitalist leaders could make this believable. At Raiford, however, Zangara told the warden that he had stalked Hoover in Washington for ten days. Assuming that this was true (which is doubtful) it strains belief that he would plan to go back to Washington in the middle of an unusually cold winter—he had often said that cold weather aggravated his stomach pains—to attempt once more to shoot a president to whom he had failed even to glimpse. And a president who would be out of office in less than three weeks.

And there is the question of the gun. If Zangara were a homicidal anarchist, would he not already own a weapon, and one of better quality than a cheap pistol? And if he had been hired to kill Cermak, why would he do it in the midst of one of the largest crowds ever to gather in Miami history? Cermak had a home on Miami Beach and was vacationing there—that fact would have offered many opportunities for a mob hit. Why would he have bought the gun before he knew Roosevelt was coming to Miami?

It would not be unreasonable to conclude that this reclusive, quiet, unemployed bricklayer, running out of money and in increasing pain, bought that gun to commit suicide in his third-floor room on Miami's 5th Street. He had told a Miami acquaintance that he was depressed by his dwindling finances to the point of suicide; he was thinking of jumping off a bridge or injecting himself with poison. It is conceivable that when, the day after buying the gun, Zangara learned about Roosevelt's visit, he decided that he could literally kill two birds with one stone: commit suicide and at the same time become famous as a champion of the downtrodden.

In his memoir he writes that hell was being sick and having to work; Zangara did not like working even when he was well, or as well as he ever was. Why die an anonymous death in a rooming house attic when you could kill yourself and achieve fame at the same time? Zangara seemed to enjoy those days of fame and attention; his execution was perhaps the centerpiece of his dull, obscure life. It is not surprising that he wanted it photographed.

The question remains of Zangara's legal and clinical sanity. Florida followed, and still follows, the M'Naghten Rule, which holds that a perpetrator must know the difference between right and wrong and understand the nature and possible consequences of his action. By modern interpretation of the rule, which has been refined in some respects over the past decades, a person who has acted under a delusion, even if he is not actually insane, may have a good legal defense as long as he has a diagnosable mental illness as well. There seems to be no question that Zangara was legally sane, that he knew what he did was illegal and considered by society to be wrong. He certainly may have had a personality disorder, but his captors found him likable, even engaging, and rational except for his political "theory" that he had a right or duty to kill heads of state in order to effect political change. He had, after all, murdered one person and injured four others in an attempt to kill the president-elect of the United States. He seemed to recognize that his ideas were not well-considered; he admitted that he had read nothing about political philosophy. Nevertheless, he was adamant about his right to commit murder for his cause. If he sincerely believed in this cause, today he could be called delusional.

John A Spencer, Ph.D., a Florida clinical psychologist who is often called to testify for prosecutors, has found, after examining all the material on Zangara—including his memoir—that he did not show signs of psychosis. Dr Spencer thinks that Zangara might have been a clinical hypochondriac, but was not a paranoid personality. Further, the psychologist feels that Zangara's attitude toward capitalism and politics reflected the "parroted primitive ideology of a disenfranchised working-class malcontent" but not delusional paranoia. "He clothed, and thereby disguised, his suicidal intentions," Dr Spencer writes, "with the eminent respectability of ideological martyrdom."

In considering whether Zangara met the legal standard for insanity by the modern interpretation of the M'Naghten Rule, Dr Spencer concludes that Zangara knew his actions were illegal because his behavior was designed to effect a particular end. While he may have had unrealistic expectations about the probable ramifications of his actions, and "miscalculated the magnitude and immediacy of the impact a political assassination may have had . . . he clearly understood that such an action was proscribed by law and was punishable by the state-sanctioned execution of the perpetrator." Hence, according to Dr Spencer, who, as a prosecution-oriented psychologist, may be more conservative than others, Zangara was not delusional.

George W. Barnard, M.D., Professor Emeritus of the University of Florida Department of Forensic Psychiatry, defines M'Naughton more broadly than Dr Spencer. He believes that a person can be legally insane only if he suffers from a diagnosable mental disease which prevents him from knowing the nature and quality of his act, or at least from knowing it is legally or morally wrong. Dr Barnard is not sure that Zangara knew that his actions were morally wrong. A case could, he thinks, be made at least by modern standards that Zangara was legally insane.

Dr Barnard notes that the two court-appointed psychiatrists who examined Zangara diagnosed him as a "psychopathic personality" but did not express an opinion about his legal sanity, as the court had requested they do. He found it significant that twenty years later, Dr T. Earl Moore, one of the two psychiatrists, told an interviewer that he had considered Zangara a "paranoid character, if not a true paranoid." This, Dr Barnard says, is "certainly inconsistent" with Moore's earlier diagnosis but, if true, means that Moore thought Zangara was suffering from a "paranoid personality disorder or a delusional disorder" and, if so, it could be argued that he had a "diagnosable mental illness" which meets the first requirements of today's M'Naghten standard.

On the question of whether Zangara knew both the nature and quality of his actions, and its moral wrongness as well as its illegality, Dr Barnard says that in his opinion, today "a case could have been made that, as a result of his delusional belief, Zangara did not know the moral wrongfulness of his acts since he consistently argued that he was right in what he did."

Thus, it is a question of Zangara's sincerity: both Barnard and Spencer agree that that if he was sincere in his beliefs, he was delusional and therefore legally insane. Dr Spencer thinks he was not sincere; Dr Barnard thinks he may well have been. Dr Barnard acknowledges that the M'Naghten argument would probably not have been accepted or even entertained by the court in 1933, and that the highly charged atmosphere would have given Zangara no chance of acquittal by reason of insanity.

There was the question of Zangara's pain, which was undoubtedly real and longstanding. He said that doctors had told him it was chronic and incurable. The Secret Service verified that he had had an appendectomy years earlier, an operation intended to alleviate his suffering. He was certainly too poor to pay for proper diagnosis and treatment. The authorities showed no inclination during Zangara's five weeks to make a definitive determination about his health. All we have is the newspaper report from the autopsy that Zangara's gallbladder was "chronically infected" and bound to the liver with scar tissue.

Dr K. Rajender Reddy, an associate professor of medicine at the University of Miami medical school and a specialist in heptology—the study of the liver—examined all of the available material on Zangara's abdominal condition and concludes that there was probably nothing wrong with Zangara's gallbladder, but that he most likely suffered from peptic ulcer disease. His complaints may have been due to "gastritis or dyspepsia associated with altered stomach motility." The "heart attack" symptoms about which Zangara complained to his uncle might have been the result of "an acid reflux

disease" in which acidity irritated the esophagus, causing symptoms that mock a heart attack. Dr Reddy thinks it remotely possible
that Zangara had acute intermittent porphyria, a hereditary disease
characterized by recurrent bouts of abdominal pain and associated
with mental abnormalities ranging from simple confusion to psychosis.

Dr Robert A. McNaughton, a Harvard-educated Miami gastro-
enterologist who had practiced in his field for fifty years, also examined Zangara's records. He considers porphyria a possibility, but
an unlikely one. He, like Dr Reddy, thinks Zangara had peptic ulcer
disease. "In an emotionally unstable person," Dr McNaughton says,
peptic ulcer disease "would be magnified and would be blamed for
many of his misfortunes." This condition can, the doctor says, last
for a long time without necessarily causing serious complications,
or physical or pathological changes in the body. He believes that
might explain why the doctors at the autopsy could find nothing
wrong with Zangara other than "chronic indigestion." Dr
McNaughton rules out recurrent gallbladder or pancreatic disease
because these would have been detectable in a post-mortem. A gallbladder bound by adhesions is not unusual and has little significance.

Robert Donovan commented in 1954: "In 1933, hardly any
thought was given to whether Zangara's mental condition had, as
he insisted, been caused by his stomach ache; today, several psychiatrists have suggested that his stomach ache had very likely been
caused by his mental condition."

In any case, it was obvious that Giuseppe Zangara enjoyed the
limelight. It was obvious, too, that he suffered almost constant pain
and may well have believed that he had only a year or two to live.
He had no wife or children, no friends, and believed only, apparently, in the rights of the poor with whom he identified. The evidence is compelling that he thought he could end his life that was a
burden to him, and at the same time attain the recognition and atten-

tion that had always been denied him. When to his surprise he survived the shooting, he made it clear that he was not afraid to die: he refused to express remorse and seemed to feel no concern for his victims. Although he did display anger when the judge sentenced him to death, he seemed to accept his fate readily, plopping himself into the electric chair and even giving instructions to his executioner to "pusha da button."

Whatever the circumstances, it seems clear that Giuseppe Zangara had suicidal tendencies and wished to die a hero's death. It seems obvious, also, that the state was intent upon killing him: his defense team was incompetent, and the press and public generally seemed to consider that this uneducated Italian immigrant was greatly inferior to them. One must remember, too, that it was in the depths of the Depression that Zangara made an attempt on the life of the one man who represented hope and faith in the future for the American people. If he had succeeded, Giuseppe Zangara would indeed have changed the course of history.

APPENDIX I

THE ARMOUR ACCOUNT

The following was found among the papers of the late Thomas Armour. It was handwritten in pencil. It has been edited for punctuation and spelling.

As the Roosevelt car stopped, it seemed like everybody stepped up on their seats in a standing position which put their heads above mine, cutting off our entire view of Roosevelt. I was standing on the ground in the aisle while the bench people were chair height. Roosevelt's car was about thirty feet west and a trifle south from the point where I was. Anxious for my boy to see Roosevelt, I got him to crowd in at the end of the second bench from me. I supported him with my right hand with arm extended full length. While standing in this position on tip toes with my neck stretched the limit, I tried to see Roosevelt myself. Standing on tip toes with my neck out so far as it could go, I tired just as Roosevelt had finished his short speech and had handed back a long line of telegrams to a committeeman on his right. He leaned forward and turned his head to his left acknowledging greetings, I presume, to Mayor Cermak. It was at this point that I tired, relaxed back on the flat of my feet, satisfied that I had seen all of President-elect Roosevelt that I wanted for this time, if it took all that strain to do it. Immediately, I noticed about three inches of a gun barrel exposed in the hand of a man, with the handle and cylinder concealed. The exposed part of the gun appeared to me as a toy.

Let me explain my position from the would-be assassin. There was a young woman about my height with her right shoulder almost touching the left side of my face. She was against the end of the bench, south of the gunman. Another woman was standing up on the bench immediately behind the gunman. My right foot was about in the center of the space between the bench the gunman was on and the next row of benches. [I was about] two and a half feet from the gunman. The benches ran east and west making both the woman and I east of the gunman and at his back. He [was turned to his right toward] Roosevelt and his car, which was headed west, placing Roosevelt's back to the gun.

The crowd had been congregated for fully one and a half hours talking and poking back and forth while waiting for the arrival of the President-elect. It was almost out of the question to suspect such a murderous attempt. [It was for this reason that] I did not [become] suspicious [of the gun barrel, and] also I'm no sleuth.

I saw the gun held in the hand [level with the gunman's] hip. It seems like in the time it takes to snap your fingers he raised it above the heads of the people in front of him, raising himself on his tip toes. In a split second I sprang and caught his arm just a moment before the explosion of the second shot, thus diverting the aim of the second shot. It was at this point that deep sorrow gripped me as I realized that with murderous intent he was aiming to kill our dearest friend, Franklin D. Roosevelt. The horror flashed through my mind of Roosevelt waiting for a chance to bring us out of this depression, of hard, hard times, only to be shot down, murdered by a murderer of the lowest type.

The first shot was on his tip toes above the people's heads. On the instant, all heads in the path from the would-be assassin dropped down as I caught on to his arm. I sighted across the barrel of the gun. I remember very clearly the sight of the gun, its direct aim was at the back of Roosevelt's head and the clear channel or path [caused by the dropping crowd created a] clear view of Roosevelt's head. Although it was a split second sight, I recall it as the best view I had had of Roosevelt. I caught hold on the muscle of the right arm between the wrist and elbow, which held the gun, thus breaking the direct aim, but the shot was [fired] at that level. I elevated the gunman's arm before the third shot which caused the gunman to pause [for just a moment]. That pause has been corroborated by many people who listened over the radio and by witnesses at the park.

My grip was on the muscle between the wrist and elbow leaving the wrist free. Zangara took advantage of this and bent his hand down for the remainder of the shots, [causing them] to go where they may, trusting that one would hit his intended subject. As I held on, the thought came to me that the bullets were bound to hit someone in the crowd of people in front of the gun. As I looked at the hand tip down, [I thought] goodness gracious, he's going to keep on shooting. My nose was so close to the explosions I could smell the powder and I could see the flash of fire from the [pistol]. This picture, I don't believe I will ever forget. But what else could one do but hold on with hopes the gun was elevated high enough for the bullets to pass over heads. As I had his arm up and I saw him tip his hand down and keep shooting, I felt the report of each shot through his arm. I did not know definitely how many shots were fired.

While I was on the witness stand testifying for the state in the Zangara trial, I was demonstrating the occurrence [when] one defense attorney shouted at me, "Why didn't you jump on him and stomp him down." But from the time the pistol left Zangara's hip until the explosion of the first shot [occurred in an instant]. [Then the shots] went one, two, pause, three, four, five. There was no time to hesitate. It was on the split second or goodbye.

Just before the fifth shot exploded some man to my right, seemed to me he was standing on a bench to the right of Zangara, caught on [with both hands] and pulled [both our arms] down at about a right angle position to Zangara's arm [just as the last shot was fired]. He was about to get the gun when an officer plunged in head first over four rows of benches, his body striking Zangara's extended arm. [It seemed to me that he dived and was grasping for the gunman's arm. I think he got the gun. The gunman released the gun and jerked his arm loose]. With the man to my right and I both holding on, the jar of [the policeman's] body broke our hold and knocked Zangara off the bench. [Thus he was free but as he stepped backward I caught him with my left arm around his back and straightened him up lifting him off the ground]. I [was carrying] all of his weight and it flashed through my mind how light he was. He turned his head slightly to the right and hollered, "Get away," exposing his face to me for the first [time]. At the moment he had spoken these words, some fellow about my own age grabbed Zangara by the throat with both hands from the back, pulling him down with me still holding on. [When we were] about two-thirds down, the officer who had plunged in regained himself and plunged in a second time breaking my hold and knocking me into the bench to my right and crushing Zangara to the ground with the officer on top. I straightened up quick to be knocked down again by Officer Jackson as he rushed by. This time I went to the ground.

As I was getting up I saw a woman [Cross] frantically trying to release her foot which was caught in a bench that had been turned over. As she tried to step off the bench during the melee, her foot got pinned in the bench so she was about to break her ankle as she was so excited. I got her quieted and then released her foot. By this time officers Jackson and Clark subdued the crowd as they were making all kinds of threats to kill Zangara on the spot. [The officers] handcuffed Zangara and picked him up, one at the head and the other at the foot, and placed him between the trunk and rear end of a car. Zangara was well secured there with Det. Sinnott, who was wounded inside the car. Clark and Jackson, in this dangerous and hazardous position, hung on to Zangara and onto the car as it sped at 60 mph through town. Sheriff Hardy [sic] stood on the running board of the car on one side while Officer Crews [stood on the other side.] Jackson lost his month's wages during the melee but was reimbursed by the city.

After releasing the lady's foot, I started brushing dirt from my clothes and realized that I had lost my hat. I wondered about my boy when I heard him calling for me to come get away quick for fear someone would take a shot at me. [He shouted: "Daddy!! Come on! Come on! Let's get away from here! I asked him why and he said someone will shoot you. I then realized that in the excitement I had forgotten about my boy.] I convinced him there was no danger and to wait until I found my hat. Finally, I saw some tall, elderly gentleman with gray hair holding it, looking it over like he was about to decide that it would be a good souvenir. [I laughed and told him it was mine]. As it was pretty well knocked out of shape, I thought of Roosevelt telling {Democratic Party Chairman} Farley that he had too many hats. It would be a fine way to show their appreciation for the trifle part I [played] by sending me one [of Farley's hats].

By this time people were pretty well gone. The crowd got away fast. But I did not care to make it known that I had anything to do with it and was [about to leave]. Up on the platform of the bandstand I could see a crowd of people crowding around some woman listening to what she had to say. A fellow by the name of Bauss came to me [and told me] to go up and make [myself] known. He told me they were taking pictures, and [listening] to some woman talking into the Movietone machine. He advised me to go over and see what it was all about. After some persuasion, I told my boy that I had probably better. I drifted over still on the ground level. This woman was standing on the [bandstand] platform about four feet from the ground in front of the Movietone machine. She looked my way and recognized me, and exclaimed as she pointed, "There's the man who pushed the hand of the gunman up in the air." [She insisted] that I should be in the picture with her. But the confusion was terrible; everybody was talking and hollering; the lights were going off and on which interrupted the movie machine, [so] I was left out of the picture. I seemed to [have been] ignored by the movie man. [But] I was caught in one picture which was a surprise to me when it was shown in the [movie theater]. I was never asked any questions but there was not much chance because the woman held the floor. It was hard for me to let this go on but I decided that I'd rather tackle Zangara than cause any dispute. I consoled myself with the fact that the truth is bound to come out. If the deed was deserving it would be proven [by those who were] actually on the spot. At the park and at police headquarters, dozens pointed me out.

Of course, this has been thoroughly investigated. Proof of the truth is now in the hands of the committee in charge of awarding national recognition. The proof is in affidavit form, under sworn oath. I have not had the slightest advice nor notification from the authorities in Washington that I am considered or that I am the one. [But] I can truthfully and safely say that local officials believe in me from the proven facts and are ready to back me. Some have forwarded their opinion to Washington favoring the credit to me.

I have been trying to get affidavits from eye witnesses to the shooting. I have found no one so far who saw Mrs Cross holding the would-be assassin's hand. I can't understand why she has gotten so much credit for averting the shots. She was not present at the trial of Zangara and so I have not heard her testify [but] she was questioned before the trial by a city official and she contradicted herself five times.

I am not seeking publicity but would like the public to know as they are demanding the real truth about it. I'm not taking the issue from a selfish standpoint; nor for self gain; nor to antagonize what has been published, but to prove to you Truth is bigger and better even though it is slower to develop. This could have been ironed out on the spot with all embarrassment and disputes kept down [because] at least fifteen people pointed to me, recognizing me as the first to spring and grab the murderer. All [of these people], who stood immediately around Zangara and I, were strangers to me. [They] emphasized that I saved the life of President-elect Roosevelt when we were [gathered after the shooting] to be taken to police headquarters [to give our] statements. Even at police headquarters I was pointed out. But you would be surprised [by the number of] publicity seekers [who tried to take credit.] This alone almost caused me [to let anyone who wanted it] have the publicity. But the pangs of knowing the untruthfulness [of what was being claimed] was tough to endure. Everyone who actually did do their part has been pushed aside.

APPENDIX II

THE CHAPMAN MANUSCRIPT

The following are excerpts from the unpublished manuscript of the late Leonard F. Chapman, Sr., Superintendent of the Florida State Prison at Raiford from 1931 to 1956. The first section contains an earlier version of the manuscript and is included to illustrate the change in Chapman's thinking over the years as well as details the author omitted in his final version. The manuscript was probably written over the years from 1940 to 1970.

FIRST VERSION

Zangara seemed to be an enigma to every one except me. By the time he sat in the chair for his execution, I was satisfied that there was no mystery about him. Nothing to this day has changed my opinion. So far as I am concerned his life and action in attempting to kill the president-elect is an open book.

Zangara was merely a crack-brained product of socialism in its extreme form and he had no connections anywhere. At that time, that was not known. And that fact died slowly. Years later Walter Winchell announced that he had positive information that Zangara was acting for the thugs of Chicago.

. . . he was not insane. No one who talked to him for long could question his sanity. He was a lone wolf. No one who read the transcript of his trial could doubt it; and no one who questioned him for long in the death cell could doubt it, especially after reading his "book."

My talks with him indicated plainly that he was actually trying to kill Roosevelt. He was a lone wolf and had no accomplices whatever. Nor was he the agent of any foreign power in any sense. And he was as sane as any uneducated fanatic can be.

Ten years later the Secret Service told me that my estimate of the man had turned out to be correct. He really was a lone wolf.

Some interest has been shown in his writings while he was in the death cell. We gave him some stenographer's note books and pencils and he wrote the "Story of His Life" as he called it. He showed these written pages to no one and guarded them while he was in the death cell constantly.

I put the note books in my pocket and showed them to no one. They never have been shown. But there was nothing of importance in them. I refused to let the press see them because I was opposed to glamorize the murderer or to let him reach any of the compatriots he might have had.

While he waited in the death cell he wrote out the tale of his life and handed it to me as he walked to the chair. I never made it public for it was nothing but a hopelessly jumbled rehash of the socialistic jargon of that day. There was nothing of any revealing nature in it which was of any service to anyone.

His "book" never will be published. It was, of course, merely a rambling account of his life from his earliest memory, interspersed with his undigested ideas, written in pencil, utterly without punctuation, in a lower Italian patois, the lettering in a cramped school boy style. Most of the ideas have been given in far better form by radicals in every land and under all conditions. It can do no good to pass it along to the public. Nothing in it has to do with any other crimes, nor are state secrets of any sort revealed.

The contents of the books never have been made public for these reasons but I am printing them in full now so as to divest them of all mystery and to show that my conclusions about him were correct. (Chapman includes the entire Zangara memoir in his final manuscript.)

The guards had completed the strapping. The hood was drawn across the face. When for the last time his voice came out, muffled by the mask, "Viva the poor people! Viva the Camora! [sic] Good-bye all poor people everywhere!" An instant's pause and then with a voice both irritated and boasting he shouted, "Push the button, go and push the button." It was his last word. Sheriff Hardie replied, "Just a minute, Joe." After an instant, "Good-bye, Joe," and threw the switch. His body gave an upward heave, but the Italian was gone. His heart beat for ten minutes, but the switch only kept the current on for forty-five seconds. A tragic figure in a way. I cannot doubt that he sincerely believed that he was a martyr to a cause that was worthy of his life. I believe he wanted the picture as much to create interest among people who sympathize with the doctrines of Communism, as to prove that he bravely died. He weakened not at all. He did exactly what he said he would do, walked to the chair by himself.

The execution of a man is unbelievably simple. No smoke, no burning flesh, no odor. Just a rigid body and shortly death. Witnesses quiet. Newsmen taking notes. Usually a few words spoken by the condemned man while the straps are tightened, and the electrician adjusts the lodes to head and leg.

I have pictures taken after the autopsy, showing the top of the head removed—rather gruesome but effective answers to the ridiculous charges that he was shielded even in his death by mysterious but powerful friends.

Some peculiar things developed. A Dr T. Earl Moore in Miami claimed to have the brain. Somebody in Detroit wrote a song and actually published it, protesting against executions. Looks like strange quirks take charge of the minds of some folks.

[In the smoke on the train platform, I heard someone say,] "I know all about that guy. He sure got the man he wanted. He wasn't shooting at Roosevelt at all. The underworld in Chicago put him up to it. And he sure made good in a big way."

I looked out of the window and thought of the two times at least that Walter Winchell mentioned in his column—the last time just a year or two ago—that he had learned from the underworld that Zangara was gunning for Mayor Cermak and had had no thought of killing Roosevelt. Because of this glaring inaccuracy, I have lost interest in Winchell's column. If he writes merely rumors, I care nothing for them. And the talk in the smoking room on the train—no wonder arm chair generals should be told to shut up. The fact is that Zangara never had been in Chicago and never had heard of Cermak. He asked me about him, talking in his broken English, and expressed regret that the Mayor had died.

The point of the whole sorrowful episode, the killing of Cermak, the threat to the President, and the execution of the foreigner will be lost by the American people if they pass the affair as a Chicago underworld spot, in which Mr Cermak was put on the spot in modern fashion, or is passed by as a sad but unavoidable flare of a crazy man.

The same conditions that produced Zangara may produce another. If social morasses be not recognized, the birthrate of such men will continue. The education of the foreign-born in the ideals and heritage of America or exclusion until their ideas are naturalized seem to be just as important as the prevention of crime by the banning of hidden firearms.

SECOND VERSION

CHAPTER XXII
ZANGARA COMES TO RAIFORD

Zangara has always seemed something of a mystery to the American public who were shocked by his attempted assassination of President Roosevelt. Theories sprang up thick as weeds including one that his immediate target had been Mayor Cermak of Chicago.

Zangara was under my protection in the death cell for ten days, and I witnessed his execution. During that time I learned a good deal of what made him the kind of man he was.

There was excitement from the moment he was slipped secretly into Raiford by Sheriff Hardie of Miami immediately after sentence of death had been pronounced for fear that accomplices might attempt his release on the 400 mile journey.

The sheriff breathed a sigh of relief as he saw him enter the death cell. "I'm glad that job's done," he said. "He's yours now!"

I didn't know another moment of peace. Raiford became the center of interest of the nation. Newsmen swarmed over the place. Photographers assailed the prison ramparts. Secret Service men and the FBI literally camped there. Fearing that Zangara had connections with the underworld of large northern cities, the governor ordered squads of National Guard to take charge of the outside rim of the prison. Every car that approached the prison was stopped and searched and the occupants questioned.

For two weeks I scarcely slept. The telephone rang at all hours of the day and night. The idea was prevalent that the underworld of Chicago would assault the prison itself to free Zangara. There were even some people in Washington who believed that Italy, through him, was taking a hand in the future of the presidency of the United States. Most people believed that Zangara was merely a tool of some larger interests.

I talked with him every one of those ten days he spent in the death cell while the death warrant went through all the legal routines. Most of the time I took along my secretary [Rose Lee Dunbar] to make notes of everything he said.

I felt it was my duty to find answers to four questions which were agitating the FBI, the Secret Service and the general public to an amazing degree.

First, did he actually try to kill Roosevelt or was Mayor Cermak of Chicago his intended victim? After all, they had been sitting side by side when the shots rang out so unexpectedly at that great rally in Miami.

Second, was he a member of a gang who had concocted a scheme to kill the newly elected President?

Third, was he an agent of some foreign power? Or a member of the Camorra?

Fourth, was Zangara insane?

To settle any doubts, I wrote an article for a national magazine which may be worth quoting here:

A warden looks at life through the prison—and finds the prison a very good telescope, or microscope, or for that matter a test tube.

Even national trends may be noted, as for instance when early on a morning in March 1933, while a heavy rain was falling, a tiny little man, 33 years of age, was electrocuted in the death chamber of the Florida State Prison.

This diminutive fellow, who weighed scarcely 105 pounds and whose education was fragmentary, might have changed the whole history of the nation and of the world. For he shot at President Roosevelt and killed Mayor Cermak of Chicago, instead.

. . . Roosevelt himself might have died before ever he had taken the oath of office and mayhap the long chain of events in national and international affairs might have been greatly different.

. . . Zangara—the frail Italian—boldly marched to the electric chair and died when the switch was thrown, defiant to the last, sustained by a misguided instinct and fully regretful that he did not succeed in his terrible attempt.

How explain this affair? How analyze the mental quirk of a man whose broken English expressed regret that Mayor

Cermak died, saying, "I'm sorry for him—what's his name? Yes, I sorry, but he should not have been there," and at the same time defend his right to try to kill the leader of a nation because, "Everybody should be equal and nobody be above anyone else."

. . . What chain of unhappy events could have led to the assault on the nation's chief? What could Zangara have hoped to gain? He remained in the death cell 10 days, awaiting his execution. I asked him to explain his motive, saying that in case he succeeded in killing the President we would have selected another, and so no gain could be recorded. His reply was given in broken English: "Sure, you get 'nother one. Then somebody kill him. And somebody kill the next one—and bye and bye nobody will be willing to be president and then everybody be equal."

Thus spoke the little man, who was born in the Province of Calabria in the toe of Italy's boot, not far from the city of Naples where the Camorra was born among discharged prisoners almost a hundred years before—the Camorra whose dark and bloody deeds have marked the Italian history for a century, and whose whole passion is revenge. Revenge—personal and individual—in the darkness of the night and at the point of a stiletto.

. . . [Zangara was] a being utterly unassimilated, a foreigner wandering in a strange land and making no effort to understand that land; practicing the hatreds which came natural to him; bent on the ancient wheel; bringing to flower the code of the Camorra; attempting to correct a fancied wrong by wreaking personal vengeance.

So he shot at Roosevelt. His bullet might have turned a national trend down another channel.

Well, what is to be done? How handle such matters? It seems to a warden that here the remedy suggests itself—namely, to educate the incoming masses in the way of American life before ever they are made free to follow their own unsavory ways. It is required that newcomers have support of some sort for at least six months and a modicum of education. But of the mysteries of American life, of the deep springs which furnish the ideals and motives of Americans, of devotion to the great values characteristic of our nation, no instruction whatever is given. So, the small figure of the peasant Italian stiffened in the electric chair when the current flashed through his body and the incident of Biscayne Bay was ended in due and legal form. The law had taken its toll for the murder of Mayor Cermak of Chicago. The body was buried in the prison cemetery, and his monument is a number on a steel marker. . . .

For in the past of Southern Italy may be found the sources which finally pulled the trigger in Bayfront Park. It was no sudden impulse—not the inspiration of the moment—not the resistless temptation of an upheaval unpredictable. It was born with the Camorra in Naples and followed the course of the years in a channel as clear as an arroya secha on the desert.

In the case of Zangara, for instance, he loitered in Rome to shoot the king of Italy, but failed as he said because, "the guards were big and the king—he is little fellow." He lingered about the White House for 10 days to shoot President Hoover but failed because, he said, "Hoover never walked out—always got in car and rode fast."

Had this been known before that fateful day in Miami! Had he been known for what he was—an irresponsible egotist, whose untutored mind was controlled by half-baked communistic ideas. He proved again that "a little learning is a dangerous thing."

CHAPTER XXIII

ZANGARA DIES

One wintry March morning in 1933 while the hardest rain of the winter was falling, I walked to the death chamber with Hon. Nathan Mayo, Commissioner of Agriculture for Florida, and with several newsmen representing the Associated Press, the International News Service and the United Press. Our mission was to attend the execution of Giuseppe Zangara. Several physicians were in attendance. They planned an autopsy to determine what caused the pain in his stomach of which he had complained and which he said caused him to shoot at the newly elected president.

The witnesses took their places in chairs directly in front of the heavy oak electric chair. Zangara entered the death chamber in front of the guards, glanced at the witnesses, and walked directly to me to hand me three stenographer's books which he had filled with comments on his life, his ideas and his plans.

They were written by pencil in an almost illegible, lower Italian dialect in a cramped school boy hand and entirely without punctuation.

With a courtly bow, reminiscent of the days of old Italy, even with an almost ironical grace, he handed me these books, making the calm and confident announcement as if he were leaving for the ages a legacy of priceless value: "This is the book."

Turning toward the chair, he hesitated a moment as his eye fell on it, and the guards stepped to his side. He waved them back with a gesture of his left hand, saying sharply, "No touch me. I no afraid of electric chair. I go sit down all by myself."

The guards stepped back. Without further hesitation, the wiry little Italian who weighed only 105 pounds and who stood only five feet and one inch in height, walked to the chair, faced the witnesses and sat down without touching the arms of the chair.

I feel sure that he thought the chair was charged with electricity and that the instant he sat down, he would die. It was a cool and determined act. In that act, there was not much of the bravado. If one can imagine a cornered rat deliberately walking into a trap and instant death, when there remains no chance to fight, one can know something of the steadfast nerve of this little man.

There was surprise evident on his face as he looked about the room while the guards were adjusting the straps. With a sudden rush of words, he shouted, "Where the picture men? You going to take my picture?"

When he was told that no pictures would be taken, his eyes flashed and his face grew solemn as if he were hearing an incredible thing. "What! You no take picture? You not take picture when the great Zangara die?"

There was a moment's pause while this unbelievable thing settled into his mind. Then he blurted in a low and intensely vicious voice and with a helpless, suppressed wrath, "No take picture! Capitalists ——! Lousy, dirty capitalist ——!"

Silence settled on the room. All eyes were fixed on the smallest figure that ever had sat in the chair at Raiford. The electrician had difficulty in adjusting the cap because of the smallness of his head. The hood was drawn across his face, and the guards stepped back. For the last time his voice came out, somewhat muffled by the cap.

"Viva Italia! Viva Camorra! Goodbye all poor people everywhere!"

After an instant, his voice sounded again, charged with irritation and boasting.

"Push the button. Go on and push the button."

Sheriff Hardie threw the switch. His body gave an upward heave, but Zangara was gone. He had not weakened at all. He did exactly what he had said he would do—walk to the chair by himself.

Dr Ralph Greene of Jacksonville, Dr C.K. Whitaker, the prison physician, and Dr J.J. Kindred of New York City performed an autopsy and found a chronically diseased gall bladder which accounted for his "stomach pains." His brain was removed by these physicians and found normal on gross examination. It was sent by them to Dr C.D. Dandy of Johns Hopkins Hospital in Baltimore for microscopic examination [and the report showed that the brain was as normal as any brain save some indications of heavy drinking in previous years.] His body was buried in the prison cemetery.

Zangara's act was the act of a madman, but he was not a madman. There was no insanity evident from the first to the last. Always, save for the moment when he sat in the chair and heaped imprecations on capitalists, he was the smiling, cheerful, dapper little Italian. Only once in the court room did he flare out for an instant.

There was a method in his act which is evidence of the coolest sanity. He shot into the crowd because crowds had balked him each time he had endeavored to kill a "capitalist." He tried to kill the king of Italy but could not see the king over his "big" guards. He lingered about the White House for ten days to kill Mr Hoover but could not aim on account of the

President's escort. At Miami, the crowd protected Mr Roosevelt. Not to be thwarted, however, Zangara shot wildly. It was his chance, and he took it. He shot with no apparent remorse, commenting, "Sorry for those folks, but they ought not to have been in the way."

What he hoped to gain by the mad act was another matter. But a warden learns to discern insanity. It is part of his daily work among hundreds of men of all degrees of mental virility. I have taken part in the examination of scores who were delivered to the hospital for the insane at Chattahoochee. I have testified in court for a man whose electrocution was set for four days later. Mine is not a scientific approach but a practical one. Wardens learn much by experience, and they rarely miss their diagnosis.

Zangara was not insane. Physicians, lawyers and the court in Miami adjudged him sane. For ten days I watched him closely, talked with him every day on all sorts of subjects. My stenographer took down every word he said. I have his "book." Every day the guards reported his speech and conduct both by day and by night. I have no more doubt of his sanity than I have of that of the farmer on the next farm or the storekeeper at Lawtey. The charge made that the State of Florida rushed him to his death merely for the sake of wiping from the slate the perpetrator of a dastardly deed, without regard to his legal rights or to his sanity, is baseless in fact and in justice.

To explain him, I need only say that he was an intense Italian, with all the Latin's volatile temperament, unfortunately transplanted to colder America where the methods he knew and the feverish ideas he evolved were neither understood nor even examined. He was the product of years of struggle against the odds of illness and ignorance, a dreadful combination. Natively he had a keen brain. Mentally he had a certain restless talent. Being what he was, having lived as he did, having the natural mental energy to resist what he regarded as a sorry experience, he reached the conclusion that one bold stroke would even the betting odds with fate and perhaps in some way bring an easier existence to others. That the leveling of the betting odds with fortune would mean death to him was a trivial consideration if only others would make similar sacrifices to carry on the struggle.

The environment which shaped Zangara can easily produce others with a perverted point of view. If the nation calmly dismisses the shooting as the act of a madman, and therefore merely unfortunate and unavoidable, the whole lesson will be lost. The way will be left open for a repetition of the act. The Zangara crime found its source in the educational neglect of the foreign born and the breach in the immigration wall that admits certain ignorant and vicious foreign elements.

Zangara was a Calabrian. This province lies in the toe of the boot which is Italy. Across the ribbon of water lies Sicily. Not far to the north was the city of Naples. In the rough, craggy, broken, mountainous country Zangara was born. His people were from the tempestuous tribes which hid in the hills and mountains and sallied forth on occasion for smuggling or raiding. They were a willful, proud, freedom loving folk. For hundreds of years they had been restive under restraint. On scores of occasions they had defied the Italian central government, retiring, when pressed, to the fastnesses of the rough country. The volatile, excitable Latin temperament flowered in Calabria.

In this kind of place, far from the refinements of modern life, Zangara was born. His home was on the second "bench" above the sea. From time to time he made his way to the shore for bathing, for fishing and "little trips in boats."

Those early years of poverty and toil on the barren farm, tending the flocks and plowing before he was six years old while "my father he go way all time and I have the hard work to do," those years of unloved childhood started the "pain" which resulted twenty years later in the theory that "the capitalists have all money and poor people no bread. I would do away with all money, burn all money. Then the poor people be just as good as the rich. I kill capitalists because I have pain in my stomach. The pain, it come because I poor child and have to work too hard. I kill President to make all the people just alike. So then I do not have pain."

One morning when he was talking freely with me, I asked him if he would try to kill the President if released from the death cell.

His reply was quick and positive. "Yes. Kill the President. That my idea. I kill him tomorrow if I get a chance."

"But," I argued, "how can people be controlled if there be no government? What would prevent people from robbing and murdering?"

"If we got no government and no money—if all money be burned up—then nobody rob because no money to steal. And nobody kill because everybody got everything just alike. Everybody have bread. What need for government if all got bread just alike?"

The mental meanderings of ignorance and suffering is a dangerous thing. Here was ignorance seeking an artificial remedy for centuries of old problems. Natural problems have never yet been solved by artificial means. However, ignorant men like Zangara can interpret problems in no other way.

Florida is hiding no secrets in Zangara's grave. He was not rushed to his death by the state in order to silence a voice that might talk out of turn as was charged in a sensational magazine article by an author who would not sign his name. Step by step the law took its course. What seemed so hurried was merely the answer to the law, to the deed of an assassin.

That he was a foreigner by birth had nothing whatsoever to do with the matter. A lawyer of Italian heritage was selected by the court to assist in his defense. Indeed, it was Florida officers who rescued him from a Florida mob at the time of the shooting.

That he was not alone in Miami, I am satisfied. That he was the representative of a secret order, I feel sure. That he was paid to do the killing, I sincerely doubt.

Ignorant, unlettered, crude he undoubtedly was. Secretive, too. Wondrously capable of holding his own counsel. But it was noteworthy that his silence was not the sullen, snarling silence of a gangster whose tongue is held in leash by the bitter code that scorns a "rat." He was cheerful, smiling, ready to talk, at time voluble.

To myself I have explained the mystery by believing him to have been a sort of traveling secretary for some secret order which was dedicated to the doubtful tenets of a bastard socialism. His talk was a strange mixture of communism and socialism with a strong admixture of fatalism and materialism.

His only employment after coming to America was bricklaying, and he was never steadily employed. After 1928, he did no work at all. Yet in the years that followed his abandonment of all work, he traveled all over America, living in rooming houses and eating in restaurants. He made two trips to the West Coast, once by way of the Panama Canal. He was in Washington where he tried for ten days to get a shot at President Hoover. He went to Tampa, to New Orleans. He lived a number of months at Miami Beach in a hotel.

Where did he secure the funds for all of this? There was nothing in his record to show that he had been a thief. He had never been arrested before that fatal night in Miami, February 15, 1933. His habits and mode of life were simple. He neither drank nor smoked nor gambled. Yet, during a winter's stay in Los Angeles, he spent each weekend across the Mexican border to "see the sights."

Had he been a bootlegger, a gambler, a smuggler or an underworld "fixer," he would have attached himself to beaten paths. His orbit would have been fixed. As it was, he seems to have been a wanderer. He always made his way back to New Jersey. Perhaps near or in this state the headquarters of this unknown but vicious secret order were established. He might have made his career as a contact man among the followers in various cities. In constant touch with the secretive strata of the social order which comforts itself by leveling shafts of invective against "capitalists," he probably conceived the idea of killing the President for the purpose of glorifying himself in the ranks of his ill-starred fellows.

I cannot believe that the members paid him to do the deed or, for that matter, that they planned the act. But an order founded for the purpose of fostering the hatred of the poor against the rich would undoubtedly magnify such a deed. The perpetrator would assume among them the proportions of a hero.

From such associations he probably gathered the vocabulary of parrot-like phrases which he used so incoherently but with such sinister meaning—"Capitalists"—"Crooks"— "Rich." In this one set of terms he found the source of every ill, even his stomach pain. In his own language he would roll such phrases over his tongue by the half-hour. His language was notable for the emptiness of its phrases.

From the moment of his arrest until the moment when he sat in the chair alone, he uttered but one illuminating word— "Camorra." This word revealed volumes. The newspaper men seemed to miss its meaning. At any rate, I did not see it mentioned in any of the published accounts.

Just before the switch was thrown and after his outbreak against "lousy capitalists," he exclaimed in a fierce and vindictive voice, "Viva Italia! Viva Camorra! Goodbye all poor people everywhere."

The word explained much to me. For more than a century the Camorra had been a vindictive, ruthless secret society in Italy. It grew up among the prisoners of Naples and was carried by those released to the dens and dark alleys of the city. Vengeance was the theme, and in the hundred years of its life it had been politically sinister. From the first, in 1823, it had been a thing of personal fear, of terror, of almost vendetta-like precision in the execution of its edicts. It was a powerful and fearless order whose genius was assassination.

What if this Italian order had seed planted in the darker sections of American cities? What if the presence of death brought forth the real Zangara—the Zangara of the Camorra? He kept his secrets well, but death is a great revealer as well as a great leveler.

"Viva Camorra!"

Granted that an American Camorra is hard to imagine in free, individualistic airs of this nation. Still, there are un-American blocks in every American city where the language and ideas, the hates and bitterness of foreign people dwell. Zangara could well have been an emissary for such a cruel heritage of far lands. That he was such, I have no doubt.

The day of his electrocution a letter reached the prison from Union City, New Jersey. It enclosed a five inch file and a note printed in ink. "Say Giuseppe. Enclose file to escape. Come to new address. Ok hiding place. 169-20 Street, Union City rear house—Tony bump off at old address. Flo, my sister, finish him August 28, 1932. Need your help. Flo-Joe."

What is this but a voice from the dark sections of American life. It is doubtless of his fellows in this society that he was thinking when he learned that his picture would not be taken while in the chair. It was a grievous disappointment. He had comforted himself with the thought that his chair picture would be enshrined in every hall, a heroic shrine, an inspiration to other dark deeds, insuring for him a sort of underworld immortality. That this should be denied him was the bitter draught which aroused him as nothing else had. . . . Camorristi. Certainly he aimed first at the President but doubtless he also intended to kill Mr Cermak also. He planned to be a double hero—a hero such as had not been seen before—one who killed two capitalist leaders at once. He was an egotist of the first rank.

He laughed when I asked him about the diversion of his aim by the lady. "No. She no knock up my arm. If she do that, why the bullets not go up in the air? No. She scared. She scream and jump and fall and this shake chair. So I miss the President."

"Was any friend with you when you shot at the President?" I asked him one morning.

"No. Nobody. It was my own idea. I think I like to kill and I shoot. Nobody else there."

"Then how could six wounds be caused by five bullets?"

"When I shoot at President, I have to shoot quick. Big crowd keep me from seeing him good. So when I see him between heads of other people, I aim and shoot quick. One bullet it hit two people in head and neck. Nobody shoot but me. I all alone."

Yet one of the eye witnesses later reported that she had sat close to Zangara for an hour, that some one had been with him, that they talked in low, mumbling tones much of the time while waiting for the President.

It did not occur to me to ask him what had become of his automobile. He had told me of buying one in New Jersey. Vague reports have come in that he had often been seen in a car in and about Miami. Was this his car? If so, perhaps that other man had slipped out of the crowd in the excitement of that hectic night while the attention of the populace was centered on the man who was captured with the smoking pistol in his hand and who freely admitted his guilt. Perhaps there were six or seven shots, after all.

If there were others, Zangara with a black sort of egotism wanted all the "credit." He regarded himself as a figure of distinction. He cannot be understood if this trait is ignored. His vanity in the sad deed is hard to imagine but not to recognize. I have never encountered anything like it before.

The day before the electrocution he said to me, "Jesus Christ, he good man. He die for poor people when he thirty-three years old. I thirty-three too. And I die for poor people."

Yet he professed to believe in no religion. "Everything here. Nothing up yonder," he said with many Latin gestures to illustrate his words.

The morning of the electrocution the prison chaplain, Rev. Sheffield, went to his cell at the request of Mr Mayo and myself to minister to the lonely little figure, but Zangara would have none of him. He immediately lost his look of loneliness, dancing about his cell at a lively rate, shouting with a great clamor, drowning out the words of the minister and demanding that he leave. This, I think, was just another expression of his egotism.

Nervy? Yes. The consistency of his conduct after his arrest was noteworthy. He asserted from the first that he was not afraid of the chair, and I could see no sign of fear whatsoever. Only a slight nervous, tense excitement.

When Sheriff Hardie told Zangara that he was to be moved to Raiford, he proposed that the prisoner should be taken from the jail in a box or disguised in women's clothing in order to avoid a lynching.

The dapper little Italian scorned the very suggestion. "No. No dress. No box. I no scared of mob. I no fraid to die. I go just like I am."

The Sheriff said that he did not seem in the least disturbed as they approached the prison. Pointing to some convicts working in the fields, the Sheriff asked, "Joe, wouldn't you like to do that for the rest of your life?"

"No," was the prompt reply. "I rather die than be locked up the rest of my life and have to work all day. Me no fraid of the chair."

Zangara's death did not end the questions nor the speculations. I got letters from all over asking for specimens of his handwriting. In several cases, the handwriting was to be "psychoanalyzed." Several wanted the signature to add to collections of "famous signatures." Visitors came who wished to see the grave. Others wanted proof that Zangara was actually dead and had not been revived after execution and so released.

They wrote or came in droves—crackpot writers of every description, nuts who had had visions, sadists who wanted minute descriptions of his facial expression when the current hit him. There seemed to be no end of them. After a while, I refused to answer any more letters and even denied permission to visit the grave.

Still the speculations continued. Ten years after the execution, I boarded the ACL (Atlantic Coast Line) train at the little station to attend the Sheriff's convention in Ocala. As I entered the smoking car and took a seat, I noticed a group of men just ahead of me.

One of them said, "This is Raiford where that guy was executed who killed Cermak."

I looked at the speaker and failed to recognize him. Neither he nor any of the group recognized me, either. The speaker was the heavy set, thick necked, positive type whose form is familiar to every group of strangers. His voice was harsh and domineering, permitting no dispute. The group turned to him, though, as if he were an authority.

"I know all about that guy. He sure got the man he wanted. He wasn't shooting at Roosevelt at all. The underworld in Chicago put him up to it. And he sure made good in a big way."

APPENDIX III

THE ZANGARA MEMOIR

The following was included in the Chapman manuscript as a carbon copy, cut and pasted to bond stationery. The whereabouts of the typed original is unknown but it is probably in the lost Secret Service file. The typing appears to be professional with few typographical errors. The translation has been slightly edited to improve readability.

Stapled to the first page is a note handwritten by Superintendent L.F. Chapman: "Here is the history of himself written by Zangara in the death house. It has never been published. I felt that he might have 'reached' some other 'crack-brain.' It was written in Italian in some note books furnished by my secretary."

RAIFORD FLORIDA.
MARCH 1933

This is the first Chapter of the true story written by Giuseppe Zangara.

FIRST CHAPTER:

My name is Giuseppe Zangara. I was born in the town of Ferruzzano, Province of Reggio Calabria, Italy, on the seventh day of September 1900. My parents' names were Salvatore and Rosina Zangara. My mother's maiden name was Rosina Cafaro. I wish to write the story by starting from the day I was born.

The first day I was born the doctors found a sickness in my ears and decided to operate on them at once. When my mother heard about the sickness she said I was bad luck. I do not remember my mother. She died when I was two years old while giving birth to a child. The child died also.

This finishes the first chapter of my life.

SECOND CHAPTER:

When I was three years old, I remember falling down two flights of stairs in the house where we lived. The stairs were built of stone and when I was picked up everyone thought I was dead.

This finishes the second chapter.

THIRD CHAPTER:

When I was four years old, I remember falling into a fire and burning my leg. Thus my bad luck continued. Also, this was the first time I remembered my name and realized that my mother was dead. I remember this dimly just like a dream.

This finishes the third chapter.

FOURTH CHAPTER:

At the age of five, while visiting one day at a house of a friend of my aunt, I fell down the stairs and broke my wrist. I remember my aunt telling everyone how unlucky I was and mentioning to them all my hard luck and all the accidents I already had.

This finishes the fourth chapter.

FIFTH CHAPTER:

When I was five years old, I remember my father was in America. He returned the same year, however. While he was away I started to school. When he found out about this he told my aunt not to send me to school anymore because he needed me to go into the fields and help with the stock. My aunt replied that I had to go to school but father said he was the boss. However, my aunt told me to go to school and so I went. The next morning my father got me out of bed early and took me with him into the fields.

I also remember my father not having much money in those days to buy animals. At one time he bought one cow and rented another one for three years from a man by the name of Antonio Romeo. During the next three years I worked for that man. He worked with the livestock and I had to do the hoeing. This work was too heavy for me at that age. One day we lost one of the cows. When my father found out about it he beat me and kicked me like a dog, and told me I was not working hard enough. From that day on he worked me so hard that I became sick. I was beaten and starved and over-worked when I should have been going to school and eating and sleeping like other children. That was when my stomach trouble started.

This finishes the fifth chapter.

SIXTH CHAPTER:

When I was nine years old, my father decided to go to America. Here I was, at the age of nine, and could not read or write. I wanted to go to school but my stepmother told me that my father had told her that I should be kept working on the farm. He never thought of me and thought only of himself. He bore me no affection. I had to work always and win my health.

My father went to the United States four times. He went there first for six months; the second time he stayed ten months; the third time he stayed a year; and the last time he stayed for two years.

This finishes the sixth chapter.

SEVENTH CHAPTER:

When I was eleven years old, my father bought two more cows and he sent me out into the fields again. He believed that at that age I was able to do all of the work on the farm. I continued to do this work for the following two years but in the meantime my sickness got worse.

When I was thirteen years old my father bought a piece of property and we planted a vineyard there. I had to do most of the work and my stomach got worse all the time. I worked three years on this property. I had no happiness in my life because I was always thinking that I had to suffer with that sickness and work all the time. I had no affection for my father. I wanted to leave the town I was born in. At that time I was sixteen years old and understood the good from the bad.

This finishes the seventh chapter.

EIGHTH CHAPTER:

In this chapter I am going to write about the bad points of my father and the treatment I received from him.

I was supposed to arise early one morning and pasture the stock but I overslept and this infuriated my father. He took all of my clothes off me and beat me with a piece of wood unmercifully and left me nude on the farm.

Another time I remember he ordered me to do something but I was slow in obeying him, so he gave me many blows with his fists and kicked me around like a dog.

Another time I remember my trousers were torn and my father would not have them repaired. When I fixed them myself he kicked me all over for doing it.

Another time I was watering the cows at the fountain. My father saw me and became very angry because I was watering them there. He struck me with a heavy piece of wood he was carrying. He hit me so hard on the head that I was knocked unconscious and had to lay in bed for two weeks recovering from the blows.

Another time he saw a broken vine and blamed me for it. He hit me with a hammer on the head, cutting me three times.

This is what I received from my father and the very reason why I wanted to leave home for always.

This finishes the eighth chapter.

NINTH CHAPTER:

I will now tell you of my experience from my seventeenth year on.

On reaching the age of seventeen years, I left my home and went to work in the town of Giamato, Cotrona, Province of Catanzaro, for a short time. After working there I worked in different cities and towns in Italy but was always suffering from the stomach ache.

I was always thinking that if my father had not worked me so hard when I was young, and had not treated me so cruel, I would not have to suffer from this malady. It also came to my thoughts that the government ought to make all the arrangements for the poor children to get an education so they can have the same rights as the money class has.

But I only see that children of the Capitalist's class getting the education and the sons of the poor have to go to work.

"This is wrong" and is my conclusion.
This finishes the ninth chapter.

TENTH CHAPTER:

I will now write about my eighteenth year.

I did not have any desire to stay in the town I was born in. I always wanted to travel and was very restless.

In the town where I was born, I was always coming in contact with people who considered themselves better than the poor working man. They always wanted to be addressed with the title of "Signore" or "Maestro" or "Signorina." That is one of the reasons I could not get along and was always worrying. I was always discontented. Always on the move, working here and there. Sometimes I would not have any money and would have to sleep outside many nights.

The Capitalist government is to blame for this. When the laboring man is out of work, he is out of bread.

At this time war was going on and I was sent to the front lines to build trenches. These were hard times. There were plenty of people starving and miserable. While their sons were fighting for the country their families were having hard times.

I was stationed near a place called Monte Grappo, Dalmatia. I did not have any ill feelings against the Austrians and did not consider them my enemies. My real enemy was the Capitalist Government that we were fighting for. The Capitalist is to blame for all wars and the suffering of the poor. I was always suffering from my stomach ache.

After the war was over, I worked in a city that had been bombarded by the enemy and helped to rebuild it. I returned to my hometown shortly after.

This finishes the tenth chapter.

ELEVENTH CHAPTER:

I was nineteen when I returned to my hometown where I was born. During the war I had picked up some knowledge of the stonemason's trade. When I returned home my father wanted to build a house out in the country. After I built the house for him, I tried to get work in town but nobody would give me work as a mason. They said I ought to work on the farm with my father. Thus, my hard luck continued.

This finishes the eleventh chapter.

TWELFTH CHAPTER:

In Italy, military service is compulsory. When I reached the age of twenty-one, I went to serve my time in the service. I was not physically fit or able but they took me anyway.

I was assigned to Company Four of the 70th Infantry. We were stationed in Tuscany. We drilled and marched every morning. This was hard on me because I was always suffering from the stomach ache. I had a special examination by the doctor and he said my sickness was Chronic. He also asked me how long I was suffering from it. I told him ever since I was six years old. I asked the doctor what the cause of it was. He said it was caused by me working too hard when I was young and he said there was no cure for it.

I blame the Capitalist Government for my sickness. Because if I had the same opportunity as the children of the Capitalists, my father would not have had me work when I was so young and I would not be suffering from this sickness.

The Capitalists have no consideration or feeling for the poor but only think of themselves. The government and the state are always controlled by them. This is another reason why I am against the Capitalists.

While I was in the service, I heard that King Vittore Emanuele of Italy was coming to visit his son. I was at the station when he arrived. I intended to kill him. I had a gun hidden on my person.

When the King arrived in his special car, however, the guards got in front of me and I could not get a shot at him. Because the guards were over six foot tall, I could not even see the King.

About four months after I was transferred to Rome (Military College.)

This finishes the twelfth chapter.

THIRTEENTH CHAPTER:

At the military college in Rome, I was detailed as the captain's attendant. The captain was forty-five years old and his wife was twenty years old. His former attendant stayed there a full week instructing me in my duties. My duties as the captain's attendant were many. I had to take care of his clothes, shine his shoes and boots, and besides, I had to do all of the house work. I also had to cook and prepare his food and wait on him. When he had visits from other officers, I had to wait on all of them. This was very hard for me because I never received a minute's rest.

The officers were all sons of the Capitalists and the men all sons of the laboring people. I did not like this work and asked the captain if I could not be transferred to another post because I was not suited for that kind of work. He told me to stay another week and informed me that we would leave for a camp in another week and that my duties there would be much lighter.

My duties at the camp were not many. I had to wake my captain every morning and bring him water three times a day. Otherwise, I had plenty of time to myself. The colonel's orderly and I used to go to the village and pass away the time fooling with the loose women of the town.

One morning I was late in waking the captain and was put in the guard house for a day and night without food. After a month at the camp we returned to Rome, to the military college. There I took up my duties as before, doing all of the house work, etc.

This finishes the thirteenth chapter.

FOURTEENTH CHAPTER:

I asked the captain for a different detail one day and told him that I was tired of being an orderly, doing housework. He asked me what work I could do. I told him that I could do masonry work and that I knew something about farming. He replied that I could have the post of gardener if I wished. I told him that I would like to do that kind of work.

My duties as gardener were to take care of the gardens at the military college. There were many different kinds of plants and flowers in the gardens.

The quarters where I was living was a single story building of stone. The colonel suggested that I build a two story building of stone as he had found out that I could do that kind of work. I built this house and worked as gardener at the same time for the next three months. I then asked the colonel for another post and he gave me guard duty.

This finishes the fourteenth chapter.

FIFTEENTH CHAPTER:

The guard consisted of one corporal and three privates. We stood a watch of two hours and were off for four hours, day and night. Our duties were to guard the paymaster's office where the payroll was kept. When I used to get off watch at night my stomach always bothered me and I could not go to sleep for three or four hours. The result was that I got very little sleep and was always nervous.

I often thought that my stomach bothered me the most when I had a rifle in my hand. Whenever I saw the paymaster handling the money, I used to think I would like to take the money because I needed it for my suffering.

I used to roam the streets of Rome hoping that I should see the King. I never saw the King, although I saw many superior officers.

All the time I was a soldier I saw nothing but the sons of the Capitalists as officers and the sons of the working people were the common soldiers. That was why I wanted to kill the head of such a government. Because I thought that this was the only way to help the poor working people.

The officers always ate at the table and were served by the common soldiers. They ate the finest food while the poor soldier was treated like a dog. I could not see why the officers should be treated any better just because they are sons of the Capitalists. I believe everyone should be treated alike.

This finishes the fifteenth Chapter.

SIXTEENTH CHAPTER:

After my term of service was over, I returned to my hometown and worked as a brick mason. I had work for the following three months. During this time I got the idea to go to America. I decided to leave as soon as possible. I did not like Italy because the poor workingman's life was too hard.

I went to Naples and from there I procured passage aboard ship. I left Naples the 19th day of August 1923, and arrived in Brooklyn, New York, on the first day of September 1923.

This finishes the sixteenth chapter.

SEVENTEENTH CHAPTER:

After arriving in Brooklyn, N.Y., I had a hard time trying to get to New York. I stopped at an Italian restaurant to get something to eat. While in the restaurant, I got acquainted with a fellow who spoke my language. I showed him the address of an uncle of mine and he offered to take me there. I was very glad to have him help me. We took an automobile and went to Paterson, New Jersey, where my uncle lived.

This finishes the seventeenth chapter.

EIGHTEENTH CHAPTER:

My uncle was living with some friends of his by the name of Francesco Caserta. My uncle happened to be out when I arrived and the people in the house suggested that I surprise him. When my uncle came home I was sitting at the table. I did not look at him but he recognized me instantly and was very glad to see me. I had not seen him for ten years.

I stayed there for two days. My uncle was working in a silk factory in Newton, New Jersey.

This finishes the eighteenth chapter.

NINETEENTH CHAPTER:

I will now write about the first day I arrived in Newton, New Jersey.

The day my uncle rented a room in a house of a friend of his and I stayed there for three days. My uncle decided to get a room nearer to the factory so we moved. In the meantime my uncle got me a job with him in the silk factory where he was employed. I worked there for two months and then I was told that there was no more work for me.

After that I was looking for work every day, but I could not find any. This was in the winter and it was very cold and my sickness got worse all the time.

I was always thinking that when I was working in the factory I suffered from the heat from the machines and always felt bad, and when I was outside I suffered from the cold. I used to think that I am going to suffer always. I was out of work for three months and then my uncle got a job for both of us in Paterson, New Jersey.

This finishes the nineteenth chapter.

TWENTIETH CHAPTER:

I wish to tell you now of my experience in Paterson, New Jersey. My uncle got work for both of us in a factory but I wanted to work at my own trade, and so I spent most of the time looking for work. My uncle and myself were living at that time at the house of Pietro Galante.

One day I met a man by the name of Giuseppe Tato. He put me to work building a stone cellar for him. I finished this after two weeks work and then was out of work again. Shortly afterward this man, Tato, who did contracting work, received a contract on a job in Bayonne, New Jersey, and I went to work for him. The first day I worked there a delegate from the local union appeared and told me I could not work unless I joined the union. He demanded ten dollars but I did not have ten dollars on me, so I asked the contractor to loan it to me. He did not have it either. The delegate allowed me until Saturday to pay him. I paid him for the following five weeks, ten dollars each week. After I had paid the sum of fifty dollars, the contractor took me to the union headquarters to get me my working card. However, the secretary of the union told me that I would have to get my first papers (application for citizenship) in order to join the union. I applied for the first papers and afterwards joined the union. After that I worked for different contractors during the spring of 1924. But I did not get much work to do in Bayonne so I went back to Paterson, New Jersey, again looking for work.

This finishes the twentieth chapter.

TWENTY-FIRST CHAPTER:

My uncle who was living in Paterson, by this time was married to a girl by the name of Giuseppa Petrie.

I could not find any work in Paterson, so I went to Passaic, New Jersey, looking for work. After some time in Passaic, I finally landed a job with a contractor as a bricklayer. The day I went to work the delegate of the local union showed up and asked me for my union card. I showed it to him but he said that I could not work as a bricklayer because the card I had only allowed me to work as a stonemason. This threw me out of a job again.

One day I met the delegate from the Bayonne union and explained to him of my difficulties. He advised me to get transferred to the Passaic local. I did this and afterwards went to work again. Later, I joined the bricklayers union which allowed me to work anywhere I wanted to.

This finishes the twenty-first chapter.

TWENTY-SECOND CHAPTER:

After I became a union man I was able to work almost any place. I remember working in New York, Brooklyn, and several other cities and towns. However, the work was very hard and the bosses very strict. If they thought a man was not working hard enough, they fired him. Or if he did not do his work just so, they would fire him also. This used to make me mad and sick to my stomach. I was always suffering from two things, the Capitalists and the stomach.

My stomach was getting worse every day. I had a very bad attack one day and had to go to the doctor. He gave me some medicine and told me to put some ice in a towel and lay in bed and keep the ice on my stomach.

I was sick for two months and could not go to work. Every time I tried to get out of bed I would stagger as if I were drunk and I would throw up a lot of green water. Nothing the doctors gave me would help me. My stomach always burned as though it was on fire and I used to think: Am I going to suffer like this always?

This was the winter of 1924 and I suffered from the cold which was very bitter. I was living on Market Street in Paterson at that time.

This finishes the twenty-second chapter.

TWENTY-THIRD CHAPTER:

I was living on Market Street at this time with my uncle. This was in January, 1925. After some time, we moved to River Street.

My stomach was still bothering me so I went to a specialist and for three visits I paid him twenty-five dollars. He told me that I had chronic appendicitis and nothing but an operation would cure me. So I went to a hospital and had my appendix removed, however I suffered much pain. The operation did not help me and I suffered right on from the same pains. I could not look for any work for about two months as the operation had made me very weak.

After a while I went to work at my trade as a bricklayer. I never was able to save any money because I used to spend it as fast as I made it in order to forget my troubles. Whenever I went out with any girls, I used to buy them whatever they wanted. My friends believed that I had lots of money but the truth is that I spent all the money just as fast as I made it because my money did me no good and I suffered all the time, so I wanted to spend my money in order for me to forget about my sickness. I am telling the truth of my life, just as I lived it. I was living with my uncle for the last five years from 1923 to 1928. I was feeling very bad and I decide to go to Tampa, Florida.

This finishes the twenty third chapter.

TWENTY FOURTH CHAPTER:

The reason I wanted to go to Tampa, Florida, was because I had heard that the climate was always warm there, and so I thought that the warm weather might help my sickness, because the cold weather was very bad for it. On the train, when I was on my way to Tampa, I met a girl and she asked me where I was going, so I told her I was on my way to Tampa, Florida. I asked her where she was going and she said Jacksonville. After a little conversation she asked me if I could play cards and I said, yes. So she took a deck of cards out of her bag and we played cards until we reached Jacksonville. There she left the train after thanking me for helping her pass the time on the trip.

I continued on to Tampa and after arriving there, I stopped at a hotel. Every morning I would walk in different parts of the city so I may get to know it. On day I happened to see the club house of the Italian society. When I entered I saw that they were all Italian people. Someone asked me how I was and I told him. I also told him how I happened to be there and also informed him about my sickness. This man told me that the climate of New Orleans was the best for that kind of sickness. I was feeling mighty bad at that time so I made up my mind to go to New Orleans because I was willing to go any where to help my sickness. I remember taking a train the following day for New Orleans, and while on the train I was always thinking about my hard luck.

This finishes the twenty-fourth chapter.

TWENTY FIFTH CHAPTER:

I will now tell you about my stay in New Orleans. I stayed at a hotel and every day I used to take long walks through the city in order to get acquainted with it. I remember that it was a very large city and there seemed to be plenty of work. I thought I would like to work but my stomach always bothered me, so I decided to have a good time and live good during my stay there.

One day I met a Spanish girl who was seventeen years old. I asked her where she was staying and she told me. She also told me that she was broke and that she needed five dollars for room rent. I asked her if she wanted to stay with me and she said yes. So I took her with me to the hotel where I was staying and took care of her during the time I was in New Orleans.

I had been in New Orleans about three weeks when the thought came to me that I had better go back to Paterson, New Jersey, because my money was getting low and I was not feeling any better. The girl did not seem to mind my leaving and we parted like ordinary friends. I went to the steamship line and bought a ticket for New York. I had a very nice trip. It took us five days before we got to New York.

This finishes the twenty-fifth chapter.

TWENTY-SIXTH CHAPTER:

I only stayed in New York one day. The next day I went to my uncle's house in Paterson, New Jersey. There was plenty of work to be had at this time. I went to work at my trade as a mason. This was in the summertime and the weather was very nice. I had decided to buy an automobile. After I had the automobile, I used to go riding on Sundays and visit my friends.

One day I visited Pietro Galante in Paterson, New Jersey. I had roomed there when I first came to this country. He had two daughters. The oldest was sixteen years old. I admired her very much and I asked her father for her hand in marriage. He was willing and so was she.

One day while I was visiting some friends of mine, I heard them talking about this girl. I heard one of them say that she ought to get married right away because she was in a bad way. They did not know I was engaged to this girl. I had intended to give her a fine wedding but after hearing this, I could not marry her in that condition. As much as I felt sorry for her, I called the wedding off.

This finishes the twenty-sixth chapter.

TWENTY-SEVENTH CHAPTER:

I had been boarding with my uncle all the time that I stayed in Paterson. I still had the car and used to drive all around looking for work. I met an Italian contractor one day who wanted two houses built. I went to work for him. When Saturday came he said, "I haven't got any money but I will pay you next week." I wanted to quit but as work was scarce, I decided to stay. I had worked for him for three months without pay. The contractor went in to bankruptcy and I could not get my money. I then went to Hackensack, New Jersey, and roomed with a friend of mine by the name of Dominic Palafrone.

I could not find any work there and I used to ride around all day long looking for work. My friends used to think that I did not need to work because I had a car, but I could not make enough money to pay for my expenses. I had heard that conditions in California were better, so I decided to leave for that part of the country.

This finishes the twenty-seventh chapter.

TWENTY-EIGHTH CHAPTER:

I went to New York to go aboard a ship to go to California. On this ship I met a woman who was traveling with her daughter and sister. She asked me where I was going and I told her, Los Angeles. She then asked me if I was traveling alone and I said yes. She then suggested that I join their party so we could go sightseeing at the different ports. This was very agreeable to me.

We went ashore in Cuba and hired a car and went sight seeing all day. That same night the ship got underway for Panama. The next stop was in Los Angeles. The people I had been traveling with invited me to stay with them in Los Angeles. They had a friend there who owned a boarding house. I stayed with them a week and then left for San Diego. I was told the climate was very good there.

After staying in San Diego a few days I caught a very bad cold and was very sick. I went to a doctor and got me some medicine, but I got worse. I finally decided to go to Miami because people had told me that the weather was always good there.

This finishes the twenty-eighth chapter.

THIRTIETH CHAPTER:

I will now talk about the time I got the idea to kill the President.

I was in Miami at this time. I was thinking about going to Washington to the inauguration to kill the President. However, on the 26th day of February, I was reading in the Miami papers where Roosevelt was coming to Miami, so I figured I would have a better chance to kill him here in Miami.

When Roosevelt arrived at Bay Front Park, I tried to get close to him but there were too many people around him. I wanted to get in front of him in order to get a good shot at him, but the people kept on pushing me back further all the time and I could not get to see him. The only people who could get near him were the officials and Capitalists and the police. When I saw I could not get near him, I decided to shoot him from the distance. While he was talking I could not get to see him because all of the people were crowding around him. He only spoke for about a minute from the car and sat down immediately after. When he did I only could see his head, although by that time I was standing on a park chair. However, the rest of his body was hidden by the car.

When I fired the first shot the chair I was standing on moved and the result was that it caused me to spoil my aim and at the distance of at least thirty feet, to miss by one foot. I then tried to get my aim again but after I had fired the first shot the people crowded around the car and I could hardly see Roosevelt's head. I saw two heads in front of the President's and figured on firing another shot between those two heads, but the bullet struck them both in the head. This is what saved his life. This was also the reason for me shooting six people with a five shot gun.

The people then tried to kill me but the police surrounded me at once and put me in a car and took me to the Miami jail. On the way to jail the police abused me and one of them had me by the collar and kept on squeezing my neck very hard. When we arrived at the jail he threw me on the stone pavement like a dog. After a while they took all of my clothes away and left me nude. A little while after they gave me a shirt and pants. A girl came to visit me and she had to write down everything I had to say. After she had left they took my shirt and pants away again and left me nude. They kept me nude until the next day. The county police then took me to a room that was just like a hotel room. While I was kept in this room, people were coming to see me day and night and would take pictures of me.

The day I went to court, I remember there was not enough room for the people to get in to the court room. I was in court for three days and the court was crowded all the time. The people could not understand how I could take things so calm and contented. And they also marveled at the way I took it. I was not worried. There were many people that took photographs of me while I was in court. They also took motion pictures of me.

I remember the judge giving me the sentence of eighty years. I asked the judge, "Why are you so stingy? Why don't you give me a hundred years?" And I told him I would die in two years anyhow and go to my rest.

I was then taken back to the same cell in the jail. I had eighty years but it did not worry me at all. I was contented. There were lots of Capitalists that came to see me. One of them wanted permission to sell the gun I had used. However, I told him that the money from the sale of the pistol did not interest me, so he left. Some of the people asked me if I belonged to any syndicate in Chicago and if they had any hand in it. I told them that my Idea was to kill the President only.

This finishes the thirtieth chapter.

THIRTY-FIRST CHAPTER:

I will now write about the time the judge sentenced me to the electric chair.

The court officers took me down to court early that morning, long before any of the people were admitted. They wanted to see what was wrong with my head. The judge asked why I wanted to kill the President and so I answered: because he was the head of the Capitalist government and I have always been against the Capitalist. I also told the judge that if I was the head of a government of "My Idea," I would kill all the presidents and Capitalists first, then I would gather all the money and burn it up. It is my belief that the people should not put money in their stomachs, but put bread there. Bread can be made without money. This is my idea. I also told the judge to think of all the people that are suffering from starvation. What is the use of all this money when the heads of the poor families have to see their children starve. I blame money for all of this. The judge next asked me what society do you belong to? I told him to the society of my own sentiment. I do not remember all of the questions. After a short while the judge read my sentence. After he got through reading the sentence, I got up and said, Judge, you have sentenced me to the chair, however, I am not afraid of the chair, for trying to kill the President who was the head of a crooked government. I was then returned to the room where I had been kept. The lawyers came up there and told me they had done all they could to help me.

Before my trial started, the judge asked me if I had a lawyer to defend me but I told him I did not need a lawyer.

Several days after, I was told by the jailer to be ready for my trip to Raiford Prison. I told him I was ready to go. They took me out of the jail after midnight and put me in a car between two officers for my last trip. It took eight hours before we reached Raiford.

This finishes the thirty-first chapter.

THIRTY-SECOND CHAPTER:

I will now write about when I was in Raiford.

When I arrived in Raiford, I was taken to the fingerprint office and had my pictures taken. Afterward I was taken to the superintendent's office where I met the Superintendent and his private secretary, and let me tell you right here, they are two very gentle persons. Every day they would come to my cell and visit me. The Superintendent told me that if I wanted anything, to ask for and he would see that I get it. One day the secretary brought me a bouquet of beautiful flowers. Another time she brought me a nice basket of fruits. I wish to thank them both for the kind treatment I received.

I find myself in a cell constructed of steel. There is a guard in the adjoining cell to watch me. There are two steel grates between us, and when anyone comes to visit me, they have to open two doors. The guards and everyone around me are very kind to me. I wish to take this opportunity to thank and "salute" each and every one of them.

This finishes the thirty-second chapter.

THIRTY-THIRD CHAPTER:

I will now tell you what I think about religion.

My belief is that all religion was invented by the Capitalists. They invented them so people would respect their property. The Roman Catholic religion was the first one to talk about HELL. The priests do not do anything and what they preach they know is false. They are like sharks, working for the Capitalist and spreading their propaganda and living off the people who go to church and believe them. They talk of paradise in the next world but there is no such thing. I believe that a person is in paradise when he has good health and plenty of money; and purgatory is a person who has good health and is working for a living. I believe that hell is when a person is sick and in misery and that death ends all. If I had my way I would put all priests in hell so no one could save them.

I believe that if all the money is burned it would do away with the priests' paradise.

This finishes the thirty-third chapter.

THIRTY-FOURTH CHAPTER:

My Idea is just. I was always against the Capitalist. This is the reason why I wanted to kill the head of this government. Because the people that run the government do not work, and the poor working people have to support them. They suck the blood out of the poor people and it is my belief that they all ought to be killed. The poor support them on their shoulders. They are no good. They have all the money tied up. The poor are willing to work but cannot because it takes money to make work. So what is the use of having money if the poor cannot have any to buy their food?

What we ought to do is to kill all of the Capitalists, burn all of the money and form a civil society of Communism. I have nothing more to say. Tomorrow I go to the electric chair to die but I am not afraid. I go contented because I go for my Idea.

I Salute all the poor of the world.

"ARRIVEDERCI"
ZANGARA GIUSEPPE

NOTES

CHAPTER 1

Pages 3–4: "Roosevelt traveled . . .": *Florida Times Union*, 13 February 1933.

4–5: "After twelve days of cruising . . .": Kenneth S. Davis, "Incident in Miami," *American Heritage Magazine*, vol. 32, no. 1 (December 1980): 86–95.

5: "After that, he was to be driven . . .": "Miami Awaits Visit Tonight of Roosevelt," *Miami Herald*, 15 February 1933.

CHAPTER 2

Information about the Bayfront Park occurrence comes from the *Miami Daily News*, *Miami Herald*, *Fort Lauderdale Florida News*, *Chicago Tribune*, Jacksonville *Florida Times-Union* and John Sewell, *Memoirs and History of Miami, Florida* (Miami: The Franklin Press, 1938).

CHAPTER 3

Pages 24, 30–32: Information about Thomas Armour comes from author's interview with Dr Thomas Armour, Jr., Deland, Florida, 1 January 1993.

Dr Armour also supplied material connected with lobbying efforts on Armour Sr.'s behalf.

25: "According to local legend . . .": Author's interview with Dr William M. Straight, Miami, Florida, 29 January 1993.

27–28: Information about Sheriff Hardie from Helen Muir, *Miami, U.S.A.* (Miami: Pickering Press, 1953).

30: "Robert Donovan, journalist . . .": Robert Donovan, "Annals of Crime: The Long Stomach Ache," *New Yorker* (27 November 1954), 118.

CHAPTER 4

Information for this chapter comes from the *Miami Herald* and the *Chicago Tribune*, February 17, 18 and 19, 1933.

Page 35: "It was during this conversation . . .": A.A. Dornfeld, *Hello, Sweetheart, Get Me Rewrite* (Chicago: Academy Chicago, 1988).

38: Headlines around the world: (Associated Press) "All World's Scorn Heaped on Zangara," *Washington Post*, 17 Feb 1933, p. 2.

CHAPTER 6

Page 46: Winchell story from Bob Thomas, *Winchell* (New York: Doubleday, 1971).

51: Interview with Judge Dixie Herlong Chastain, Miami, 4 March 1993. Dixie Herlong's mother had insisted she learn shorthand so that she could have a trade to "fall back on" in case her dream collapsed of succeeding in the law, which was basically a male profession, and indeed, she had been forced to make her living as a stenographer. One of her most vivid memories from those lean Depression years was of a lawyer asking her to lend him money to buy lunch.

She married R.B. Chastain in the late 1930s and retired to raise her family. Later she returned to the law and in 1965 she became first a juvenile court and then a circuit court judge. She became the most senior juvenile court judge in the United States. At the age of eighty-four she still heard cases.

55: The gun, manufactured by the United States Revolver Co., a defunct subsidiary of the Iver Johnson Co., a major firearms manufacturer at the time, eventually became the property of State Attorney Hawthorne, who lent it to the Secret Service for an exhibition in the 1950s. The Secret Service still has it.

58: "A few days . . . .": Donovan, "Annals of Crime."

CHAPTER 7

Page 61: The day after the shooting . . .": *New York Times*, 16 February 1933.

61–62: H.P. Woertendyke quote: "Zangara's Past in New Jersey Probed," *Newark Evening News*, 17 February 1933.

63: "The Italians told . . .": "Sarajevo Link Doubted," *New York Times*, 19 February 1933.

65: "Monte Grappo, Dalmatia . . .": Dalmatia was the coastal province of what used to be Yugoslavia. It is some two hundred miles southeast of Monte Grappa, which is in the northeastern corner of Italy, and was the scene of a major battle in 1917.

69: "Between 1923 and 1931 . . .": "Mystery Trips Mark Calendar of Joe Zangara," *Newark Star Eagle*, 17 February 1933.

CHAPTER 8

Page 83: Donovan, "Annals of Crime," 108. Lummus Park, located near the north bank of the Miami River on the perimeter of the downtown area, contained the largest shuffleboard court in south Florida, attracting tourists and tournaments for decades.

CHAPTER 9

Page 87: Turrou telegram: FBI archives.

91–93: Letters: FBI archives.

CHAPTER 10

Page 105: "A formal reading of the charges was waived." No transcript exists of the hearing. Newspapers did not report who waived the reading.

111: Donovan, "Annals of Crime," 120.

CHAPTER 11

Pages 123–28: Information on Cermak comes from author's interview with Robert Graham, Cermak's grandson, North Miami, Florida, 6 February 1993, and Carl Sifakis, *Encyclopedia of Assassins* (New York: Facts on File, 1991).

128–29: John H. Lyle, quoted in "Was Cermak Target?" *Miami Herald*, 21 April 1957.

136–37: Author's interview with Dr William Straight, Miami, Florida, 29 January 1993.

138: Author's interview with Robert Graham, North Miami, Florida, 6 February 1993.

CHAPTER 14

Information on the Cermak funeral comes from the *Chicago Tribune* and the *Miami Herald*, both papers 7 March 1933.

Page 166: K.A. Nisset letter to the editor: *Tampa Tribune*, 21 March 1933.

CHAPTER 15

Page 169: "In the late 19th century . . .": Ken Driggs, "'A Current of Electricity Sufficient in Intensity to Cause Immedtate Death': A Pre-Furman History of the Electric Chair," *Stetson University Law Review* (October 1992).

171: "Such swift justice . . .": Today in Florida, when someone charged with capital murder enters an open plea of guilty, as Zangara did, the court is required to seek the advice of a twelve-person jury to recommend life in prison with no parole for at least twenty-five years, or death in the electric chair. Before deciding this, the jury must hear evidence of the nature of the crime and the defendant's past history from both the prosecutor and the defense. And the judge is not required to follow the jury's recommendation. If he decides to impose the death penalty, he must state in his sentence the statutory rerequisites necessary to qualify the crime for the ultimate penalty. Those prerequisites include the nature of the crime as well as the defendant's criminal record, if any, and his attitude.

Since the death penalty was reinstated in the state in the early 1970s, Florida enacted eleven aggravating circumstances which would justify imposition of the death penalty: these range from commission of a capital felony while in prison to cold-blooded murders "without any pretense of moral or legal justification." The courts have further developed standards defining those circumstances and what facts constitute sufficient grounds for aggravation and mitigation of a death sentence. In 1939 the state legislature passed an act requiring the Florida supreme court to review all death sentence cases regardless of the wishes of the condemned.

172: "Dave Sholtz had made . . .": Merlin G. Cox, "Dave Sholtz: New Deal Governor of Florida," *Florida Historical Quarterly*, vol. 43, no. 2 (October 1964): 142–52. When Sholtz's term ended in early 1937, he ran for the Democratic nomination for the U.S. Senate against the incumbent, Claude Pepper in the 1938 off-year elections. Both men were Roosevelt's proteges. Because of the Zangara incident, Sholtz had developed what seems to have been a personal relationship with the president, enabling him to obtain audiences with FDR and to keep federal funds flowing into Florida. The governor admired and emulated Roosevelt, to the point of giving "fireside chats" on state-wide radio. But Roosevelt did not support Sholtz: he let it be known that Pepper's re-election "would please him greatly" ("Ex-Gov. D. Sholtz of Florida Dead," *New York Times*, 22 March 1953). Sholtz lost the primary and returned to the practice of law. He served as national head of the Elks and national commander of the Military Order of the World Wars. In 1956 he died at the age of sixty-two and is buried in Miami's Woodlawn Cemetery.

173: Harold S. Cohn telegram: National Archives. Letters to Sholtz: Florida State Archives.

174: Letters to Roosevelt: National Archives.

175: Italian government: Wire service report, 18 March 1933.

175–77: Melvin Richard/*Alligator* episode: Author interview with Melvin Richard, Miami Beach, Florida, November 1993.

179ff: Information about Warden Chapman from author's interview with Gen. L.F. Chapman, 10 January 1993, and from the warden's manuscript. After he retired, Chapman could not help but notice that during his twenty-five years of working to make a difference in the lives of the criminals sent to him, the crime rate in Florida had skyrocketed and recidivism at his prison was no better than at harsh maximum security facilities like Sing Sing, Joliet and Alcatraz. Many of the prisoners whom he released with high expectations would later return:, sentenced again for fresh crimes. He writes, "So far as doing anything about crime in Florida is concerned, I might as well have put in the quarter century sitting on the creek bank and looking at a cork."

Now, fifty years later, the "father of the Florida prison system" is nearly forgotten, commemorated only by a plaque in the prison yard.

185: "According to R.P. McClendon . . .": Author's interview with R.P. McClendon, Starke, Florida, 28 May 1993.

186: "Comm. Mayo paid a visit . . .": "Assassin Pays Death Penalty," *Los Angeles Times*, 21 March 1933.

189–90: Dr Greene's letter: Courtesy of the Greene family.

191: *"Viva Italia! . . ."*: These were Zangara's last words according to all the reporters who were there.

195: "The *Tampa Tribune* conjectured . . .": "Zangara—And Others," 21 March 1933. Texas Women's Democratic Association letter: Justice Department files, National Archives. Walter Winchell from Thomas, *Winchell*.

196: "His uncle, Vincent Carfaro . . .": Associated Press wire service story, 21 March 1933.

CHAPTER 18

201–2: Author's interview with, letter from, Dr John Spencer, Fort Lauderdale, Florida, 30 June 1993.

202–3: Author's interview with, letter from, Dr George M. Barnard, Gainesville, Florida, 15 June 1994.

203: Author's interview with Dr K. Rajender Reddy, Miami, Florida, 28 September 1994. Information also comes from a letter from Dr Reddy.

204: Author's interview with Dr Robert A. McNaughton and letter from Dr McNaughton, Miami, Florida, 19 July 1996; and Donovan, "Annals of Crime," 120.

BIBLIOGRAPHY

BOOKS & ARTICLES

■ ■ ■

Burnett, Gene M. *Florida's Past* (Englewood, Fla.: Pineapple Press, 1974).

Chapman, L.F. Unpublished manuscript of L.F. Chapman (1884-1977), Superintendent of the Florida State Penitentiary at Raiford, 1931-1956.

Clarke, James W. *American Assassins* (Princeton, N.J.: Princeton University Press, 1982).

Cooper, H.H.A. *On Assassination* (Boulder, Colo.: Paladin Press, 1984).

Cox, Merlin G. "Dave Sholtz: New Deal Governor of Florida," *Florida Historical Quarterly*. Vol. 43. No. 2. (October 1964).

Crossland, Bob. "Fifteen Seconds of Terror." *Coronet Magazine* (February 1960): 107–10.

Davis, Kenneth S. "Incident in Miami." *American Heritage Magazine*. Vol. 32. No. 1 (December 1980): 86–95.

Donovan, Robert J. *The Assassins* (New York: Harper & Brothers, 1955).

———. "Annals of Crime: The Long Stomach Ache," *New Yorker* (27 November 1954): 100–21.

Dornfeld, A.A. *Hello, Sweetheart, Get Me Rewrite* (Chicago: Academy Chicago, 1988).

Driggs, Ken. "'A Current of Electricity Sufficient in Intensity to Cause Immediate Death': A Pre-Furman History of Florida's Electric Chair." *Stetson University Law Review* (October 1992).

Elman, Robert. "Lunatic With A Stomach Ache." *Guns and Hunting Magazine* (March 1965): 46–50.

Fillmore, Richard. "I Kill All Presidents." *Startling Detective Magazine* (May 1933): 20–25.

The Florida Handbook (State of Florida, 1993).

Ford, Franklin L. *Political Murder: From Tyrannicide to Terrorism* (Cambridge, Mass: Harvard University Press, 1985).

McKinley, James. *Assassination in America* (New York: Harper and Row, 1977).

Muir, Helen. *Miami, U.S.A.* (Miami: Pickering Press, 1953).

Sewell, John. *Memoirs and History of Miami, Florida* (Miami: The Franklin Press, 1938).

Sifakis, Carl. *Encyclopedia of Assassins* (New York: Facts on File, 1991).

Simpson, Richard D. "Bloodshed at Bayfront: The Zangara Attack." *Update Magazine.* Vol. 7. No. 1 (February 1980).

Smiley, Nixon. *Yesterday's Florida* (Miami: E.A. Seemann Publishing, 1974).

Thomas, Bob. *Winchell* (New York: Doubleday, 1971).

Zangara, Giuseppe. Unpublished manuscript. March 10–19, 1933, from the L.F. Chapman manuscript.

AUTHOR'S INTERVIEWS

■ ■ ■

William M. Straight, M.D., Miami, Florida, 29 January 1993.
Thomas Armour, Jr., M.D., Deland, Florida, 1 January 1993.
Judge Dixie Herlong Chastain, Miami, Florida, 4 March 1993.
Robert Graham, North Miami, Florida, 6 February 1993.
Dan Hardie, III, Miami, Florida, 15 February 1993.
Robert J. Donovan, March 1993.

R. P. McClendon, Starke, Florida, 28 May 1993.

Gen. L.F. Chapman, Jr., U.S.M.C., Ret., 10 January 1993.

John Spencer, Ph.D., Fort Lauderdale, Florida, 30 June 1993.

Melvin J. Richard, Miami Beach, Florida, November 1993.

Dr George M. Barnard, Gainesville, Florida, 15 June 1994.

Dr K. Rajender Reddy, Miami, Florida, 28 September 1994.

Dr Robert A. McNaughton, Miami, Florida, 19 July 1996.

OFFICIAL SOURCES

■ ■ ■

The U.S. State Department archives, National Archives, Washington, D.C.

The U.S. Justice Department archives, National Archives, Washington, D.C.

The Roosevelt Library, Hyde Park, New York.

The Florida State Archives, Tallahassee, Florida.

The Alan Mason Chesney Medical Archives, Johns Hopkins Medical Institutions.

The archives of the Federal Bureau of Investigation, Washington, D.C.

The archives of the United States Secret Service, Washington, D.C.

Transcript of the "statement" of Giuseppe Zangara taken February 15–16, 1933.

Transcript of testimony from sentencing hearing, March 8–10, 1933.

INDEX